For Today's Worship Keyboardist

Intermediate Level

AF271284

KEYBOARD WORSHIP

Book 2 of 4

Applying Contemporary Chord Colors

DR. BARRY LIESCH

ISBN 978-1-7325764-2-1

Scripture quotations are from the Holy Bible: English Standard Version (ESV) Copyright ©2001 by Crossway, The NIV Study Bible New International Version Copyright ©1985 by Zondervan, and New American Standard Bible (NASB) Copyright ©1973 by Moody Press.

For announcements and more information consult worshipinfo.com

Acknowledgements

I have learned in life that friends are important. And in attempting a mammoth project of this size, a four-book series, friendships are indispensable.

In regard to *Book 2*, I am indebted to the following friends, students, and professional keyboardists and colleagues who encouraged me, read chapters, offered feedback, suggested improvements, noted errors, requested clarification, appealed for more "hand holding" ("Please explain more"), and at times (as good friends do) took me to task by putting their finger on gaps and weaknesses: Jeff Askew, Sharon Bernard, Mel Bowker, Robert Denham, Noelle Cablay (major feedback), Cliff Hulling, Bob Kauflin, Irene Lee, Jun Lee, Larry Mumford, Jon Neal, Rique Pantoja, John Redford, Ron Rogalski, John Tebay.

The play-along band pieces/tracks were created by Tom Keene and Chris Wills. The Band tracks were mixed by Iam Keene. Thankyou Tom, Iam, and Chris. All of the remaining mp3 tracks were created/performed by me. The added second "cycles" were the contributions of Rique Pantoja and Jun Lee. Drew Brooke, Elisa Walker, and Mike Watts provided technological assistance.

Moreover, I wish to express my grateful appreciation to Biola University for awarding me a semester sabbatical leave which permitted uninterrupted concentration on the project. Finally, despite technical issues limiting the formatting and physical appearance of the book due to the fixed nature of my PDF chapter files, Charylu Roberts, pianist and founder of O. Ruby Productions, skillfully guided the book through to publication. Thank you, Charylu!

Contents

Foreword for Keyboard Series

Learn, Integrate, Apply! I will be at your side as your coach, helping you to grow as a worship keyboardist. In this book, techniques will be explained in detail so you can *learn* them. Listen to the examples. Play them. Get the shapes of the sounds into your fingers! *Integrate* them into your thinking. An abundance of music examples will help you understand how they function in real musical situations. *Apply* them. Graft them into a favorite worship song, or even better, create an original arrangement.

A major objective of this book and series is to provide you with the tools to build your own musical style (language) for the glory of God.

Intermediate to Advanced Keyboardist. The four books gradually rise in difficulty. *Book 1* begins very, very simply and develops to the intermediate level. It should be useful for a basic, piano proficiency class. Book 2 begins at the intermediate level and morphs to a semi-advanced level. Books 3 and 4 are mostly advanced. In total, about 1200 music examples are presented.

On the whole, these books are aimed at college-level students who have acquired a least *a minimum of two semesters of music theory* (or the equivalent). I expect them to be useful to both undergraduates and graduates. They deal predominantly with harmonic possibilities, which are a foundational building block, and less with rhythm.

Acoustic Piano. The books do not address synthesizer capabilities or idiomatic ways of playing strings, ambient pads, or B3 organ sounds––important! It has grown out of teaching a keyboard lesson in a room with an acoustic keyboard. That's it! However, a section in each book is devoted either to playing in a worship band (in Books 1 and 2), or accompanying solo singers and instrumentalists (in Books 3 and 4).

Detailed Approach, Achievable Chunks, Audio Playback. However, if individuals do not know much music theory and their sight-reading is deficient, the book should still provide solid value. Many examples are very easy to read. The detailed commentary communicates in simple English what is going on musically and theoretically. It breaks down concepts into small, achievable chunks. Audio playback of the examples is included so you can listen and play along, and an extra, special feature will be provided for those who struggle reading music notation (see the end chapter on "What is Midiculous Software?").

Two Kinds of Students. I have been teaching keyboard improvisation at Biola University, an evangelical university of 6000 in the Los Angeles area for many years. Most of my students are music majors whose primary instrument is the piano, undergrads with "classical chops." A good number read music notation fluently. The majority, however, cannot improvise, cannot think in music, do not have a practical grasp of how sounds relate (function with one another), or do so in a simplistic, halting fashion. They don't know what to do. They have not experienced the freedom inherent in improvisation. They are most comfortable with notated music.

On the other hand, I've had other students who improvise well but read music slowly, hesitantly, and with difficulty. The differences between the two, in both background and aptitude, can be startling, extreme! The classical folk read. The improvisers seek to invent. However, the improvisers, too, are limited in their understanding of how music works. They have meager resources and lack the musical concepts to develop their ideas effectively. *This is my attempt to meet the needs of each of these diverse learners.*

Many times, I've gone back to my office after a lesson and have added another step or example to improve clarity. In other words, these materials have undergone much thought, testing, and revision in attempting to "zone in" where students need help.

Problem of Transitory Worship Songs. A major problem concerning the transitory nature of contemporary worship music needs addressing. I appreciate that young people would like the book to contain the very latest, "hot" worship songs (you'll find some). But this doesn't make much sense for a book of this sort. Unfortunately, many of the latest songs tend to last a couple of years. Then they're gone. The "turn over" rate is astonishing, unrelenting. Strange as it may seem, if this book were to major in current worship songs, it would quickly become outdated!

Therefore, I've chosen well-known hymns and worship choruses with a least some proven staying power. However, in actual lessons I have incorporated songs when students exclaim, "I love that song!" These are *their* songs of heart-felt worship. I've learned they are *really* important to them. So, I often respond "Let's look at that song too." It could be an Asian or Latino worship song. Students love this!

Fulfilling a Promise. In another worship book I wrote, *The New Worship: Straight Talk on Music and the Church* (Baker Books, 2001), I called for an outpouring of worship materials in all areas, including music, the dramatic and visual arts, and works that would embrace the theoretical, practical, and pedagogical. I pledged myself to contribute to that effort (p. 35).

These keyboard books are part of my effort to make good on that promise. I want to bless the thirsty keyboardist. If another contributor can borrow from what I have written, improve upon it, and advance the field, terrific! Nothing would make me happier.

No Greater, No Higher Function. Without doubt, many wonderful, marvelous things can be done with music. But I feel confident in declaring this without reservation. There is *no greater, no higher function* for music than to lead people in worship, and to proclaim the eternal Gospel of Jesus Christ.

Ideas in Keyboard Series

In seeking to hone our improvisational capacities, the keyboard has advantages over single-line instruments, for it allows us to think more comprehensively about music—not only melodically but also harmonically. Ideally, we need an…

Abundance of Harmonic Possibilities. We need many options ready at our fingertips. The lyrics may cry out for a precise, fitting sonority. Our chances are much better of finding it if we have an extensive, internalized array of colorful, variegated sounds to draw from. Moreover, the keyboard can help us internalize chord structures and functions. As we make music physically with our fingers, the theory behind music becomes tactile, concrete, alive—less abstract.

Abundance of Examples. The volumes employ over 1200 examples. Three kinds of examples are introduced: (1) abstract examples describe a particular chord and how it functions harmonically; (2) it is then demonstrated a number of times in different songs so you see its potential and usefulness; (3) finally, you'll be given an opportunity to use/apply the technique yourself in a piece where it can function effectively.

Transposition Exercises. The repetition of playing a short phrase, its functions and spacings over and over again in various keys, helps establish it firmly in our inner ear and fingers. The goal is to acquire the "feel" of chord shapes and relationships so we don't have to think hard about them. A seventh or ninth, for example, has to become as effortless as playing a C major chord.

Transposition greatly stimulates the thinking/hearing process. It tests whether we can apply concepts. It forces us to think in new keys and get "command" of those keys. Transposition assignments are kept short so as to be achievable (often only four measures) and employ well-known songs to make the task more enjoyable and relevant.

Modulation. Once we can play songs in different keys, the desire to be able to fashion effective transitions, and to modulate and to craft segues within and between pieces emerges. Modulations culminating in flowing, seamless worship can usually be handled more competently by keyboardists than guitarists. Therefore we'll offer detailed training in modulation techniques, and we'll discover that sus chords and "four over five" chords are particularly useful.

Chord Spacings (Chord Voicings). Students sometimes have a good idea and may have seized on a good chord progression. However, their realization of it frequently sounds bad. I often ask, "Did that sound good to you? How could we make that same chord, or sequence of chords, sound better? Let's work on that together." The problem is often excessive doubling (even tripling) of notes, particularly in the lower register, and not being sufficiently aware of the inner-voice movement. This book will illustrate many skillful spacing (voicing) options.

Guitar Keys. In worship contexts today, guitarists (who often rule!) tend to avoid keys with flats. They prefer keys with sharps. Therefore, the range of keys in these books is limited to those you will tend to use most frequently. Once we can think in the keys of C, D, E, F, G, and A, it is relatively easy to extend our thinking to the flat keys. Furthermore, this limitation reduces the "brain load," allows us to cover more material, and yet spend sufficient time on the details to truly grasp them.

Sing and Play. The ability to be able to sing and play simultaneously is invaluable when leading or accompanying worship—and it's challenging! It takes extra energy and concentration to maintain good pitch, tone, and congregational eye contact while singing, and yet play fluently and rhythmically, barely looking at the keys. A higher level of keyboard mastery is demanded. We'll be developing this skill. The words to many songs will be provided so you can practice singing and playing.

Collaborate with a Worship Band. This book is also intended to develop your arranging skills so that you can collaborate with a worship band. After exposure to so many rich harmonic possibilities, you will have musical ideas. You'll be able to pitch in and be a creative force. Imagine suggesting during a rehearsal, "How about using this chord? Would this harmonic progression add more interest? Would a modulation between these two songs create a smoother flow?" Moreover, you will be developing skills so you can create your own custom piano arrangements and worship charts.

Creative Ways to Supplement This Book When Teaching

(1) Have students bring in a hymnbook or a photocopy of a song. Added second and sus chords can be penciled in, and 3+1 and 4+2 voicings can be explored.

(2) If you have Asian, African American, or Latino students, encourage them to bring in ethnic pieces.

(3) Prior to the lesson, have students enter on their computers the song lyrics and their original chord progressions. Place the computer or ipad on the piano rack. Expand and enhance what's written. Enter the new pop symbols on the computer immediately.

(4) Have them create an original arrangement of a hymn/song. Encourage them to record on cell phones their ideas and variations immediately as they develop so ideas don't get lost.

(5) Have students record their teacher playing improvised alternatives. This becomes valuable for recall and future reference. It's often difficult to remember what was played.

What Improvisation Requires

Throughout this book I will be at your side as your personal coach, guiding to toward attaining greater competency, so you can serve the Lord confidently in any number of musical situations.

Think for a moment what improvisation requires. Improvisation is speeded-up composition. Improvisation requires knowledge and familiarity with musical processes. Improvisation requires us to "think and live in music" and to fine-tune our "inner ear" so we can imagine, conceive, and bring our ideas to fruition.

Why are many musicians so uncomfortable with improvisation? We frequently find ourselves stuck without ideas. Our processes for fashioning ideas are shallow. Our attempts seem so imperfect and unfinished! Even after we acquire some improvisational knowledge, often we become fixated on the next note in a worship song, *the absolute present,* rather than thinking broadly and freely. Given these challenges, the way we think about improvisation is important. How can we better orient our thinking?

Think of the word I-M-P-A-C-T. Our longing is to impact others for Christ through music. But what does it take? What character and musical qualities do we need?

I   Incentive–strong desire–is critical not only to getting started but to sticking with it.

M   Musicianship. Artistic sensitivity and a minimum of technical facility is required to perform decently even simple musical ideas. Build your technique! To accomplish this, you will need an acoustic piano or an electronic keyboard with *weighted keys.* When we have an abundance of technique our ideas come more readily.

P   Patience—sustained effort—is indispensable. Allowing ourselves time to develop, and a certain willingness to experience trial and error, is a precondition for growth.

A   Adaptability, being able to work in an ensemble, deal with personalities, and read the mood and needs of the congregation is essential. An openness to new styles is part of the improviser's world and required of today's Christian musician.

C   Courage, even a certain daring, is crucial for expressing yourself on the spot. This can be scary! We must be able to accept stubbing our toe from time to time. Remember the turtle: *He doesn't make progress until he sticks his neck out.*

T   Taste comes from experience and work as well as unteachable instinct. Knowing how much to do or how far to go to enhance worship without distracting from it or calling attention to yourself is a tough call. Sometimes less can be more.

Overview: Six Contemporary Harmonic Expansions

This Chapter will give you a quick thumbnail sketch of the book

Let's look at a rough outline of the six contemporary harmonic expansions which are explored in this book – and which help give worship its modern sound.

Some background. Briefly, chords based on thirds have occupied a dominant place in western music for centuries (1600 - to the present). For example, consider the basic major triad and it alternatives.

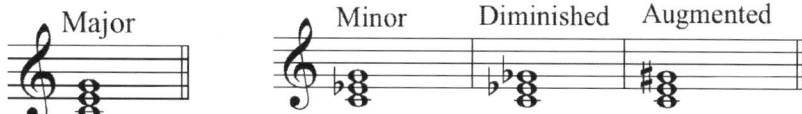

Over time more thirds were added, resulting in various seventh, ninth, eleventh, and thirteenth chord extensions. See some representative examples.

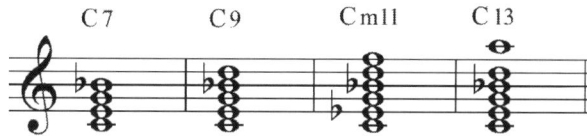

The contemporary expansions. Several different expansions have become commonplace in contemporary worship music: added seconds, sus chords, open fifths, quartals, four over five, and one over four chords. These options have introduced some new, attractive colors into worship expression, and in some cases, bold, harmonic tension (eg., I/4).

Alterations surrounding the *third* of the major triad have been important. A basic idea is that instead of employing the third of a C major chord, a second (D) or fourth (F) could be substituted.

D « E » F

Let's look at what has happened. (Not in any historical order.)

Expansion One: the emergence of Added Second chords

C:	1		3		5	Tertian Harmony (thirds)
Cadd2	1	2	3		5	Added Second with the third
C2	1	2			5	Added Second without the third

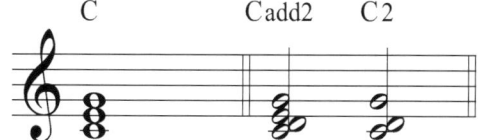

Discussed in chapters 2, 3, 4

Expansion Two: the emergence of Quartal chords (comprised of 4ths)

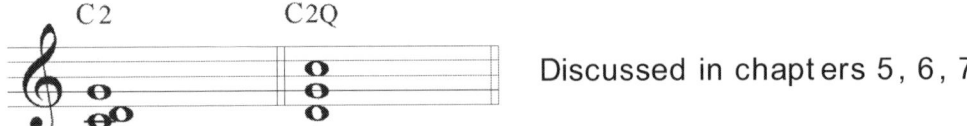

Discussed in chapters 5, 6, 7

A C quartal (C2Q, our unique symbol) will be considered an inversion of the C2.

Expansion Three: the emergence of Sus chords

C:	1	3	5	Tertian Harmony (thirds)
Csus:	1		4 5	Sus Chord

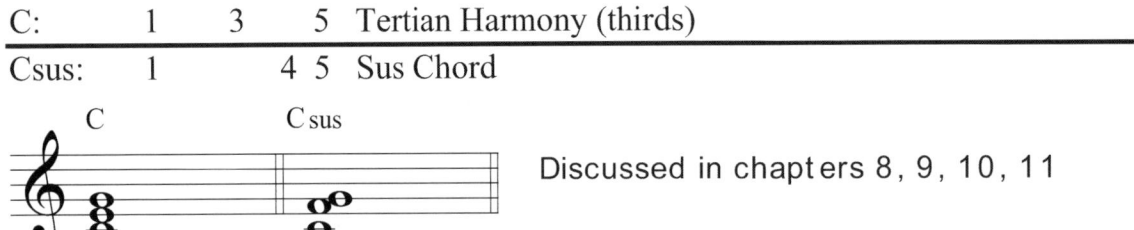

Discussed in chapters 8, 9, 10, 11

The Sus has a unique quality in that thirds can be piled on. The following may look ridiculous, but all of these sus alternatives sound good (if handled properly).

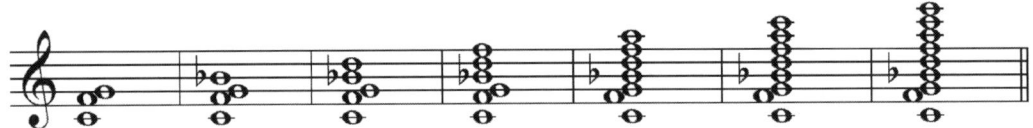

Expansion Four: the emergence of the Four Over Five chord

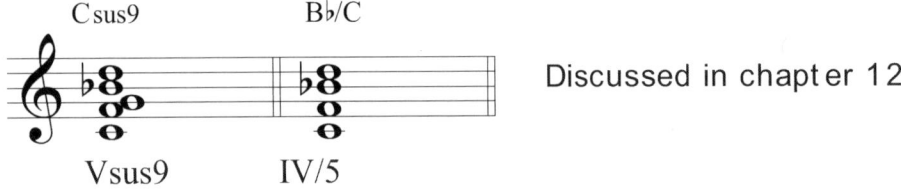

Discussed in chapter 12

Expansion Five: the emergence of the One Over Four chord

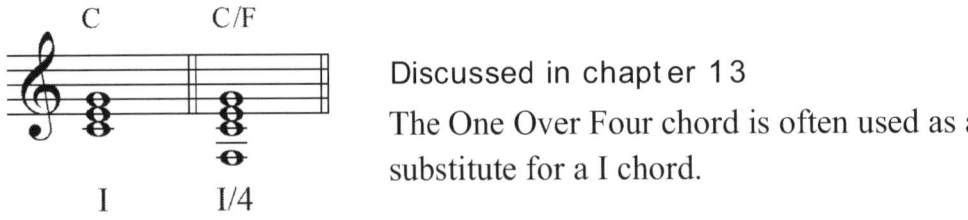

Discussed in chapter 13

The One Over Four chord is often used as a substitute for a I chord.

And finally, the simplest expansion of all!

Expansion Six: the emergence of Open Fifth or Octave Drones

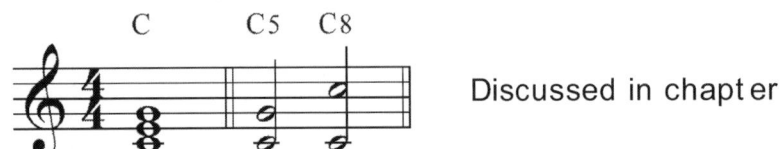

Discussed in chapter

APPLYING THE CONTEMPORARY HARMONIC EXPANSIONS

CHAPTER 1

Drones / Pedals

- 11 pages
- 23 examples

Drones are common in guitar-driven worship today. And they are a very significant part of "world music." For example, drones are absolutely fundamental to the music of India. We'll look at various ways to use them in both worship choruses and hymns. Drones can help worship materials become more accessible (easy to perform) and sound more contemporary. We'll revise the harmonies found in songs, simplifying them, and stripping them down to the bare bones.

In the examples below, often the keyboardist would be playing a right hand, sustained atmospheric "pad" on a synth (rather than an acoustic piano). Acoustic piano sounds fade away and decay too quickly. The keyboard bass part could be omitted entirely.

OUTLINE	REPERTOIRE
Applying Drones to Worship Choruses	I Could Sing of Your Love Forever
Applying Drones to Hymns	Refiner's Fire Great is Thy Faithfulness
Varying the Bass Part	Let Everything That Hath Breath
Added Second Drones	Be Thou My Vision Joyful Joyful

What is a Drone? A drone is a note or notes that are continuously sounded and held throughout all, most, or at least a significant part of a piece while other notes simultaneously being played change and develop. A drone could be the lowest note, the highest high note, or one in the middle. Drones often occur on the tonic or dominant (scale degrees one or five). When speaking about drones, single notes, octaves and open fifths (rather than triads) come to mind. The quarter note C major chord is the only measure not likely to be used as a drone.

Example 1.1 Possible Drones

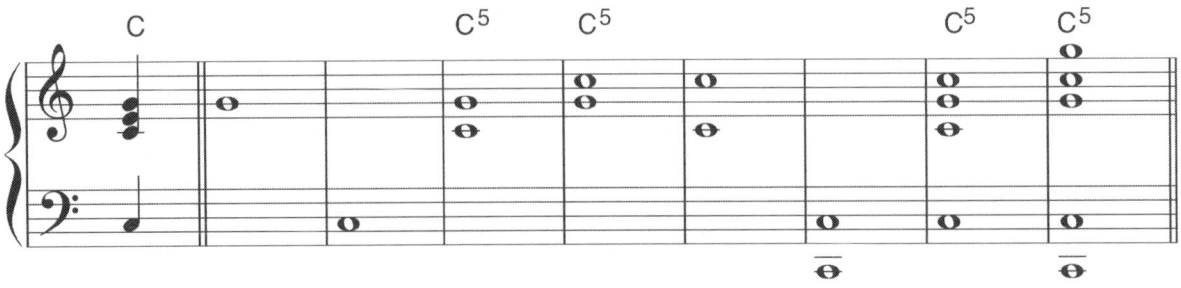

A C5 drone, because it lacks the third, results in much more harmonic *ambiguity*. Because it has no third, the C5 sound itself is *neither major or minor*. But in a given context it could imply a major or minor chord. That attribute can yield interesting results.

Drones are similar in function to "pedals" or "pedal points." The word "pedal" may have come from organists holding their foot down on foot pedals while playing on the keyboard with their hands. Pedals, in general (not always), tend to be briefer, more limited to a measure or two, or just part of a piece.

Let's draw a contrast. Hymnbook harmonies are specifically fashioned for singers and keyboardists. Below, the chords change on almost every measure—often too quickly for smooth performance by guitarists.

Example 1.2 Fast Chord Changes in *Joyful Joyful*

Chord changes can be slowed down dramatically by using *drones*.

Example 1.3 Drones in *Joyful Joyful*

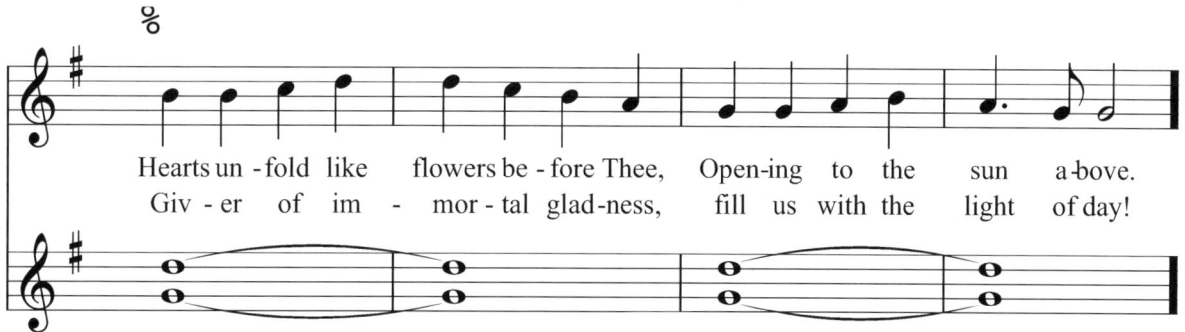

Guitarists, keyboardists, and drummers would be free to add rhythms to the drones in order to create interest.

Let's add a little rhythmic complexity. Below, bassist provides melodic movement.

Example 1.4   Bass Part with Movement in *Joyful Joyful*

Applying Drones to Worship Choruses

In the lead sheet below no drones occur. A chord progression of triads (E, C#, A2) is evident.

Example 1.5   *I Could Sing of Your Love Forever*

I could sing of your love __ for-ev - er   I could sing of your love __ for-ev - er

Using the same basic sonorities, let's apply an E5. Drones occur.

Example 1.6   Drone Version of *I Could Sing of Your Love Forever*.

I could sing of your love __ for-ev - er   I could sing of your love __ for-ev - er

Example 1.7   *I Could Sing of Your Love Forever* (Harmonic Variant)

The E5 works well with all of the bass notes in the major scale, as below.

Example 1.8   *I Could Sing of Your Love Forever* (Scalar Variant)

Try it! Improvise with the examples above. Try to open the excerpt up dynamically and rhythmically. Also, create some other drone possibilities.

Clearly, harmonic variation is possible using drones.

Example 1.9 *Refiner's Fire* (With Typical Chord Changes)

Example 1.10 Drone Used in *Refiner's Fire*

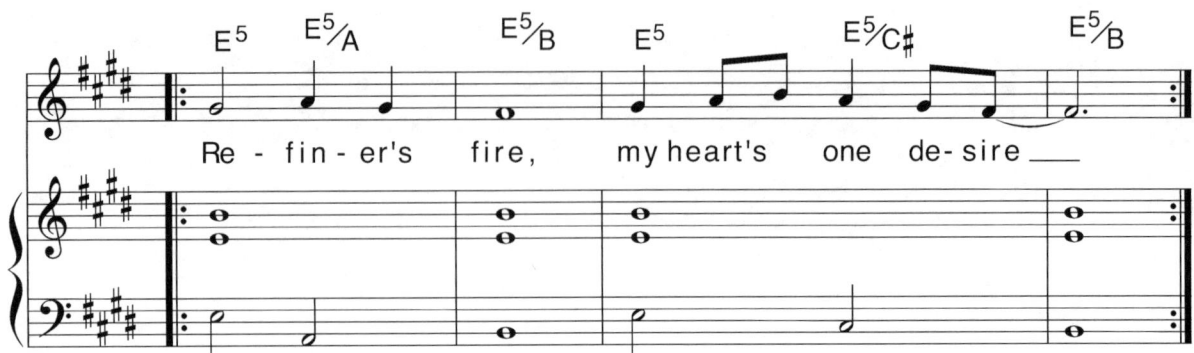

Improvise! Improvise over the four measures above. Repeat the phrase at least four times. Experiment with various bass notes and various kinds of rhythmic patterns.

Below, create various drones, repeating the melody line four times. Try various bass lines and various rhythms with the drone. Try building toward and from a climax.

Example 1.11   *Let Everything That Has Breath*

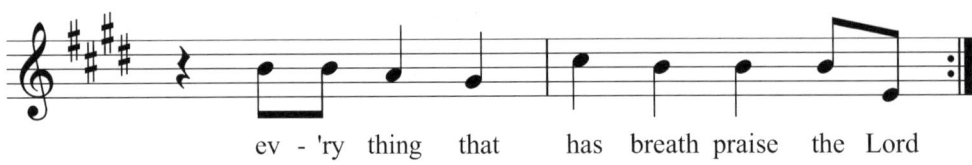

Try it! Were you aware that the bass part could have walked up or down the scale?

Applying Drones to Hymns

Two unique contributions of "the West" to music are homophony (verticalized harmony), and polyphony (horizontal, multiple, simultaneous melodies). Music in the rest of the world, on the other hand, tends to use drones to a much greater degree instead of harmonic progressions and polyphony. Drones are characteristic of "world music."

Drones are valuable. They can impart a contrasting sonic image and feeling to that found in hymnbooks. When a C5 drone in the treble clef is played against a major scale in the bass clef, it diverges sonically and harmonically from the classical, tertian system (chord composed of stacked thirds)

Example 1.12 C5 Drone with Major Scale in Bass

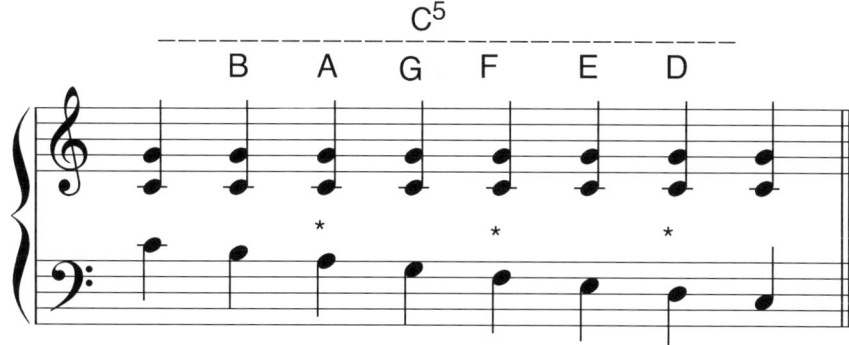

Example 1.13 Drone in *Be Thou My Vision*

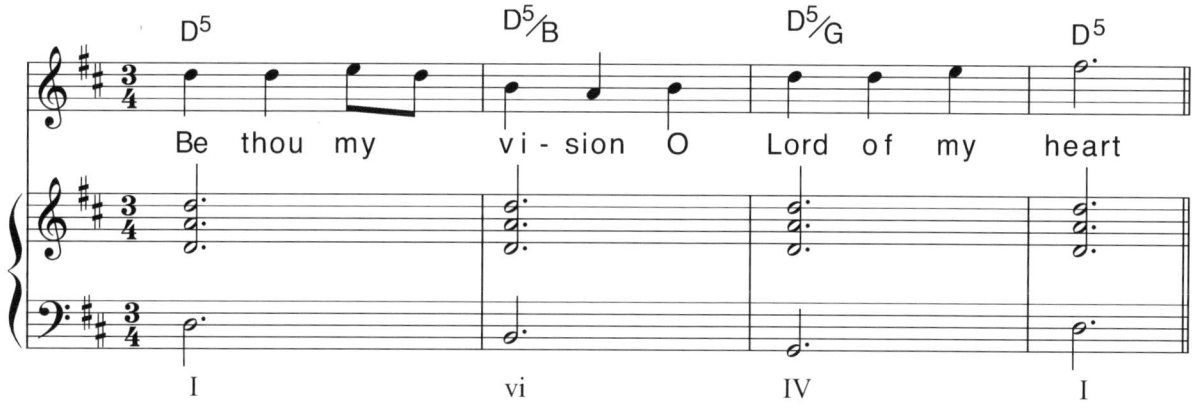

Do you like the effect? The bass provides the *changes of harmony* indicated by the Roman numerals, while the other instruments drone away on D5 (an open 5th or 4th depending how it's voiced). A G2 chord is created in measure three. The slash symbol (D5/G), though, does express the composite sound. Alternatively, the bass could have also held a D through measures one and two.

Varying the Bass Part

Develop the ability to vary parts. The examples below explore possible alterations to the bass part for lines one, two, and three of *Be Thou My Vision*. A time-honored technique, contrary motion between the bass and soprano parts, is a useful consideration.

Example 1.14   Alternative Bass Lines for 1st line of *Be Thou My Vision*

Example 1.15   Alternative Bass Lines for 2nd line of *Be Thou My Vision*

The first alternative walks the bass up the scale: a "line" was created. An "added second" chord was used as a drone. We'll talk about added seconds shortly.

Example 1.16   Alternative Bass Lines for 3rd line of *Be Thou My Vision*

Harmonic and melodic anticipations and delays are possible. Below, a harmonic anticipation (D5/G) comes in a beat early (m.1, beat 3). Also note, m.3 beat 2.

Example 1.17   Rhythmic Anticipations in *Be Thou My Vision*

Example 1.18   Drone in *Great is Thy Faithfulness*

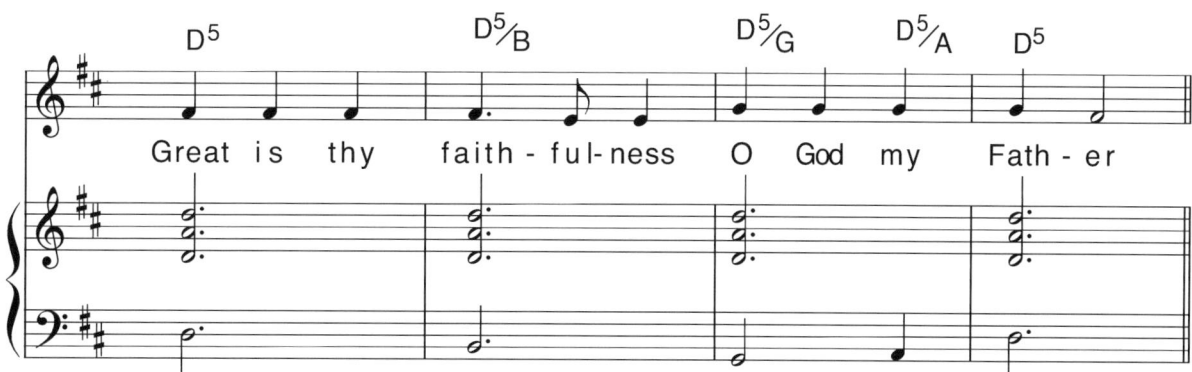

Example 1.19 **Try it!** Create Bass Lines for *Great is Thy Faithfulness*

Improvise several alternative bass lines. Experiment! Write out two bass lines you like the best. Useable bass notes are E, G, A, and B, and D. Even placing the notes in a different order can result in an interesting effect. Consider using rhythmic variation (syncopation?) for the second version. Place pop symbols in the staffs of lines 3 and 4.

Perfect fifths can be suggestive. Perfect fifth sounds can be "suggestive" of fuller harmonies, even those not typically found in hymnbooks (as below). They can be created by worship bands with a minimum of effort.

Example 1.20 Harmonies "Suggested" by Slash Chords Using Perfect Fifths

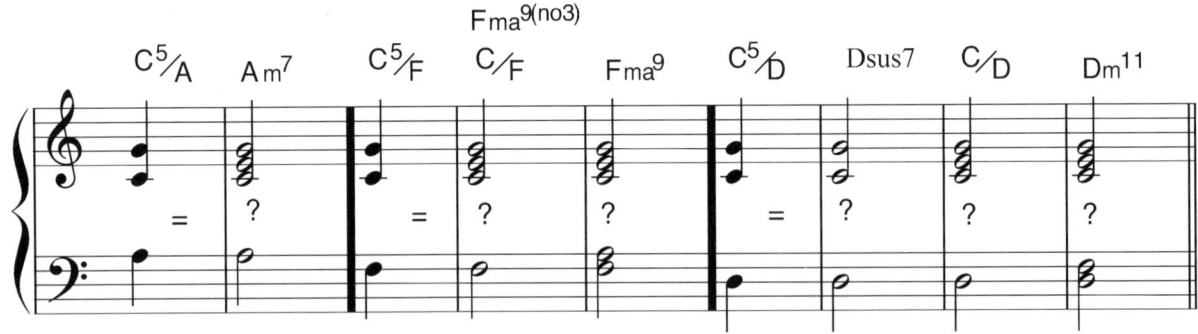

Added Second Drones

Drones with added seconds can also occur. They too can be used with all the bass notes in the major scale.

Example 1.21   C2 Drone with Major Scale in Bass

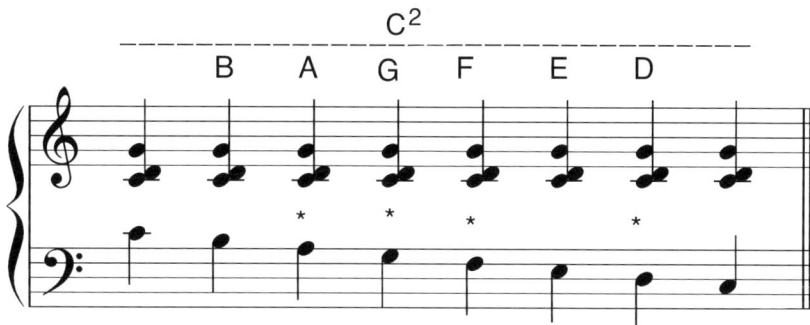

Example 1.22   Alternative Ways of Looking at the Asterisked Sonorities Above

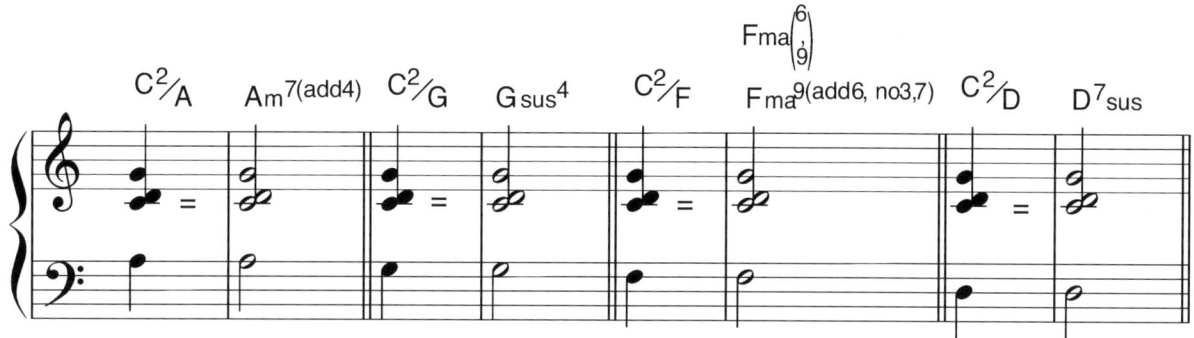

Notice, we resorted to harmonic descriptions involving added 4ths, sixths, and
 elevenths—sounds not found in hymnals

Example 1.23   Drones Used Throughout *Be Thou My Vision*

Drones are frequently employed to project a mood of meditation, even
transcendence—indeed, they can very effectively suggest these kinds of feelings,
especially when they stretch out for longer periods of time.

Below, open fifths are *alternated* with added second drones to create a slightly more
colorful result. The idea of providing slight alternations in the drone is our new thought.

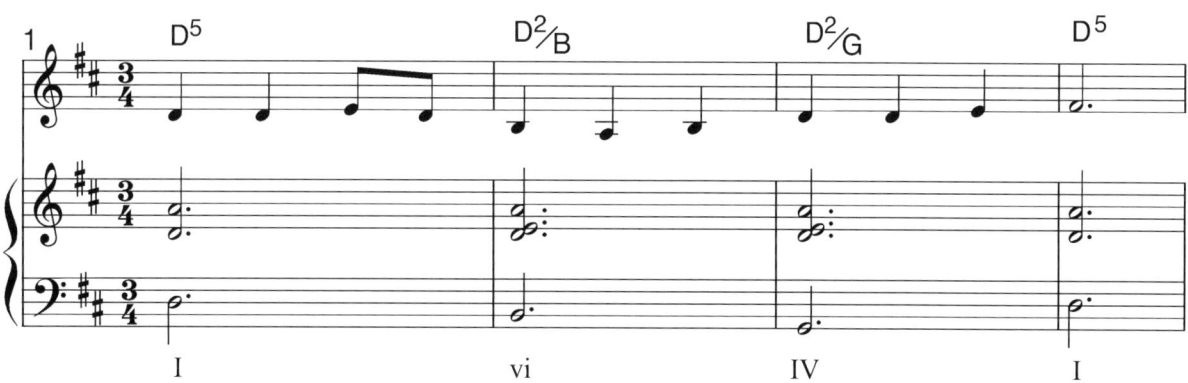

In ms. 1-4 a D drone is alternated with a D2 drone. In ms. 5-8 an A drone is alternated with an A2 drone. In ms.9-11 a B2 drone is alternated with a B minor triad.

Drones can be employed in all kinds of worship songs. Many examples of drones involving scale degrees 1 or 5 occur in Book 1, chapter 9, *Letting Go of the Melody*. Drones often use octaves or perfect fifths. Drones can slow up the chord changes, make songs more accessible, even create a contemplative feeling. "Added second" drones were also mentioned. The next chapters look at added seconds in more detail.

I can do all things through Christ who strengthens me.
Phil 4:13

CHAPTER 2

Added Seconds Without Thirds

- 11 pages
- 26 examples

OUTLINE	REPERTOIRE
Added Second Chords	Jesus Loves Me
Added Seconds *without* the Third	Holy Holy Holy
Try it!	Be Exalted, O Lord Give Thanks
How C2, F2, & G2 Function in C Major	Spirit of God Descend Upon My Heart

Both contemporary choruses and traditional hymns are in this book, for diversified worship (a worthy goal) is healthy in the long run. We recognize, however, that songs from the recent and distant past may need to be reshaped if we are to speak to the moment—if our worship is to be contextualized to our times.

How, then, can this be done? How can choruses and hymns be updated and yet have variety and musical substance? An answer (in part) can be found in the use of added second and quartal chords and the use of drones. Worship leaders should know how to integrate these sounds. When you employ them, you will immediately sense that the harmonic language has been modernized.

Added second and quartals are useful in congregational playing, accompanying soloists, improvising in a band, and when soloing. They occur in Rock, Country, and Jazz music, and dozens of movie scores—they are ubiquitous in today's music. They have wide applicability.

Think of added seconds and quartals as a colorist enhancement, an extension of traditional harmony and contemporary practice. They will not disrupt or jar the basic sound structure. The ways harmonies normally function does not need to change. For example, ii chords can continue to progress to V chords, I chords to vi chords, and so on. Subtle, not dramatic change results. Yet the modification is one of real significance! Moreover, keyboardists can incorporate added seconds and quartals into triads while other team members (i.e., guitarists, singers) play and sing straight triads. The new substitutions will not clash. A new dimension of color, however, will be injected.

We'll focus on added seconds now, for several chapters, then address quartals.

Added Second Chords

"What is an added second chord?" An added second chord is a major or minor triad with an interval of a major second added to the composite sound. The third of the triad may or may not be present. When the third is present (Cadd2 = 1235), the sound is warmer. When the third is not present (C2 = 125), the sound is leaner and slightly more biting in quality.

Example 2.1

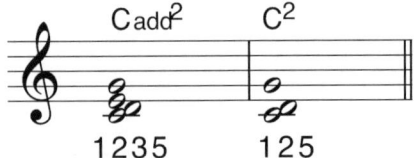

Added second chords can also be inverted, just like triads.

Example 2.2

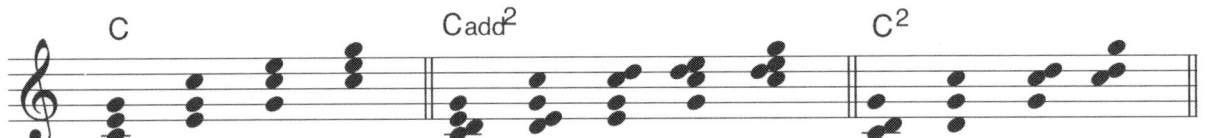

Added Second Chords *without* the Third

Added seconds *without* thirds (1,2,5), frequently occur on scale degrees I, IV, or V with the root, third, or fifth in the bass.

Example 2.3

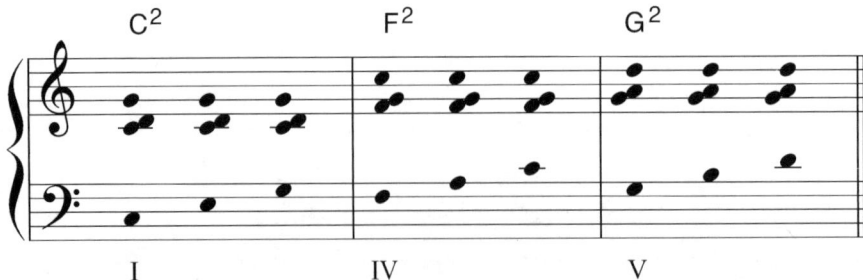

Which do you like best? The added second with the root, third, or fifth in the bass? Keyboardists often feel the third in the bass sounds particularly good. So we'll particularly pursue that option in this chapter.

An octave doubling could be used to add strength and warmth to the sound (as below).

Example 2.4

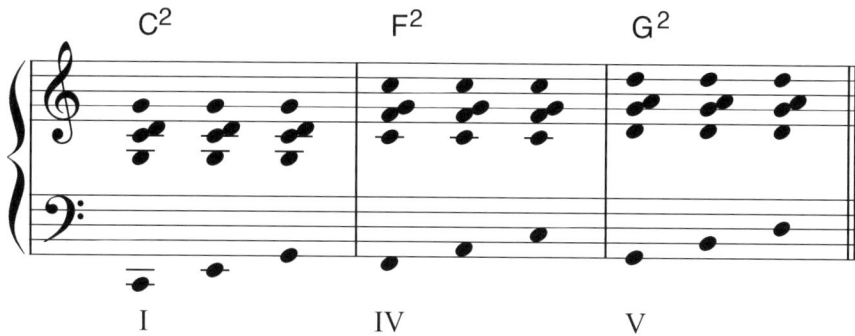

Do you like the Added Second Effect?
The example below suggests typical ways in which added seconds can be employed.

Example 2.5 *Jesus Loves Me*

Try it!

Below are two examples of a chorus and a hymn, as published. <u>Play</u> an added second chord (*without* a third) wherever an asterisk is indicated.

Example 2.6 Insert Added Seconds without the Third at the Asterisk

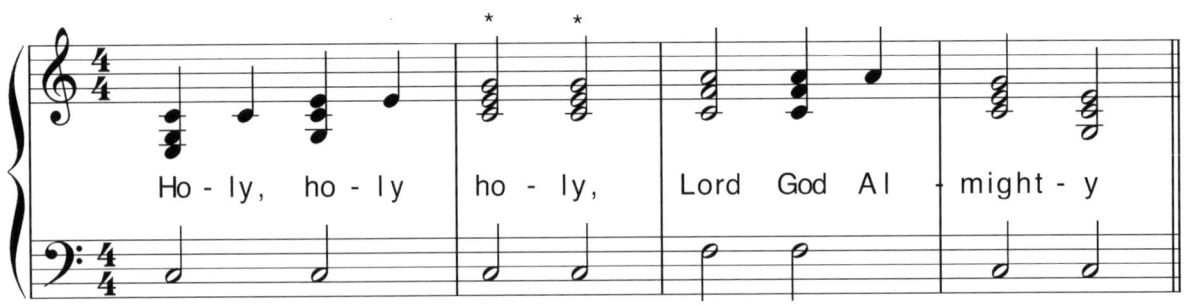

Example 2.7 Added Seconds with the Root in the Bass.

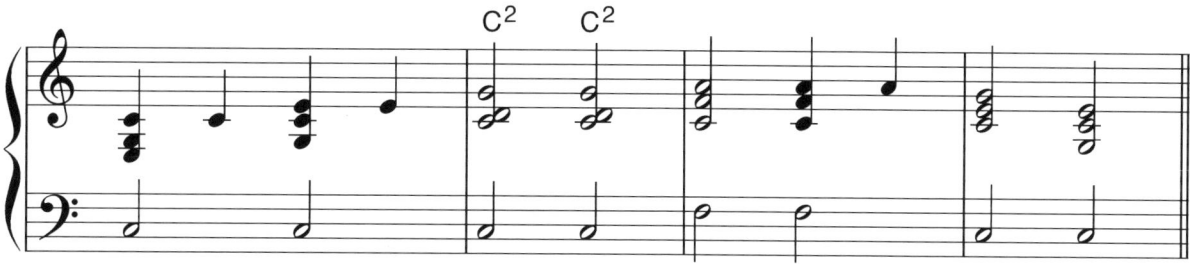

Example 2.8 Added Seconds with the Third (E) in the Bass.

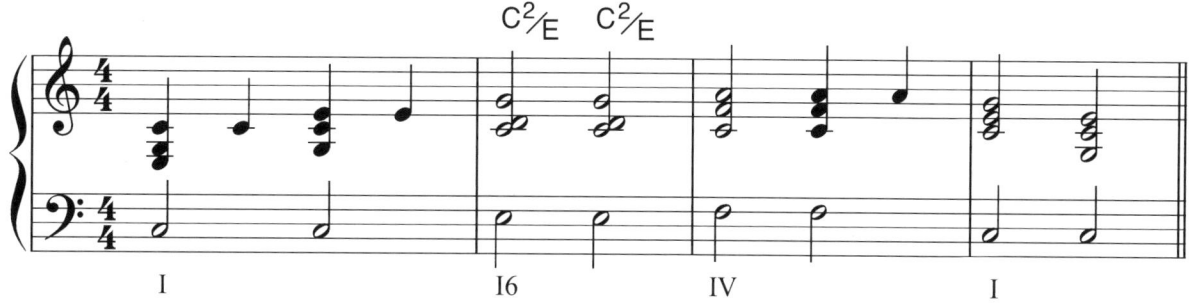

Note, the *third* in the bass sounds particularly good.

Try it! Play the above example in the keys of C, D, E, F, G, and A.

Example 2.9 Added Seconds with an Octave Doubling (bigger sound)

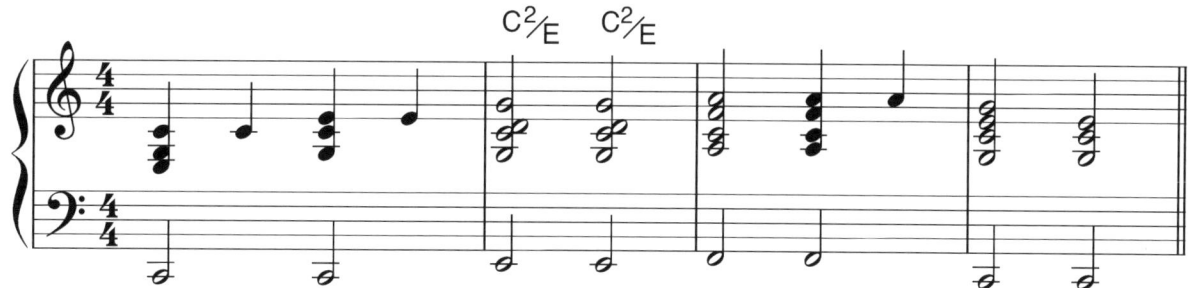

Play the above example in the keys of C, D, E, F, G, and A.

Example 2.10 Add a C2/E Chord at the Asterisk. Transpose & play in D, E, F, G.

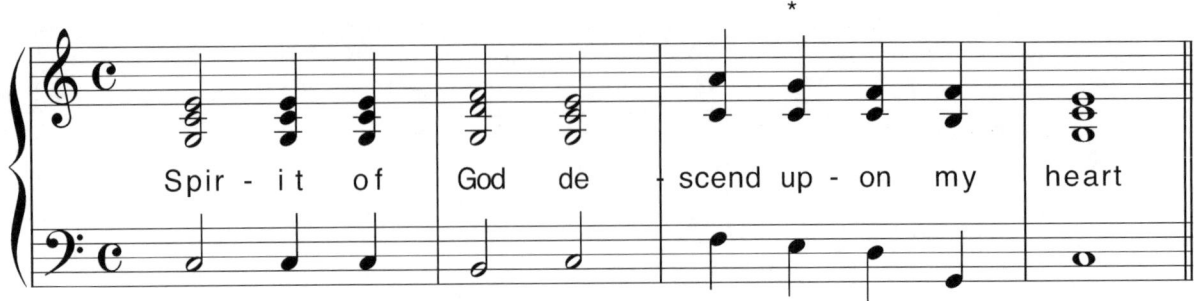

Spir - it of God de - scend up - on my heart

The example above is slightly harder. Close the book when you have mastered it.

Example 2.11 Change the Bass/Insert Added Second Chords (*Be Exalted, O God*)

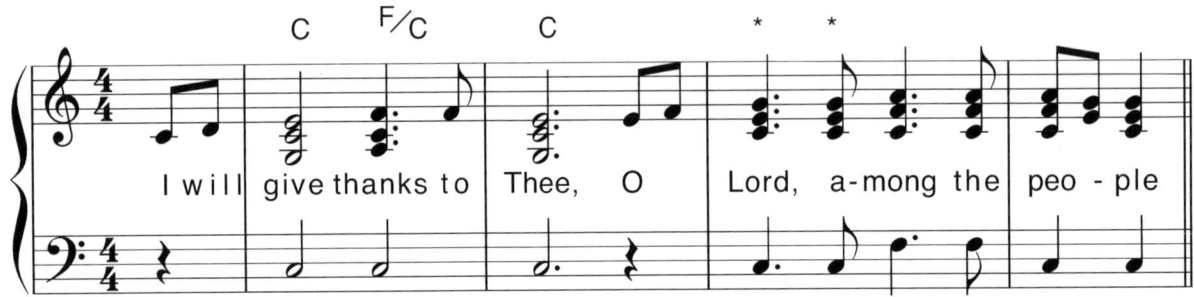

I will give thanks to Thee, O Lord, a-mong the peo - ple

Try it! Play the above in the keys of D, E, F, G, and A.

Scale Degrees ii, iii, vi.

Added second chords can occur on scale degrees ii, iii, and vi also (as below). They're ambiguous (neither major or minor). The third in the bass makes the quality minor.

Example 2.12

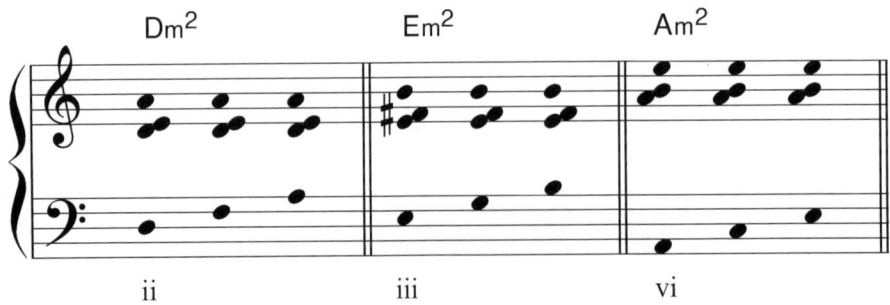

Notice above, the added second is always a major second above the root. Thus in measure two, the added second is an F#, not an F.

Example 2.13 Create Added Seconds <u>without</u> the Third *(Give Thanks)*

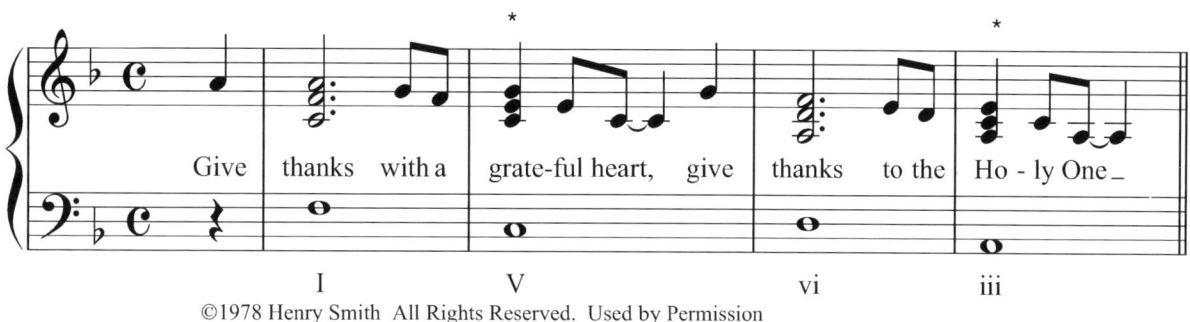

Now play the phrase again, but this time fashion some first inversion added seconds (third in the bass). The bass line can descend in a stepwise motion (F, E, D, C).

Example 2.14 Descending Step-Wise Bass Line

Stepwise bass lines are often very effective. Your solution should look like this.

Example 2.15 *Give Thanks* (Stepwise Bass)

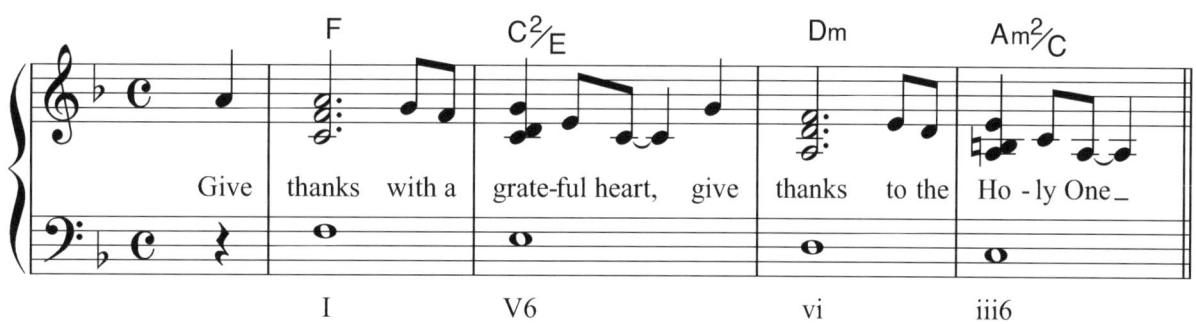

Did you forget the B natural on the iii6 in measure 4? Which solution do you like best—root position or first inversion? Play each again and compare the results. *Transpose:* play each result above (root position & first inversion) in the keys of E and G.

Next, practice the exercise in all the keys. Play the inversions (125; 251; 512; 125) through the cycle of fourths (up a 4ᵗʰ or down a 5ᵗʰ)—C, F, Bb, Eb, Ab, Db, Gb, B, E, A, D, G, C.

For variety also try arpeggiating (linearizing) the right hand. Vary the bass rhythm.

Example 2.16 Play through the Cycle (Down a Fifth or Up a Fourth)

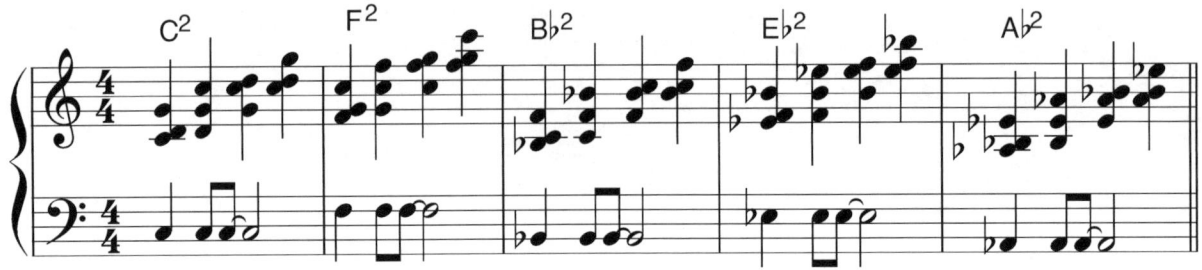

Example 2.17 Added Second with Third in Bass (Cycle: Down 5th, Up 4th)

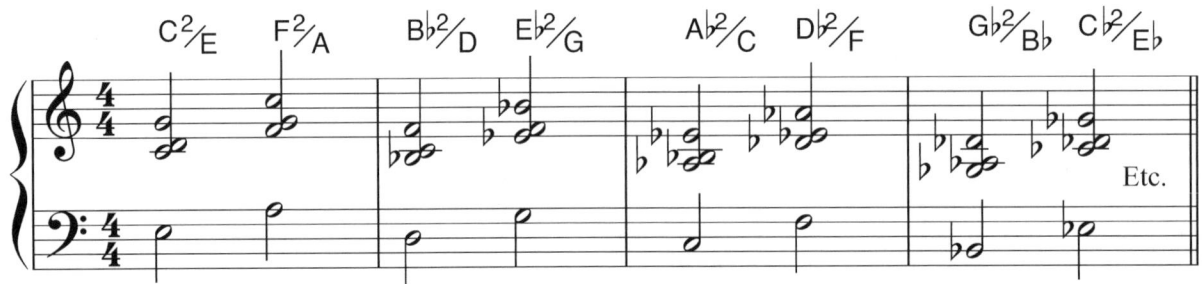

Added second chords can function smoothly and effectively in traditional hymns and choruses. Below, see some of the ways they could function.

How C2, F2, and G2 Function in C Major

When a I chord in C major is the starting point, the added second chord (*without the third*) could function the following ways. The asterisks indicate a C2 or G2 chord. A C chord is in root position for the first chord of each measure. Play the examples below.

Example 2.18 First Chord in Root Position (Play it)

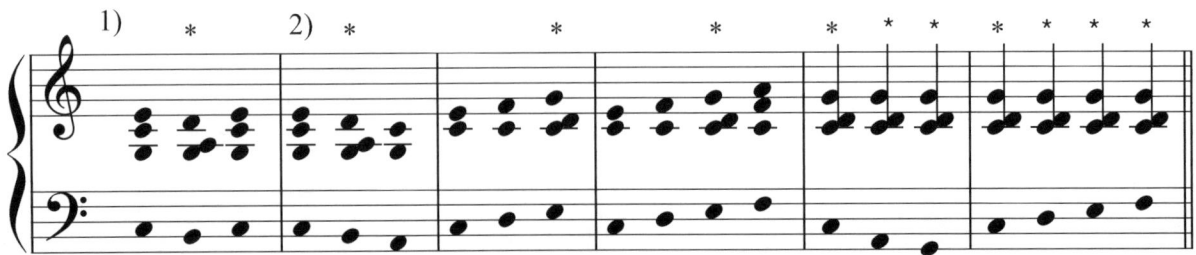

Above, examples 1) and 2) could be played on a IV or a V chord .

Example 2.19 Extending the Concept to scale degrees IV and V.

Below, the G2/B chord in example 1 functions as a neighboring chord (N). The G2/B in example 2) functions as a passing chord (P).

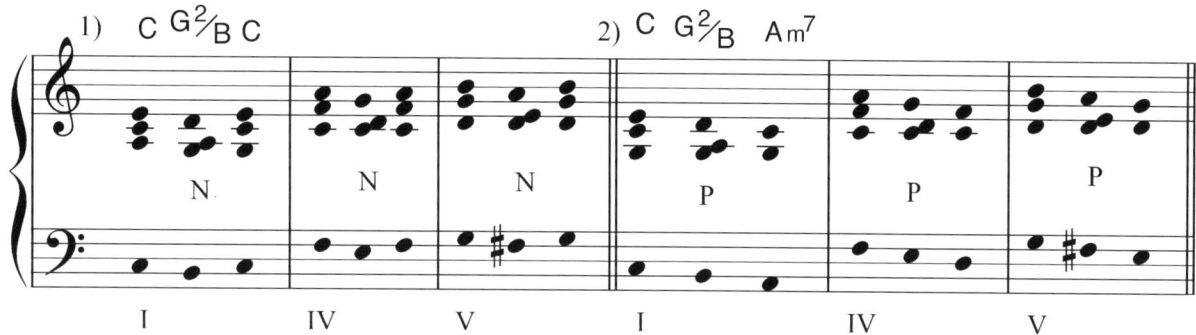

Below, the first chord in each measure is in first inversion (third has the lowest tone).

Example 2.20 First Chord in First Inversion (Play it)

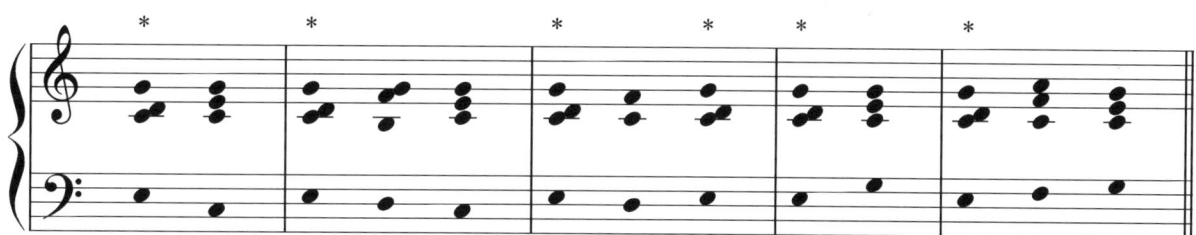

Below, the first chord in each measure is in second inversion (fifth as lowest tone)

Example 2.21 First Chord in Second Inversion (Play it)

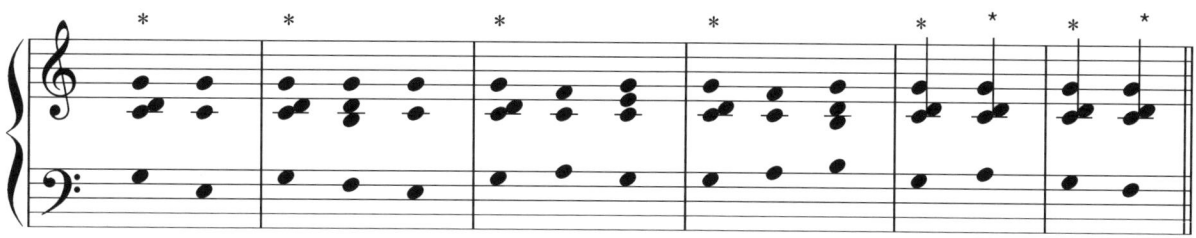

Next, a IV chord is the starting point. Added seconds function similarly.

Example 2.22 First Chord is a IV (Play it)

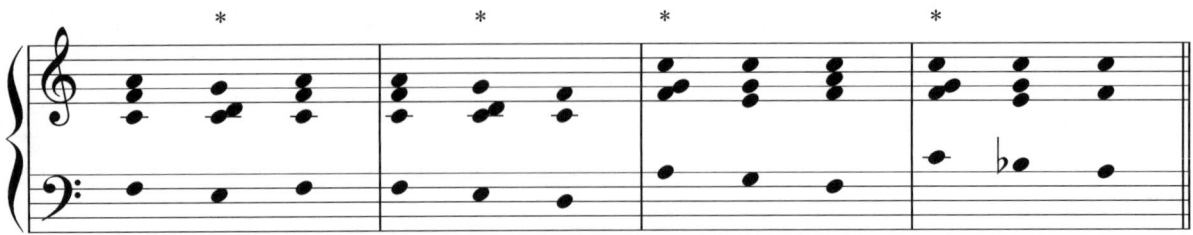

Below, a V chord is the starting point. Added seconds function similarly. In measure 4, two consecutive added second chords walk up the scale—a nice effect which becomes the subject of the next chapter.

Example 2.23 First Chord is a V (Play it)

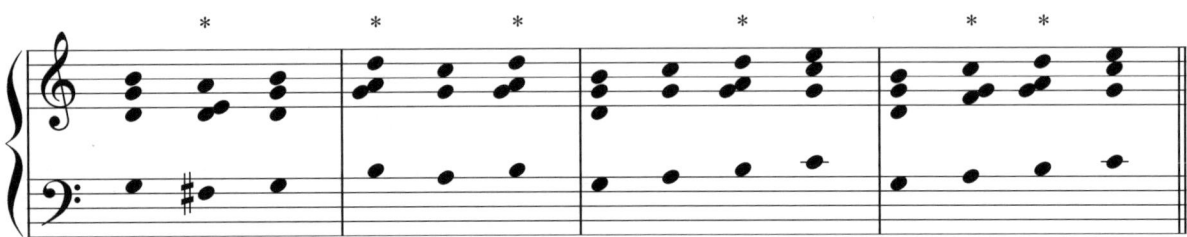

Example 2.24 Added Second Chords Through the Cycle (1, 2, 5 of Major Scale)

C	C D G	D G C	G C D
F	F G C	G C F	C F G
Bb	Bb C F	C F Bb	F Bb C
Eb	Eb F Bb	F Bb Eb	Bb Eb F
Ab	Ab Bb Eb	Bb Eb Ab	Eb Ab Bb
Db	Db Eb Ab	Eb Ab Db	Ab Db Eb
F#	F# G# C#	G# C# F#	C# F# G#
B	B C# F#	C# F# B	F# B C#
E	E F# B	F# B E	B E F#
A	A B E	B E A	E A B
D	D E A	E A D	A D E
G	G A D	A D G	D G A
Bass	**Root Position**	**1ˢᵗ Inversions**	**2ⁿᵈ Inversion**

The chart above is divided into groups of four for easy reading and performing. Practice the four rows or columns as a small group (initially) before attempting the entire cycle.

Playing the Horizontal Rows (across the page)
1. Playing <u>up</u> the chart from the bottom row results in the descending fourth cycle (down a fourth = up a fifth).
2. Playing <u>down</u> the chart rows results in the descending fifth cycle (down a fifth = up a fourth)

In this book and the others in the series, the descending fifth cycle will be more strategic.

Playing the Vertical Columns
1. Play only the root position chords up and down the column
2. Play only the 1st inversion chords up and down the column.
3. Play only the 2nd inversion chords up and down the column.

Example 2.25 A Way to Play Descending Added Seconds Through the Cycle

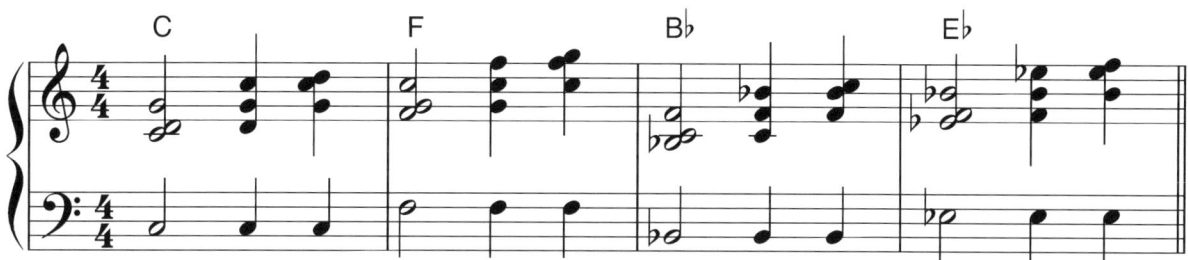

Another practice option is to go to the next closest inversion.

Example 2.26 Going to the Closest Inversion

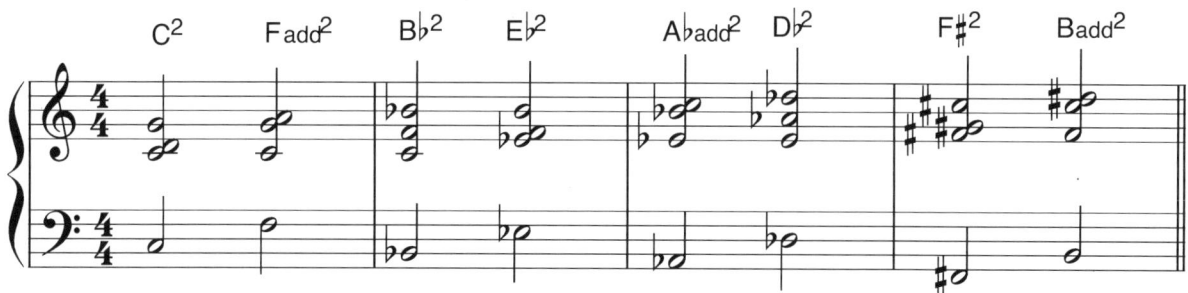

How I did weep, in the Hymns and Canticles, touched to
the quick by the voices of Thy sweet-tuned Church!

The voices flowed into my ears, and the Truth distilled
into my heart, whence the affection of my devotion
overflowed, and tears ran down, and happy was I therein.

Augustine

CHAPTER 3

Added Seconds Walking Up

- 14 pages
- 29 examples

OUTLINE	REPERTOIRE
Walking Up Using Major/Minor Sevenths	Spirit Song Immortal Invisible
Walking Up: 3 Added Second Voicings	We Shall Overcome As the Deer
Walking Up : Songs with Added Seconds	Spirit of God Descend Upon My Heart
Extensions/Drones with Added Seconds	Knowing You Be Thou My Vision
	Give Thanks Great is Thy Faithfulness
	Be Still My Soul Refiner's Fire
	Nothing But the Blood of Jesus

We continue developing added seconds *without* the third in this chapter, but show that *consecutive* added seconds can be employed in the process of walking up the scale.

Added seconds without the third tend to be ambiguous (neither major or minor) because the third is not present. Thus they are also well suited to be employed with drones.

Before we address added seconds that "walk up" the scale, we review open, closed, and shell major and minor sevenths that also walk up the scale.

Walking Up: Using Major &Minor Sevenths

Example 3.1 Four Part, Closed & Open-Spacing Harmony (Spirit Song)

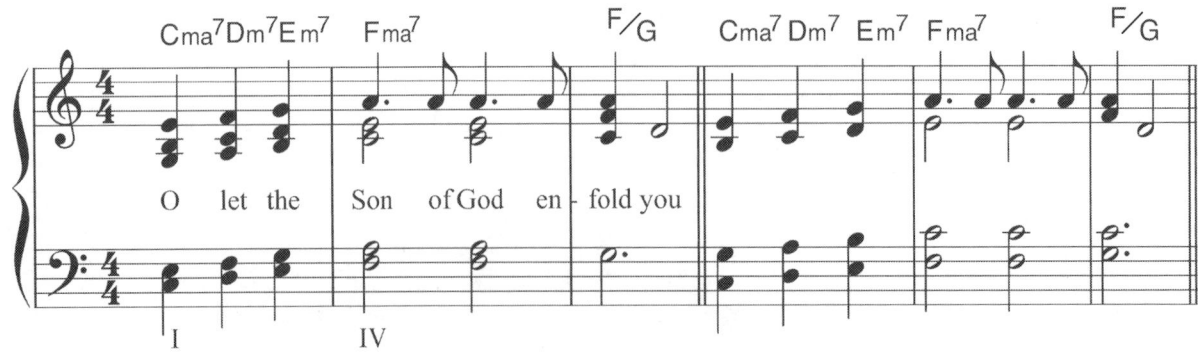

Try it! Play the above in the keys of C, D and E.

Example 3.2 Shell Spacing (*Spirit Song*)

"Shell" spacing retains only the essential notes in chords (the "bare bones"), the root, third, and seventh of the chord (the 5th is omitted).

Try it! These spacings (voicings) are important. Play them in the keys of D, E, F, G, A.

Example 3.3 Spacing for Upper Registers (Upper Octaves)

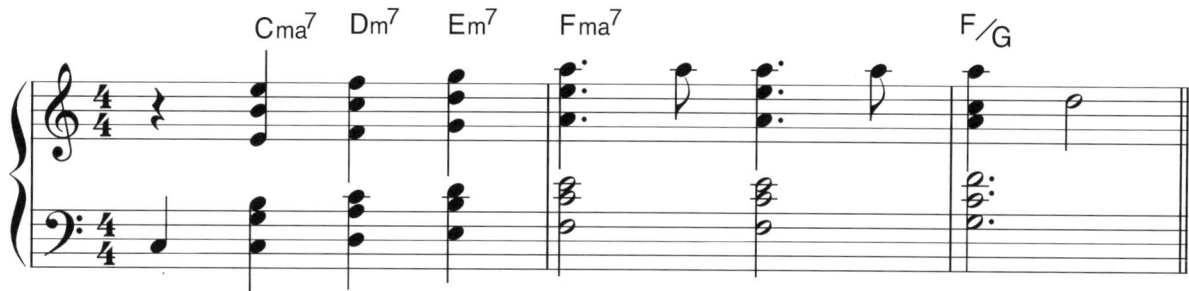

Try it! Play it in the keys of C, D, E, F.

Walking Up: 3 Added Second Voicings

You will find many opportunities to "walk up" when playing songs. Having available at your fingertips a spacing in the middle, low, and upper part of the keyboard will provide you with a repertoire of different nuances and resonances of sound.

The progressions below are a little harder, but students like the sounds.
Notice, below, that two consecutive added seconds are employed.

Example 3.4 Three Spacings Using Added Seconds for Walking Up

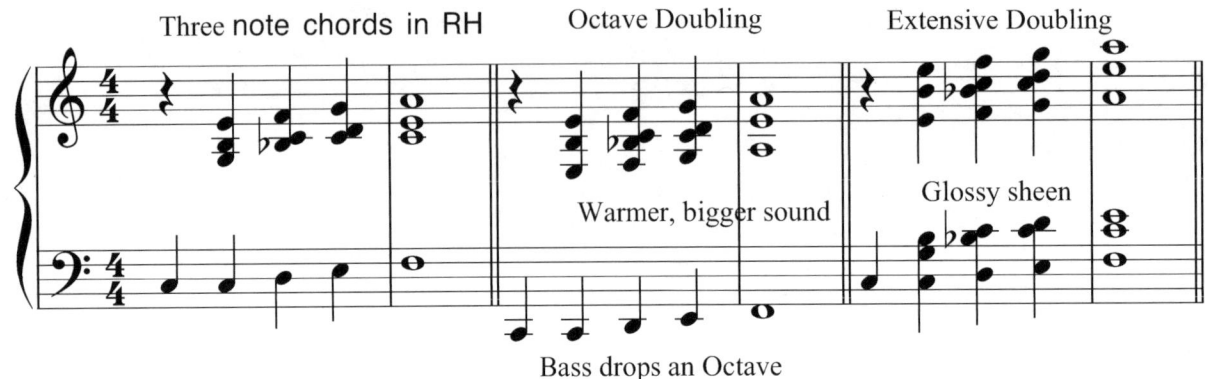

Example 3.5 *Spirit Song* **(Three Notes in RH)).** Play in keys of C,D,E,F,G,A.

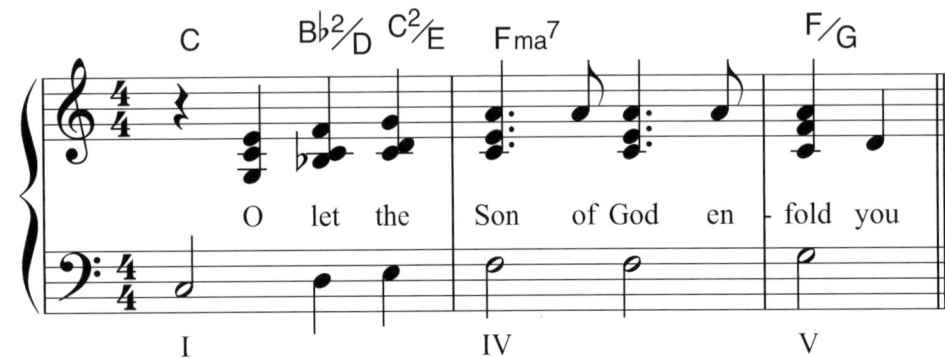

Example 3.6 *Spirit Song* **(Octave in RH; Bass Drops in LH)** Play in C, D, E, F, G.

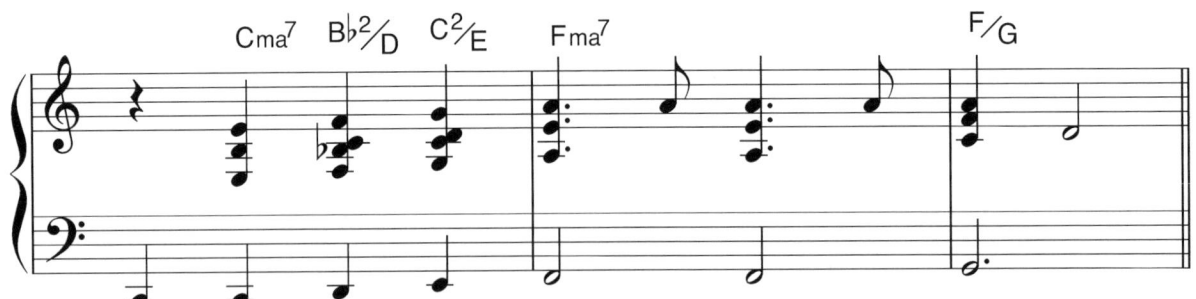

Example 3.7 *Spirit Song* **(Doublings in RH & LH)** Play in C, D, E, F, G, A.

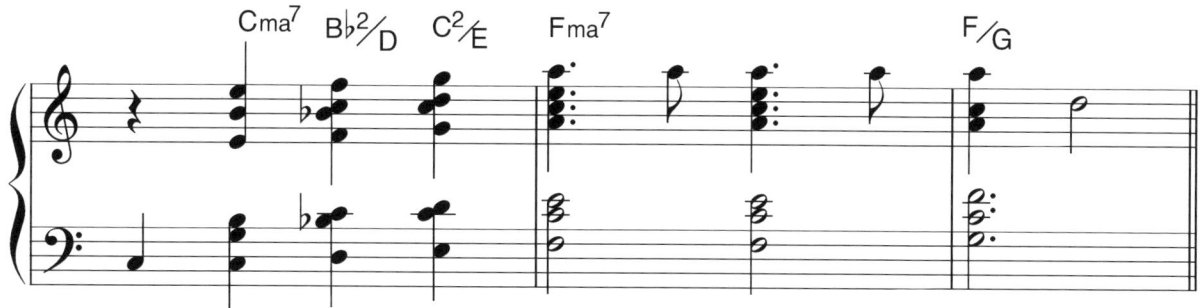

Example 3.8 *Knowing You* **(As Written in Hymnbooks)**

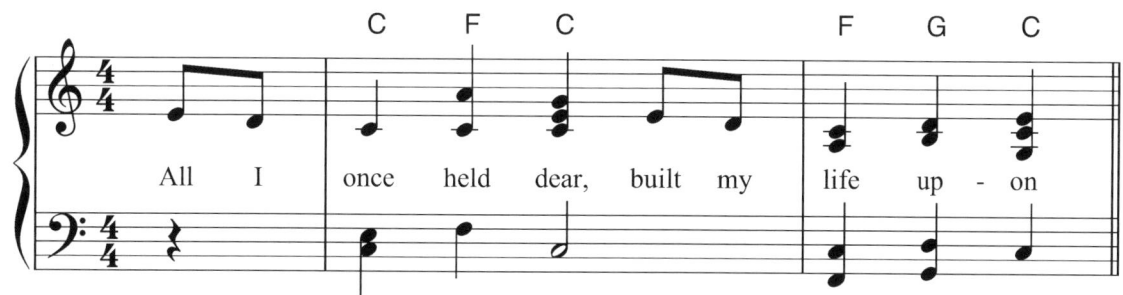

©1989 Graham Kendrick All Rights Reserved. Used by Permission

Example 3.9 *Knowing You* **(Added Seconds with Bass Walking Up)**

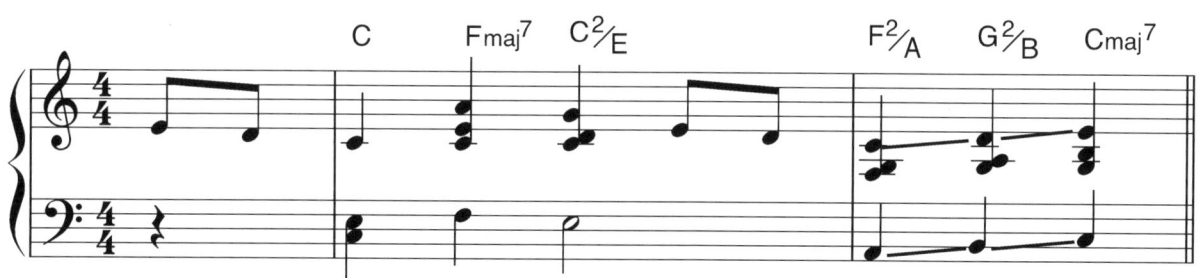

Example 3.10 *Knowing You* **(Same, but with Octave Doublings)**

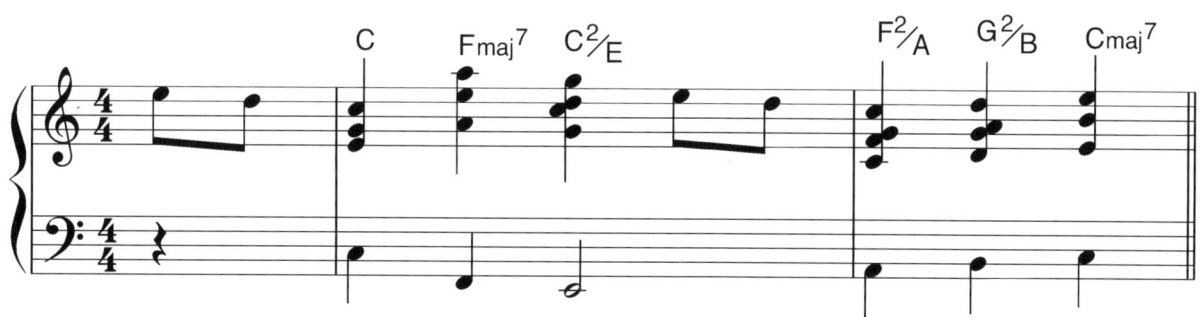

Become comfortable moving material into a different register--particularly the high and low registers. Keyboardists often remain exclusively in the middle. This is limiting.

Example 3.11 *Be Thou My Vision* **(Play with the Three Voicings in C, D, E, F, G, A)**

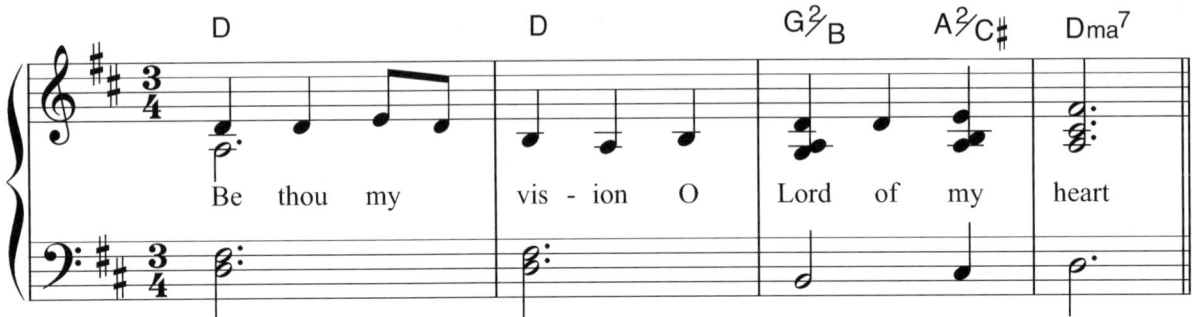

Do it! Play it with the other two voicings (octaves and doubling in LH and RH).

Below, play added seconds at the asterisks.

Example 3.12 *Be Still My Soul* (Play in C, D, and F)

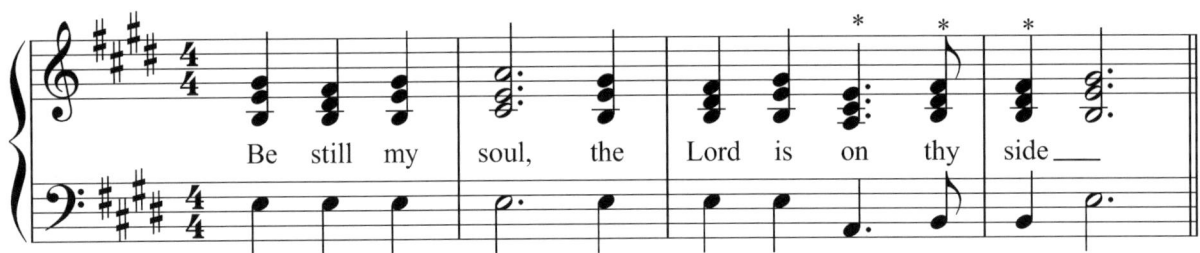

Consider the following option as well.

Example 3.13 *Be Still My Soul* (Play in C, D, and F)

The next exercise presents a problem. See if you can figure it out!

Example 3.14 Play it! Walking Up the Bass Assignment *(Give Thanks)*

This exercise is more challenging. <u>Write</u> a bass "walk up" where the "x" markings occur.
In measures two and three the bass notes should be D, E, F#, G; in measures four and
five, C, D, E, F. Use added second chords with the third in the bass.

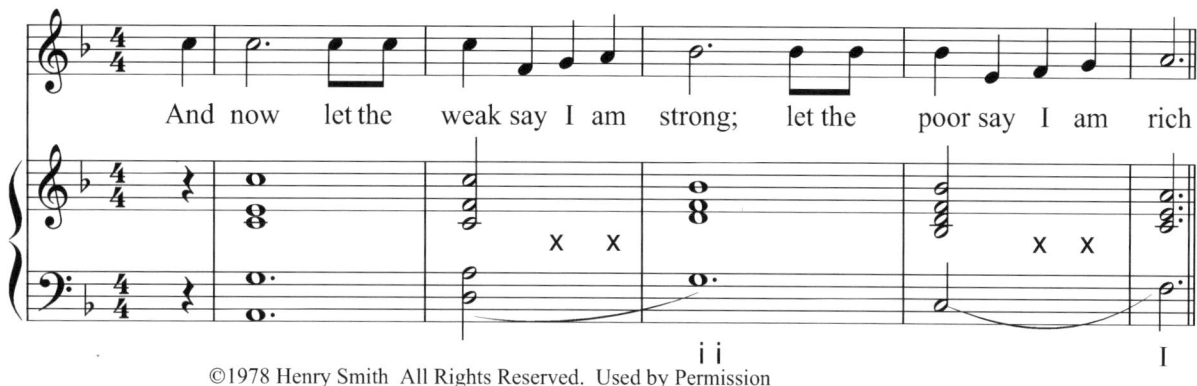

©1978 Henry Smith All Rights Reserved. Used by Permission

Example 3.15 Play it! Solutions to "Walk Up" Bass *(Give Thanks)*

A. Three Note Chords in the Right Hand for the Added Second Chords.

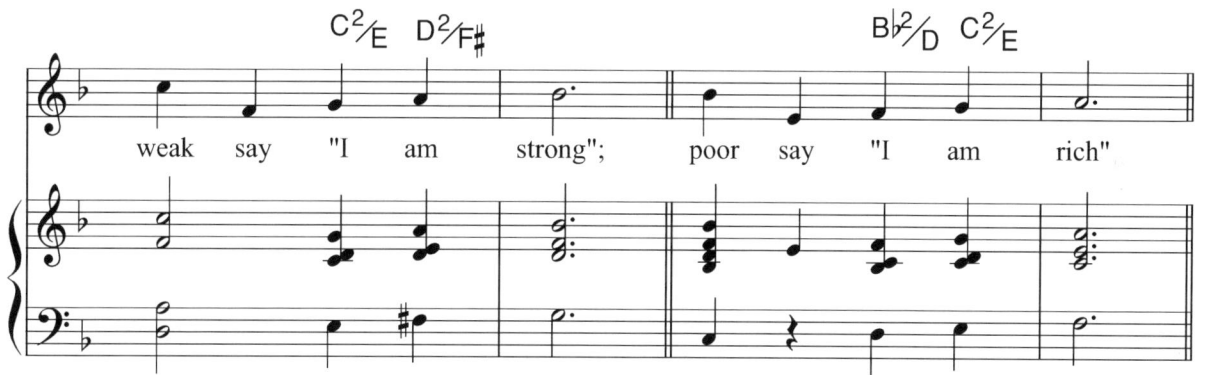

B. Octave Doubling in the Right Hand for the Added Second Chords

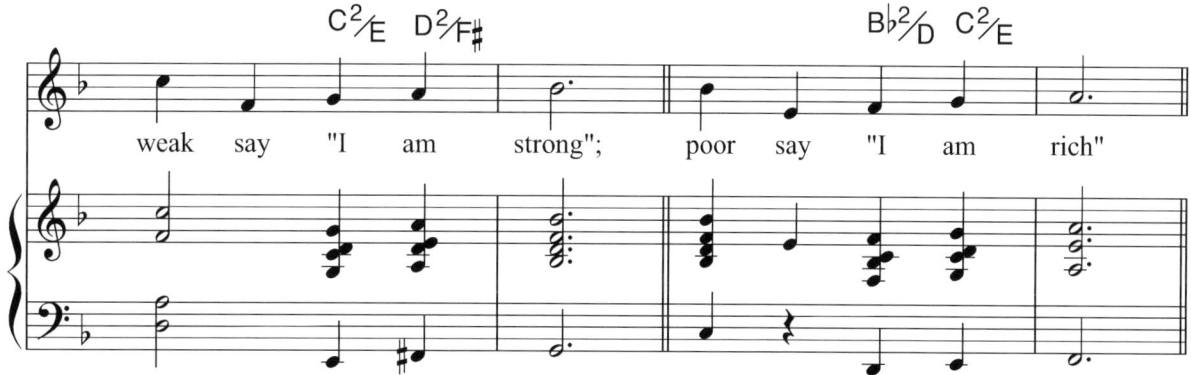

Notice (above), the octave doubling in the right hand warms up the sound.

Added second chords with the *third in the bass* sound particularly good.

C. More Extensive Doublings in Higher Registers

Remember the three types of voicings. Test their usefulness. Apply all three to the various worship songs below.

Example 3.16 *Try it!* **"Walking Up"** *(Nothing but the Blood of Jesus)*

Example 3.17 *Try it!* **"Walking Up"**   *(Spirit Song)* Play in D and C.

Play this excerpt using the three kinds of voicings for the added second chords.

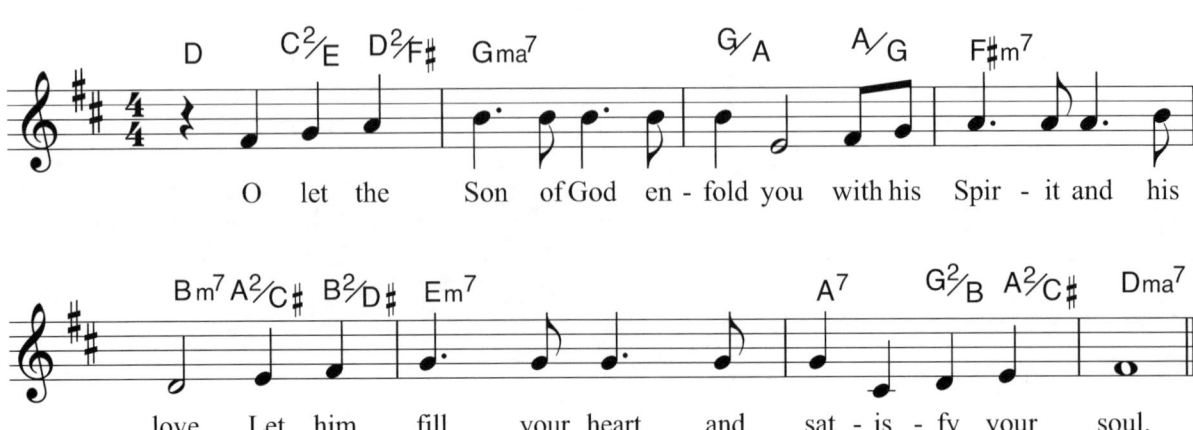

Example 3.18 *Try it!* **Walk Up Using the Three Voicings** *(Great is Thy Faithfulness)*

Try it! Play the excerpt as well in the keys of G and A.

Example 3.19 *Try it!* **Walk Up Using the Three Voicings** *(We Shall Overcome)*

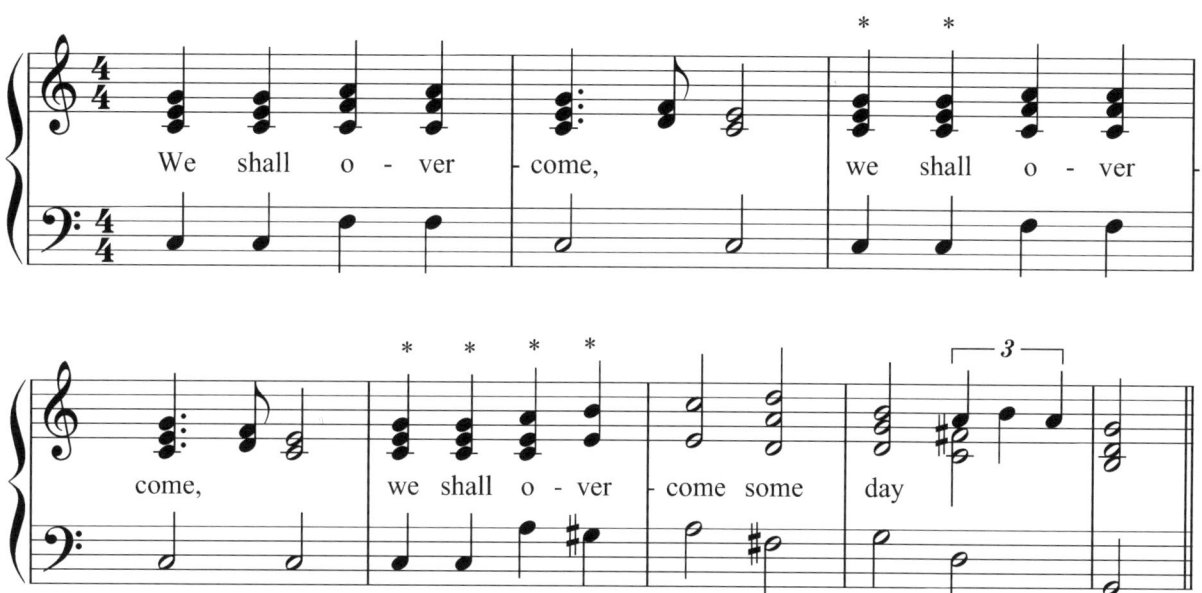

Above, play added second chords with the third in the bass where you see asterisks.
Walk up to the A minor chord in measure 6 (the bass part will be E, F#, G#, A).

Example 3.20 *Try it!* **Walk Up Using the Three Voicings** *(Refiner's Fire)*

Example 3.21 Memorize! Walk Up through the Cycle (Down 5th, Up 4th)

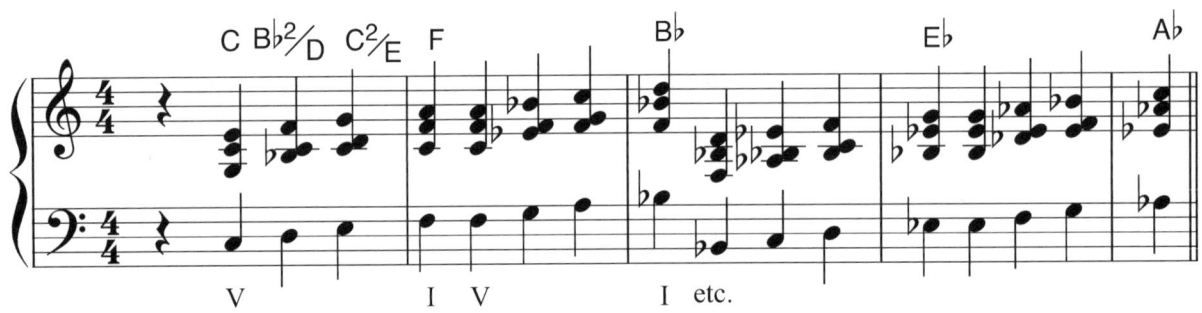

Example 3.22 Memorize! Walk Up the Cycle (Octave Doubling in Right Hand)

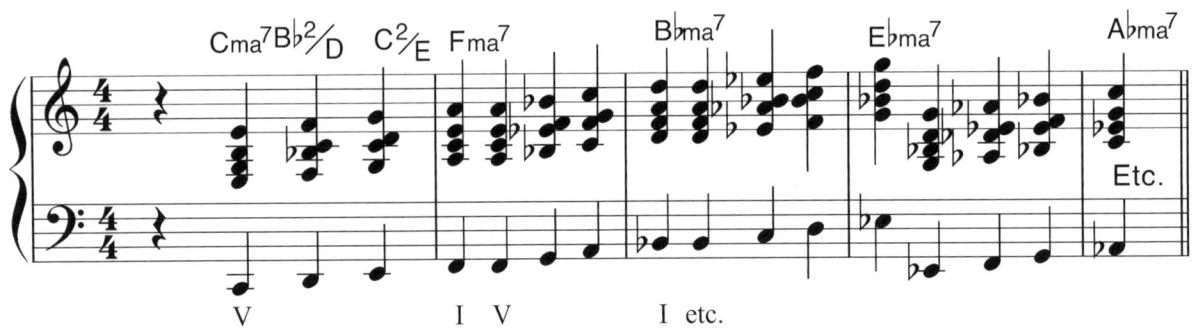

Example 3.23 Memorize! Walk Up the Cycle (Extensive Doubling)

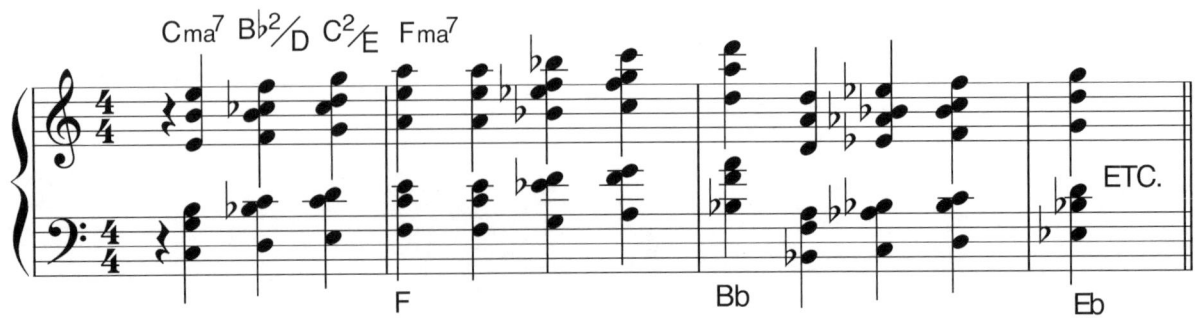

This is a lot of work, but it will help get the sound into your ears, and the shape/feel of the chords into your fingers.

To be effective, we need to have a number of voicings that we can use, readily, instantly, depending on the nature of the piece and the kinds of effects and feelings we are striving to project. Using just these three voicings, alone, can make a big difference.

Below, harmonize the example. First, just chord (no melody). Then chord and sing.

Example 3.24 *Be Thou My Vision* **(Flesh out the Chords)**

Try it! This time integrate the melody (an octave higher than written) with the chords.

Next, see how broken and arpeggiated seconds could be employed in a hymn. Some fingerings are suggested for this much more technical rendition.

Example 3.25 Broken and Arpeggiated Seconds *(Immortal Invisible)*

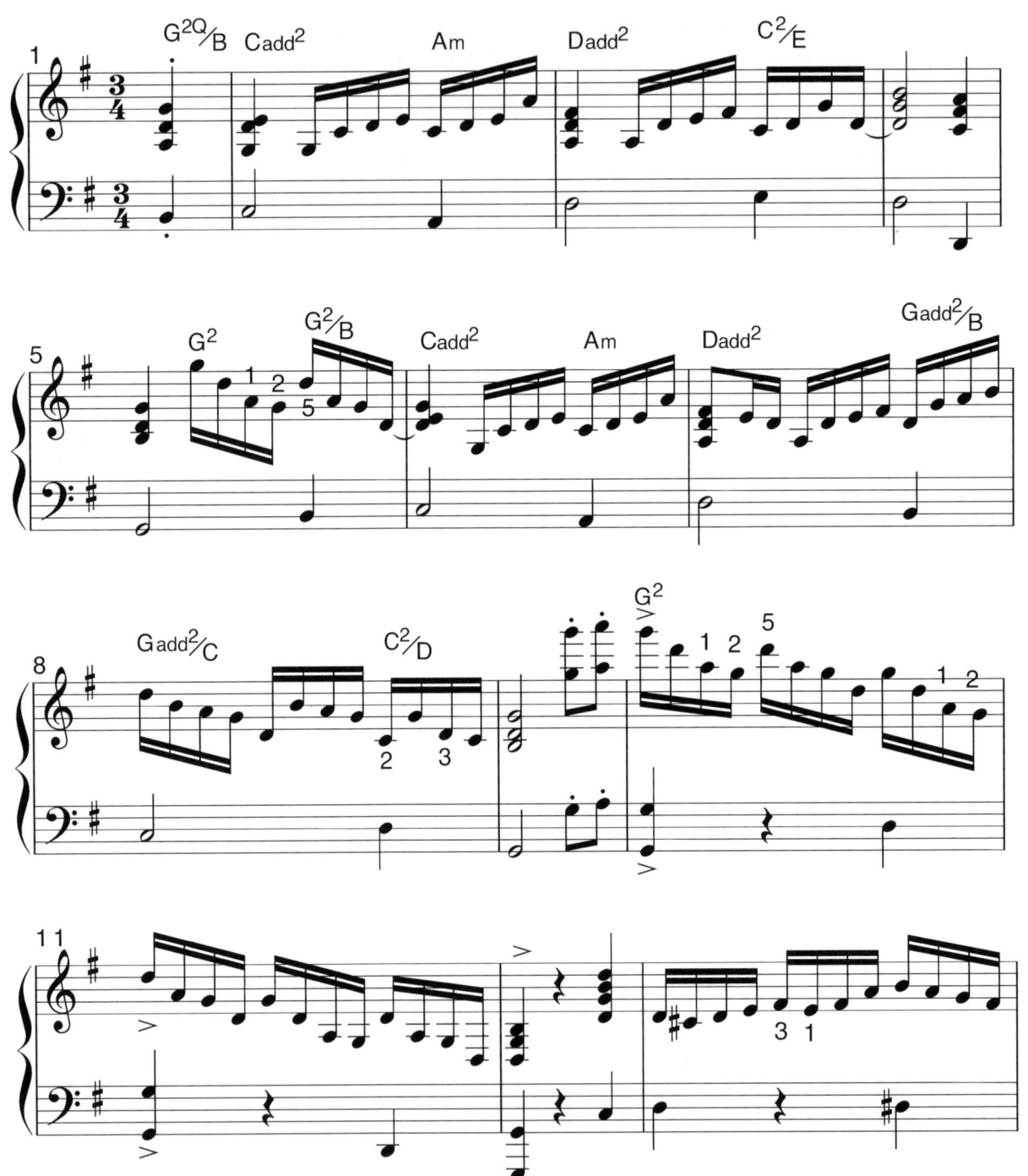

Try it! Sing the lyrics along with the recorded example above.

Extensions/Drones with Seconds

Drone passages (pedals) are popular in today's worship—especially in guitar-led worship. Let's see why added second chords *without a third* function better in droning contexts than major triads. Below, see a comparison between a C major chord (the drone) and a C2 or C5 sound (also a drone) when the bass notes change. All the chords from both examples below are useable.

Example 3.26 C vs C2 Drone

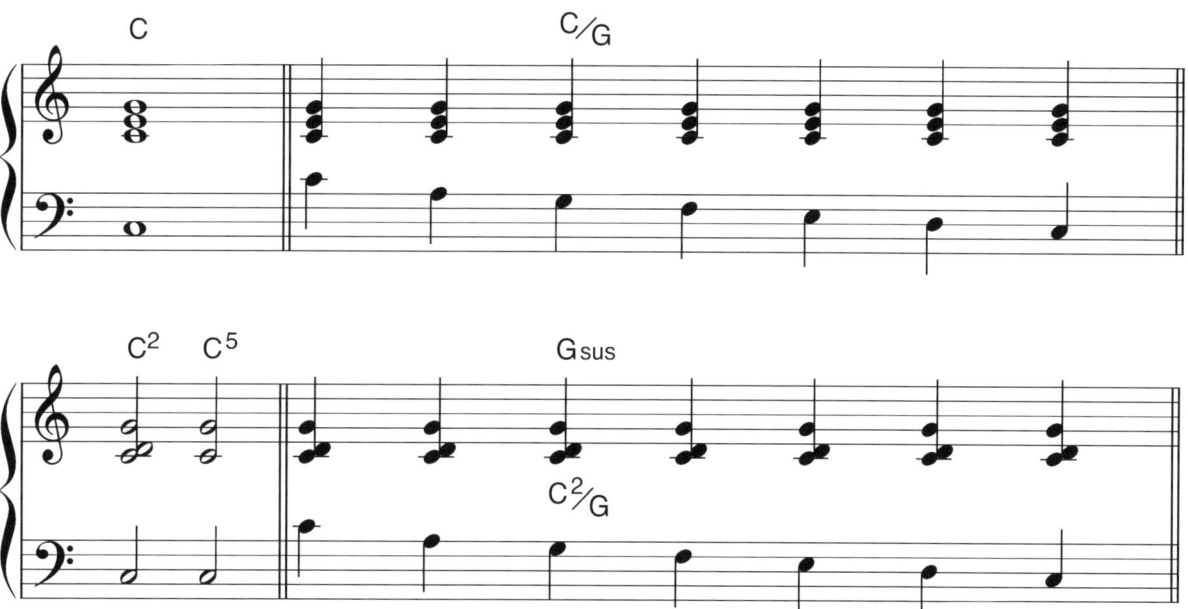

Compare particularly the chords with G in the bass. C/G has one meaning, a C chord in second inversion—or expressed differently, a C chord with the fifth in the bass.

On the other hand, the C2/G is *more ambiguous* and also more flexible. It can have *two* meanings—(1) a I chord with the fifth in the bass, or (2) a V chord (Gsus) with the root in the bass. That is, the C2/G can have a dominant function, whereas the C/G can't.

Example 3.27 Asterisk Chord Can Have Two Meanings

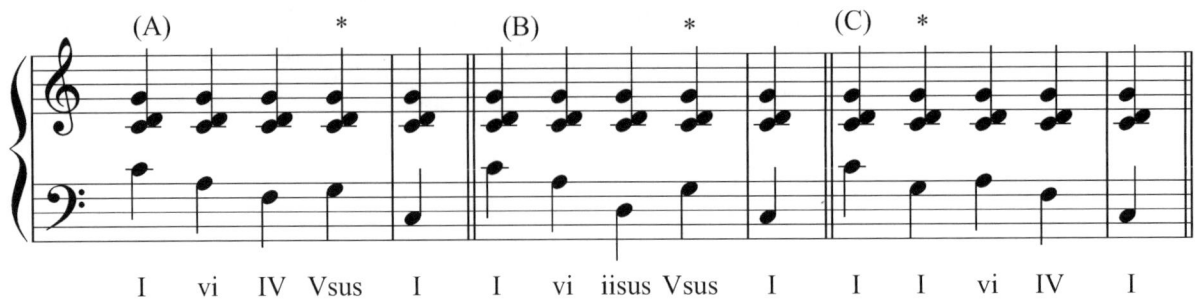

In (A) and (B) above, the chords with G in the bass act as V chords in a V-I cadence, whereas in (C) the second chord (C2/G) clearly functions as a I6/4 chord (not a V).

When using C2 drones, any number of chord progressions—even traditional chord progressions such as I vi ii V I—can be created without any clashes. For these reasons, guitarists often drone on an added second chord without a third, or an open fifth.

Example 3.28 *As the Deer* (Drone Version)

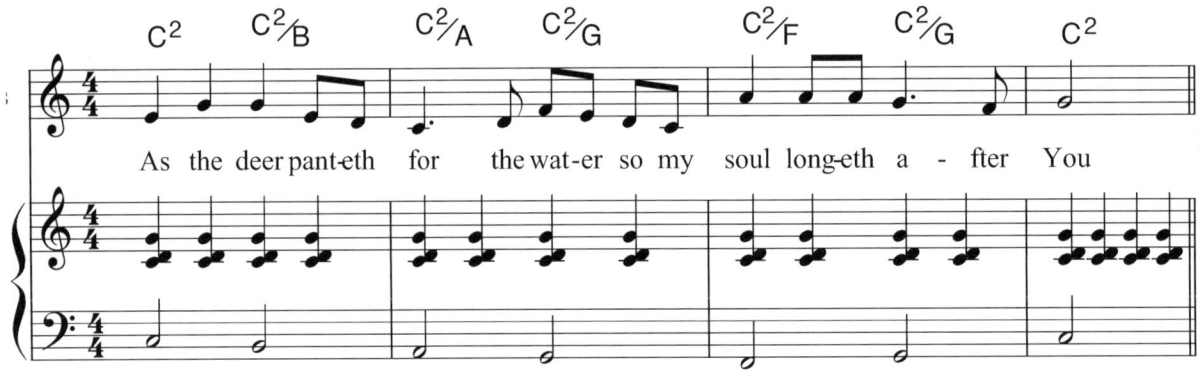

Example 3.29 *Be Thou My Vision* (Drone Version)

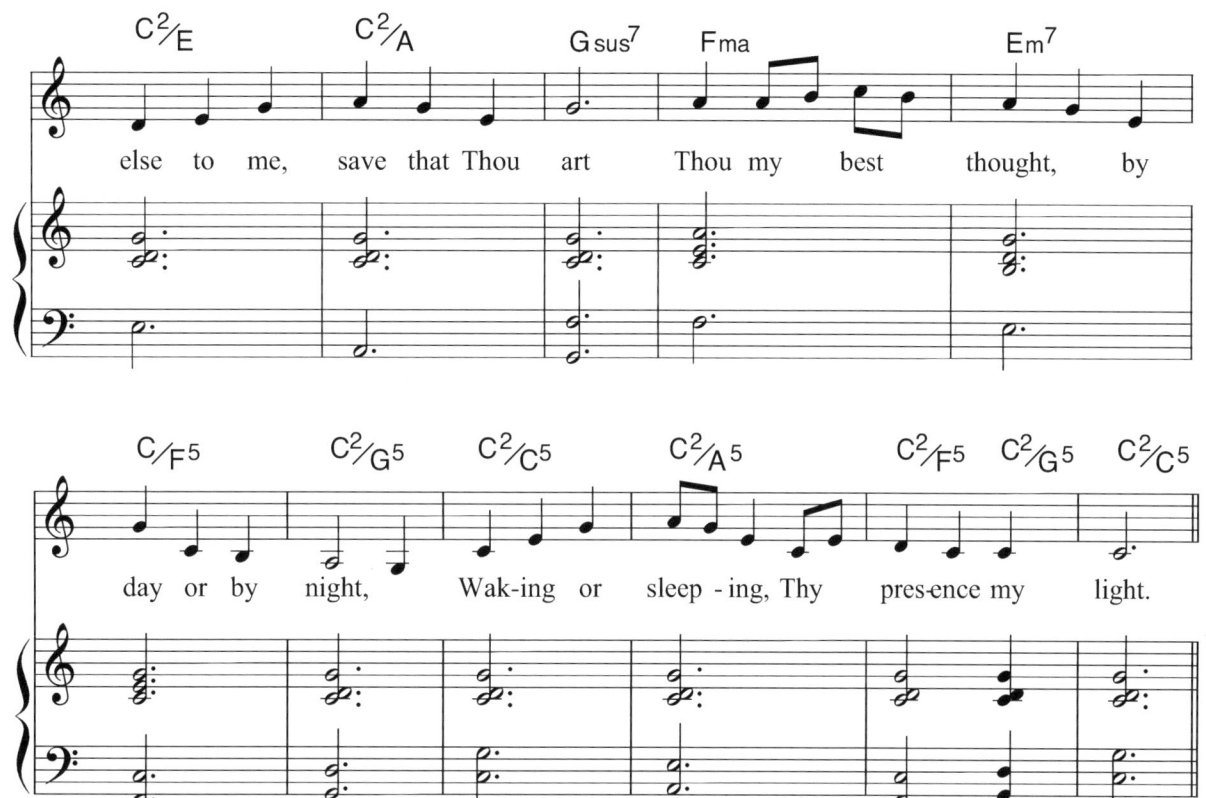

A Trap We Often Fall Into

Our identity as musicians can be driven more by our last performance (good or bad) than our standing in Christ, as Rory Noland shares below.

Many of us work hard at keeping up the impression that we have it all together. This is a trap that a lot of performers fall into because we always have to put on our best face. We have to appear confident even when we're not. This self-generated confidence then causes us to be defensive toward anyone with constructive criticism. Sometimes it feels as if whether we're gifted or not depends on how people respond to our latest endeavor. "You're only as good as your latest outing," is not true, but sometimes that's how it feels.

Rory Noland *(The Heart of the Artist)*

Added Seconds with Thirds

- 13 pages
- 25 examples

OUTLINE	REPERTOIRE
The Difference between Dadd2 and D2	Give Thanks Jesus Your Name
Added Second Chords *with* the Third	The Old Rugged Cross
Added Second Fills	Amazing Grace Holy Holy Holy
As the Deer	The Lord's My Shepherd
The Faithful Worship Leader	As The Deer

The Difference between D2 and Dadd2

First, let's look at voicings of the D2 symbol (without the third).

Example 4.1 D2 Voicings (With <u>No</u> Third Above the Bass)

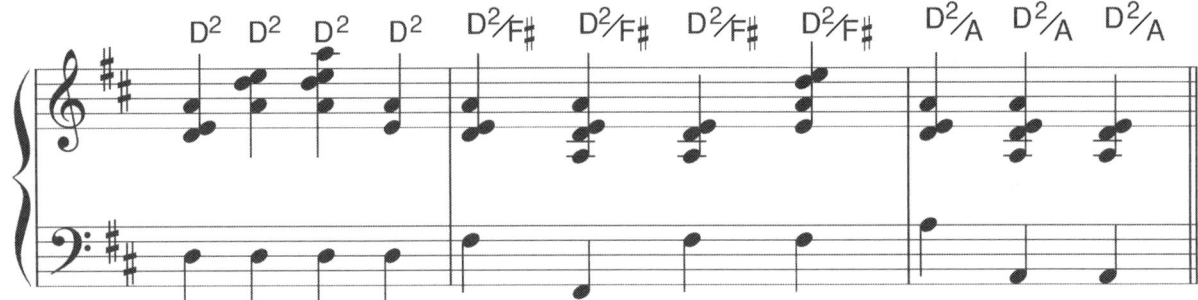

However, the Dadd2 symbol instructs the performer to play a D triad (D, F#, A) and to *add* a major second (E) to that composite sound. Here are some possible spacings.

Example 4.2 Dadd2 Voicings (<u>With</u> the Third) in Root & Second Inversion

Above, in chord 3, an F# is included in the tenor but not the RH. Why?—doubling the F# (the third) with both hands results in a less clean sound.

Comparing the two types, the D2 sounds crisper and has *more bite* than the Dadd2 sound. On the other hand, the presence of the third in the Dadd2 creates *warmth* and helps the chord to blend with other chords.

Added Seconds *with* the Third

In order to establish added seconds *with* the third firmly in your mind, play the inversions (1235; 2351; 3512; 5123; 1235) through the cycle of fifths (up a 4th or down a 5th)—C, F, Bb, Eb, Ab, Db, Gb, B, E, A, D, G, C. Vary the rhythms.

Example 4.3 Play through the Cycle of Fifths (Major Quality)

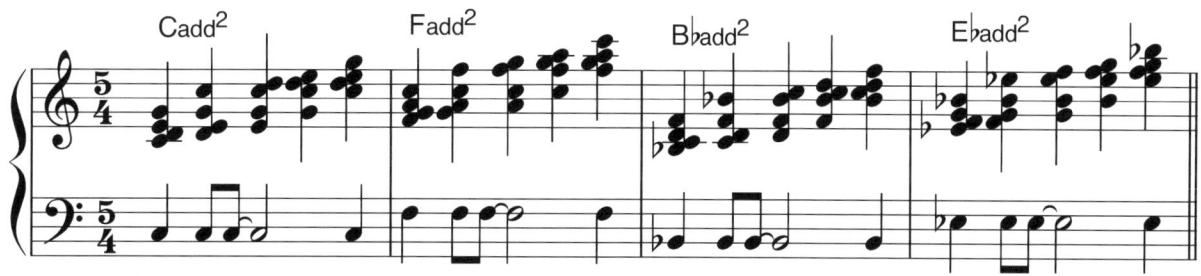

Example 4.4 Play the Cycle of Fifths (Minor Quality)

Note, the added second is always a major second—never a minor second. Let's apply this idea by starting simply as possible. The added second chord doubles the bass.

Example 4.5 *Give Thanks*

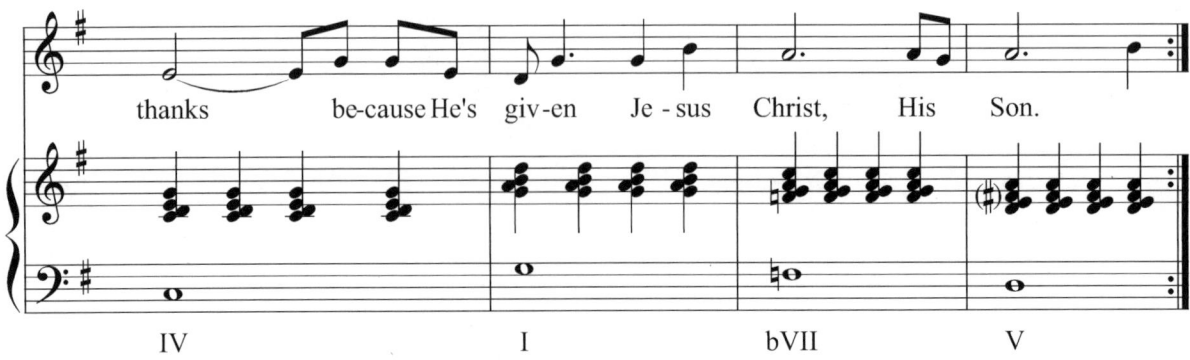

Play it! Perform this "chording" in the keys of C, D, E, and A. Avoid looking at the notation above. Instead, focus on the sequence of Roman numerals below:

I V vi iii IV I bVII V

Example 4.6 Give Thanks (With more Variety)

Added Second Fills

Added second material can be used as fills when the chords are linearized.

Example 4.7 Added Second Fills

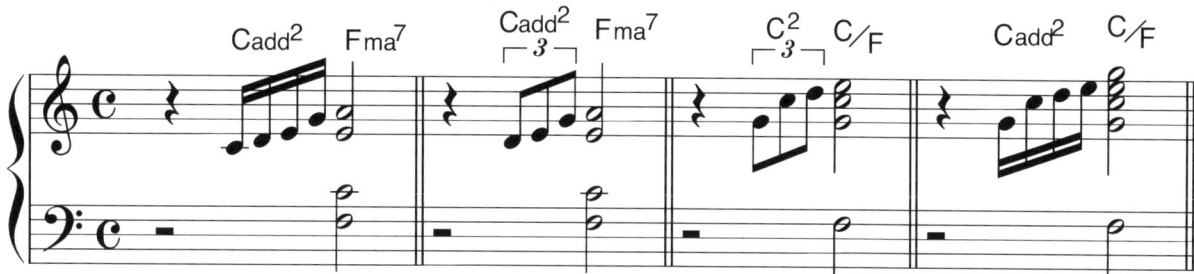

Try it! Now, add some melodic movement to *Give Thanks,* breaking up the added second chord or creating arpeggios (as below).

Example 4.8 Scalar and Broken-Chord Added Second Fills *(Give Thanks)*

Example 4.9 Arpeggiated Fills *(Give Thanks)*

Try it!   Create your own arpeggiated fills for *Give Thanks.*

Example 4.10 *Jesus Your Name* **(Warm Result)**

We could also use various permutations of the 1235 and 2351 as fills (as below)—experiment! Create permuted fills for *Jesus Your Name*.

Below are added second fills. Play them and add the chordal accompaniment as well. Then create some of your own.

Example 4.11 The 1235 and 2351 Shapes Used as Fills

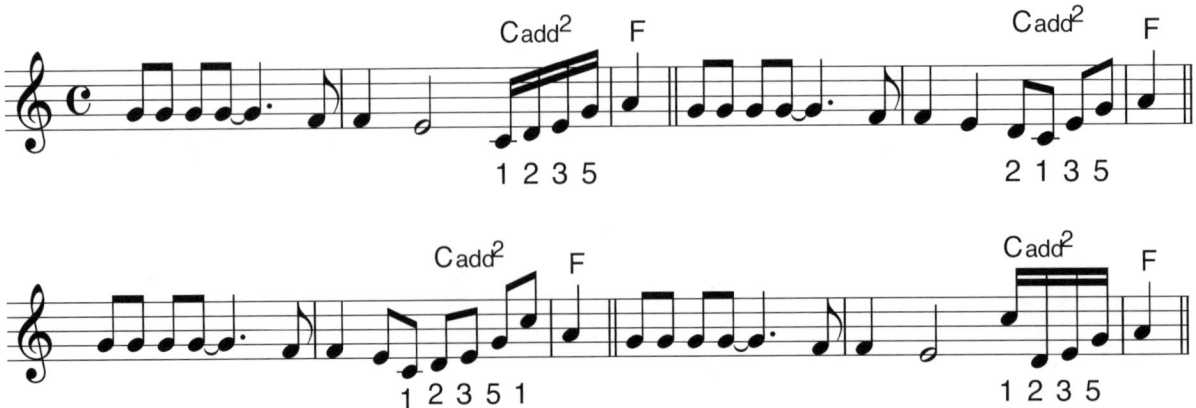

Example 4.12 Fill-in the Added Second Chords *(The Old Rugged Cross)*

Example 4.13 Model Example *(The Old Rugged Cross)*

Play it! Transpose the excerpt above into the keys of Bb and A.
Below, contribute at least two added second fills.

Example 4.14 Play the Added Seconds and Add Fills *(Amazing Grace)*

Example 4.15 Possible Answer to Above

Example 4.16 *Holy Holy Holy   Create 2 Added Second Fills*

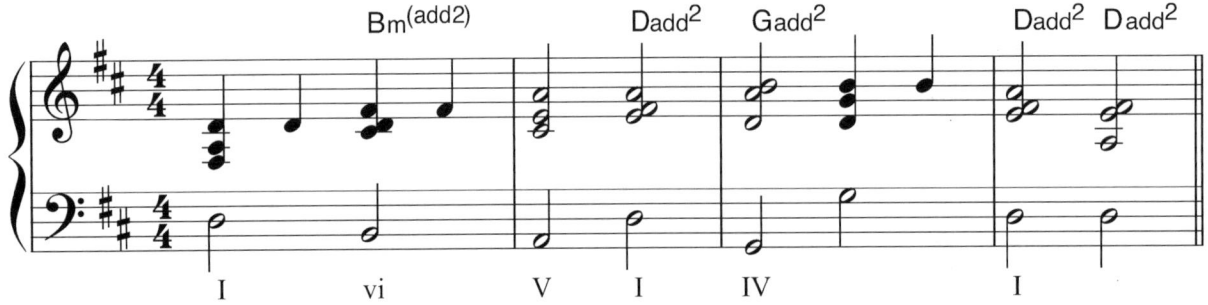

Play it in the keys of C, E, and G using Roman numerals as your guide.

Example 4.17 Rocking Motion with Pastoral Feeling *(The Lord's My Shepherd)*

Measure one employs a Dadd2, but when the bass moves to F# (m.2), the cleaner D2 is used in the right hand. Test this out for your self. Play a Dadd2 and then a D2 in measure two and compare the difference.

Above, the rocking motion has a pastoral effect. The RH third (F# in m.1) contributes warmth. Ms.1 & 2 use the 1235 shape, while m.3 employs the 5123 shape.

Example 4.18 Combination: Rocking Motion & Added Second Fills *(Give Thanks)*

Example 4.19 Combine Rocking Motion with Added Second Fills *(Give Thanks)*

As the Deer

Another wrinkle. See asterisks. The added second (added 9th) is approached by an arpeggiated leap in the LH. A nice effect! Also look at measure 2, beats 2 and 4. The added second chord (B C E) resolves while the root, the bass note (A), is sustained by the pedal. The G on beat 3 is a passing note (on the way to F).

Example 4.20 Added Seconds in the LH Transverse a Ninth

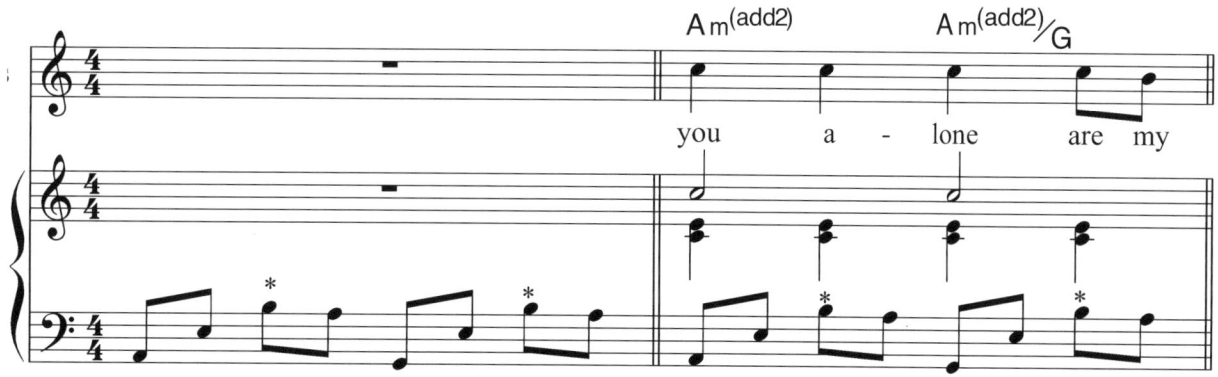

Below, the longer excerpt uses added seconds with and without the third. The rocking motion helps create a feeling of longing. Note measures 5 and 9 where the added second is intensified emotionally by means of the leap in the bass of a major ninth (A to B).

Try it! Complete the example below. Create interesting lines.

Example 4.21 *As the Deer*

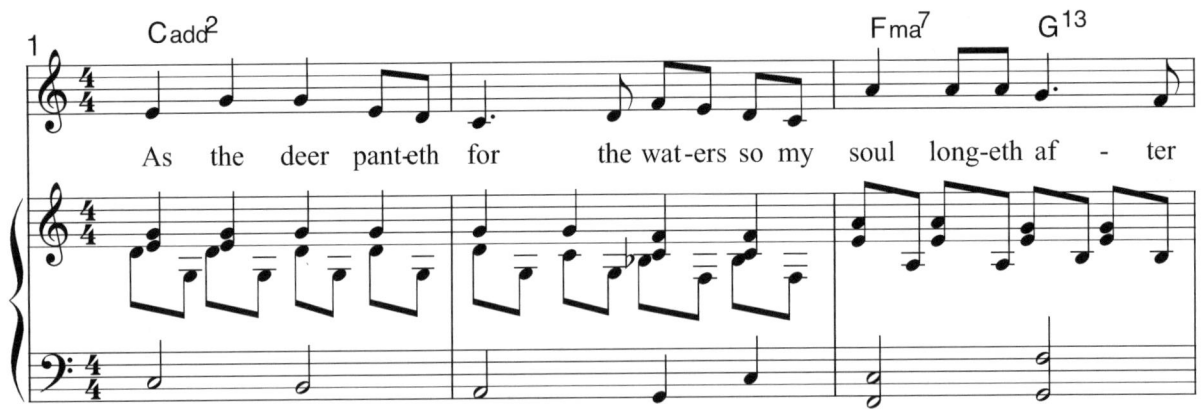

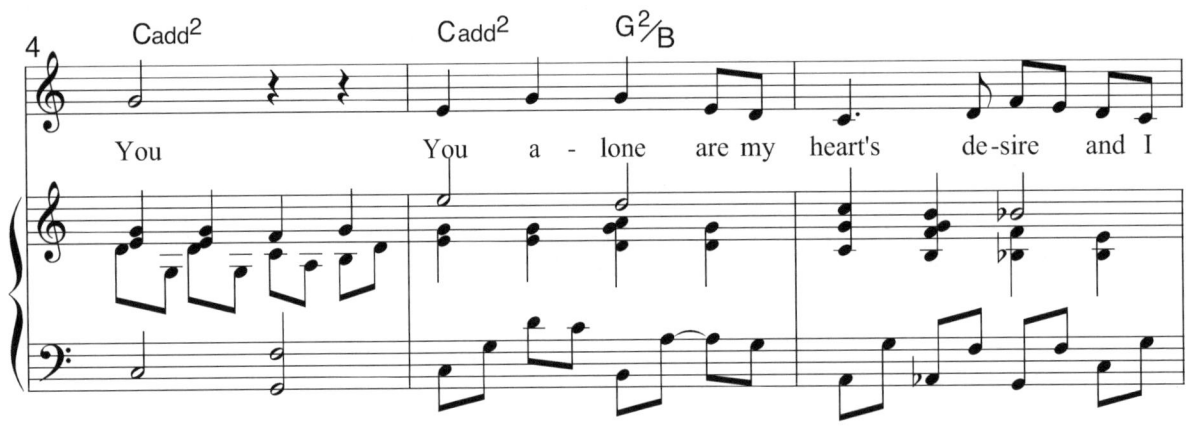

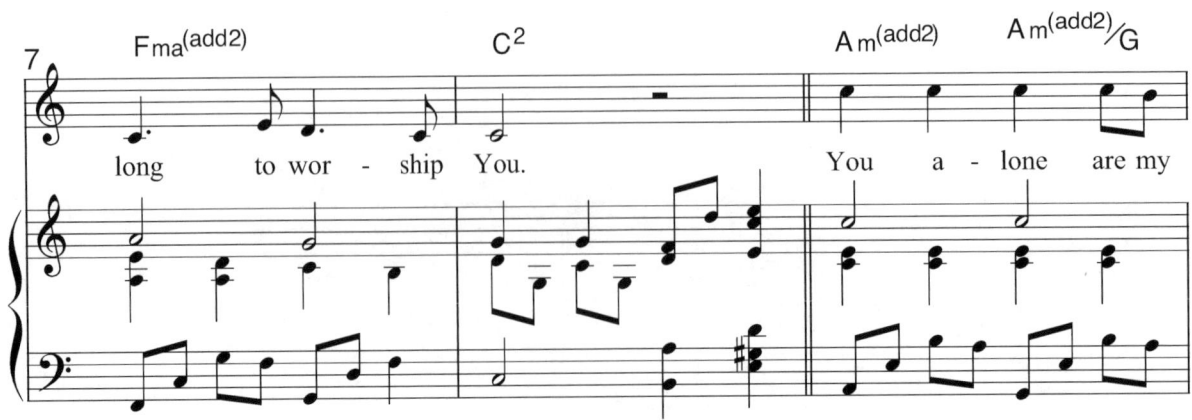

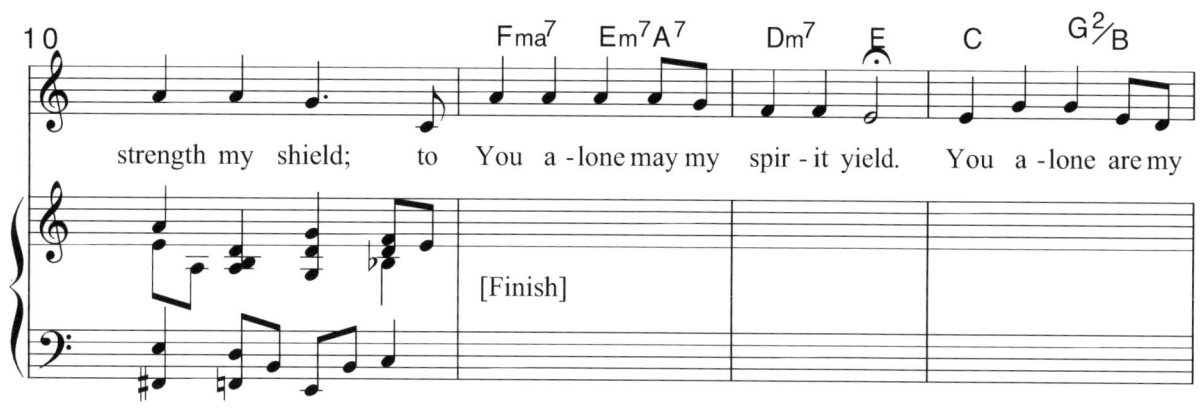

Example 4.22 Realize the Lead Sheet *(As the Deer)*

Below is a possible realization of the Lead Sheet above, with a few minor changes.

Example 4.23 Basic Realization *(As the Deer)* **Improvise!**

Do it! Improvise. Attack the above piece in these ways:
(1) Practice the chord changes until they are fluent.
(2) Sing and play the example.
(3) Create fills of various kinds and thus add energy and atmosphere to the piece.
(4) Then play the song more elaborately as a (a) solo and (b) as a possible accompaniment, using your fills to complement an imaginary live singer.

Example 4.24 Transition to the Chorus *(As the Deer)*

The transition to the chorus (m. 8) deserves our attention if we want the congregation to sing out on the high C ("You alone"). We have a whole measure (4 beats) to provide a fill. Create 5 different ways to play that measure and a couple following. To spark your imagination, you are provided you with some harmonic variations below.

Example 4.25 Possibility Worked Out (based on m.2 variation directly above)

A faithful worship leader
magnifies the greatness of God in Jesus Christ
through the power of the Holy Spirit
by skillfully combining God's Word with music,
thereby motivating the gathered church
to proclaim the gospel.
Bob Kauflin *(Worship Matters)*

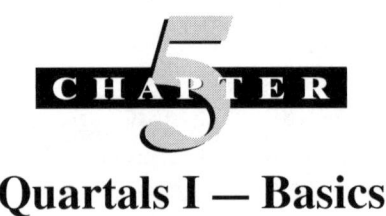

Quartals I — Basics

- 12 pages
- 25 examples

OUTLINE	REPERTOIRE
Quartal Chords (258)	Emmanuel More Precious Than Silver
Using Added Seconds and Quartals	His Name is Wonderful
Quartal Chord Substitutions	Refiner's Fire Great is the Lord
Answers	Spirit of God Descend Upon My Heart
	Be Exalted O God Shout to the Lord
	Sing Praise to God Who Reigns Above
	Great is Thy Faithfulness
	The Solid Rock Holy Holy Holy

In this chapter we continue to build on the added seconds learned in the previous chapter, but our focus will turn more to the introduction of quartal chords—chords comprised of perfects fourths.

Like added seconds, quartals are useful when playing congregationally, accompanying soloists, improvising in a band, and when soloing. They have wide applicability.

The color (sound) of quartal chords, however, is distinctly unique, modern, and instantly recognizable. Think of them as a *coloristic enhancement* to traditional harmony and contemporary practice. They need not disrupt or jar the basic harmonic structure.

We'll work directly from the published versions of hymns and choruses and show you how to modify them. You'll get practice creating your own alternatives.

Quartal Chords (258)

Traditional harmony is tertian (composed of thirds). The concept of quartal harmony in this book is limited to chords composed of intervals of a *"perfect fourth"* (that is, no augmented fourths or tri-tones).

Notice the *second chord* below (2,5,8) has a sound distinct from the other two. For this reason, we've given it ***our unique, custom symbol C2Q,*** which means it can be derived from a C2 chord, and that it is composed of perfect fourths (quartals or "Q").

Example 5.1 Unique, Custom Symbol (C2Q)

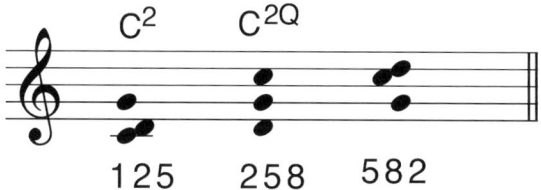

Chords typically take their name from the root note (C above). However, in the second chord above, the lowest tone (D) is an added second (a color note), while the soprano is the root. Because the soprano functions as the root, we must call it a C2Q, not a D2Q.

Major quartal chords frequently occur on scale degree I, IV, or V. The root, third, or fifth of the chord can be in the bass. All three work. Which sounds best to you? Quartals with the root, third, or fifth in the bass?

Example 5.2 Quartals on Scale Degrees I, IV, V

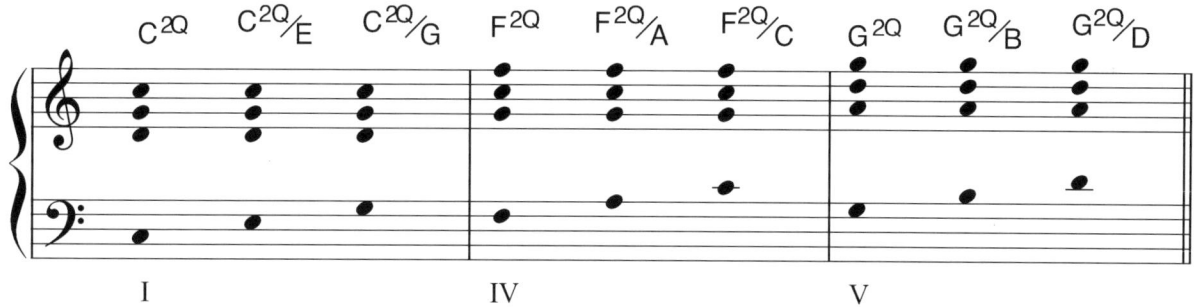

Above, the quartals are the three-note, stacked chords in the RH.
Below, keep the root of the quartal in the soprano. Keep the root of the chord in the bass.

Example 5.3 Write it! Quartals with the Root in the Bass

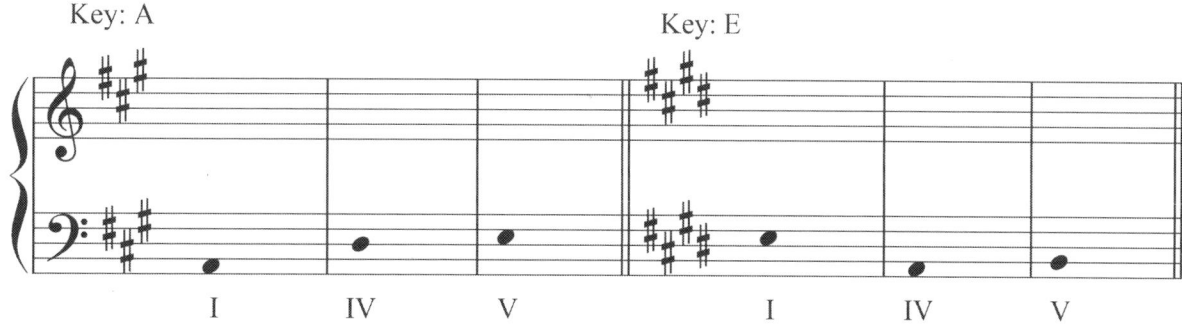

Example 5.4 Write it! Quartals with the Third in the Bass

Practice writing quartals in the right hand with the third in the bass (already supplied).
Keep the root in the soprano. Indicate the appropriate Pop symbol.

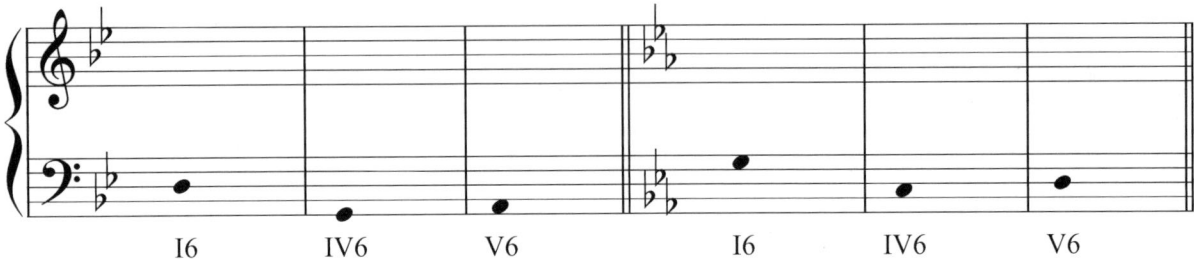

Quartals function similarly to added second chords, as demonstrated below.

Example 5.5 Perform it! Test the Sound

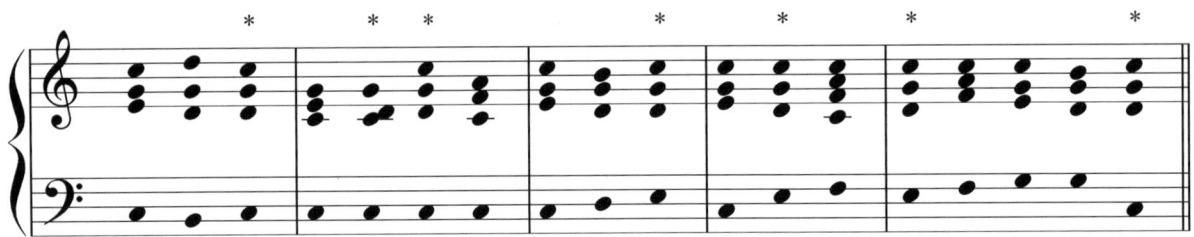

Let's apply that idea to a couple of songs.

Example 5.6 *Emmanuel.* I6 to IV movement in the bass. Play in D, E, F, G.

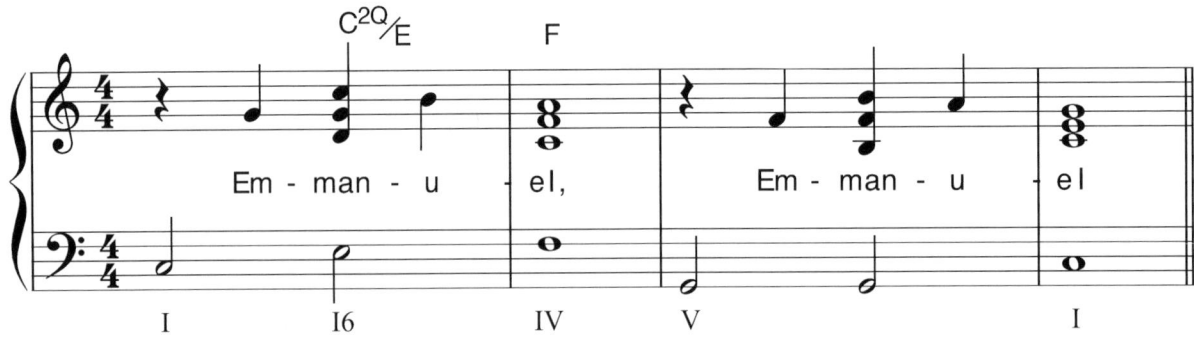

Example 5.7 *His Name is Wonderful.* **Bass movement (V6 to I). Play in D, E, and G.**

Example 5.8 *Be Exalted O God* **Bass Movement (V6 to I, V6 to IV6 to V7)**

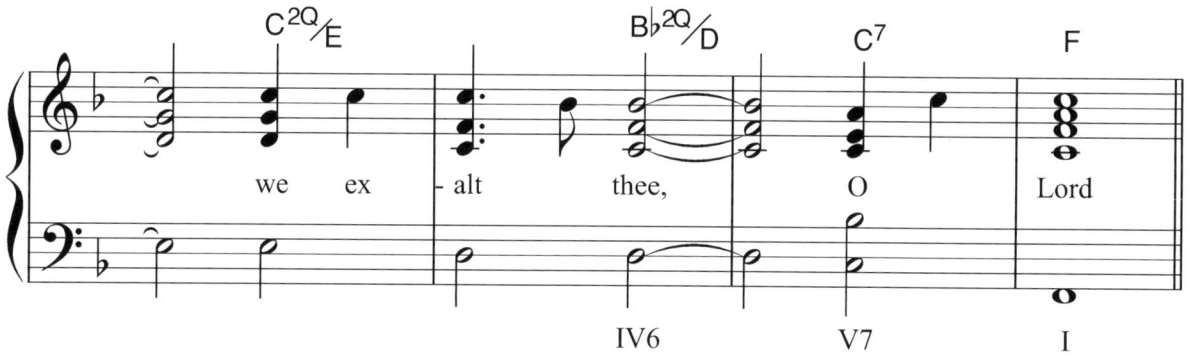

Using Added Seconds and Quartals

Example 5.9 Hymnbook Version of *More Precious Than Silver*

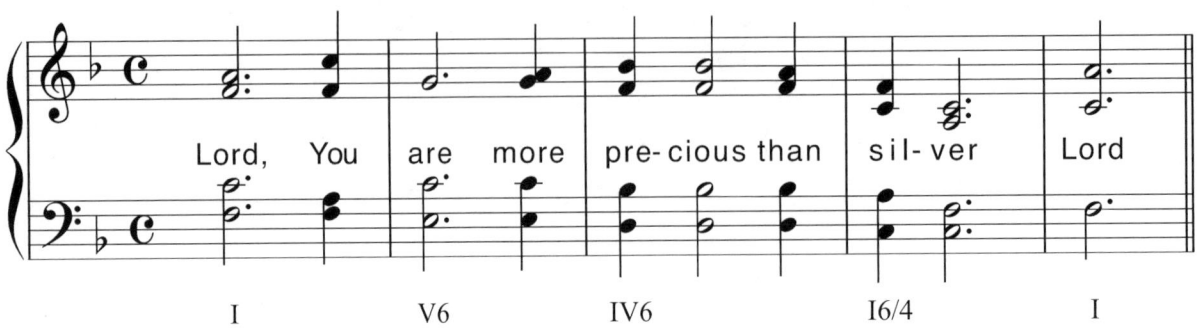

Notice (above) the movement in the bass (F-C). Bass lines are so important in creating beautiful music. Recast this excerpt with added seconds and quartals, placing single bass notes in the left hand and three or four note chords in the right hand. When you're done, look below.

Example 5.10 Quartal and Added Second Substitutions *(More Precious Than Silver)*

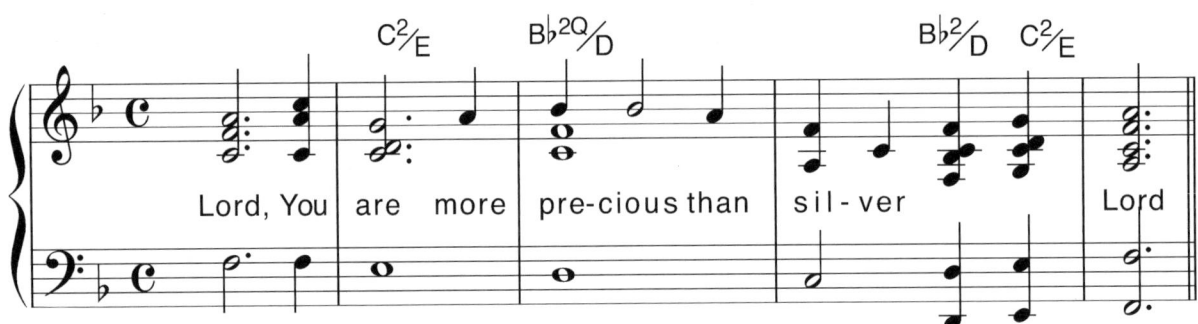

Focus on the last two added second chords above. They act as a kind of fill, walking up from C to F (in the bass). Notice the bass and soprano notes are both doubled, which gives the chords strength and warmth. This "walking up" can be used effectively again and again. Memorize the feel of walking up the scale with added seconds.

Improvise! Play (and sing) the above example in the keys of E, F, and G.

Quartal Chord Substitutions

Now let's apply quartal chords (also called "fourth chords") to some hymn and chorus fragments. Below, change the chords to fit the written-in symbol substitution.

Example 5.11 *Refiner's Fire.* **Play it in the keys of C, D, E, F, G, and A.**

Example 5.12 *Great is the Lord* **Play it in the keys of C, D, E, F, G, and A.**

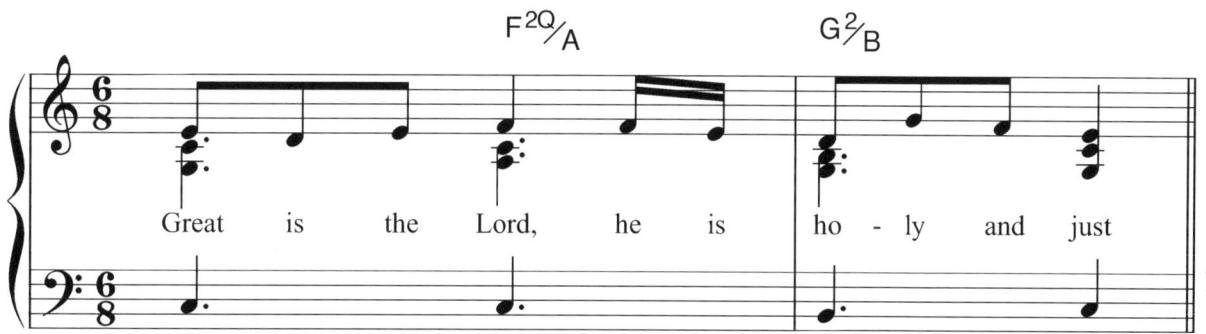

Below, can you create a quartal chord on the word "thanks?"

Example 5.13 *Be Exalted, O God*

The harmony goes from a C to an F/C to a C chord—with a pedal (C) in the bass.

Idea: whenever you see the root of a major triad in the soprano, a quartal chord substitution is probably a possibility. Above, the root of the F chord is in the soprano.

Example 5.14 Quartal Substitution *(Be Exalted, O God)* **Play in D,E,F,G, A.**

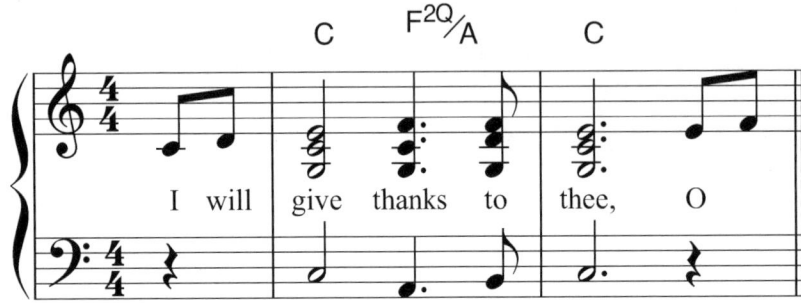

Try it! An F quartal chord substitution results in a more modern sound.
Close the book. Play the above in D, E, F, G, and A major. A good way to learn how to think in music is to take a short phrase (like the above) and play it in various keys.
Play it. Play and say out loud the Roman Numerals. Play & sing the words.

The exercise below should help make the process of learning the quartal chords easier.

Example 5.15 Quartal Exercise (Play through Cycle: Down 5ᵗʰ, Up 4th)

See m. 1 above. The bass moves from E to F, from an altered V6 to a I chord.

Example 5.16 F Substitution *(Spirit of God Descend Upon My Heart)*

Below, a two-measure excerpt is repeated. Could a quartal substitution be integrated into the first two measures? Yes. The first step involves sensing that the F chord (of measure four) could be substituted for the G7/B (measure two).

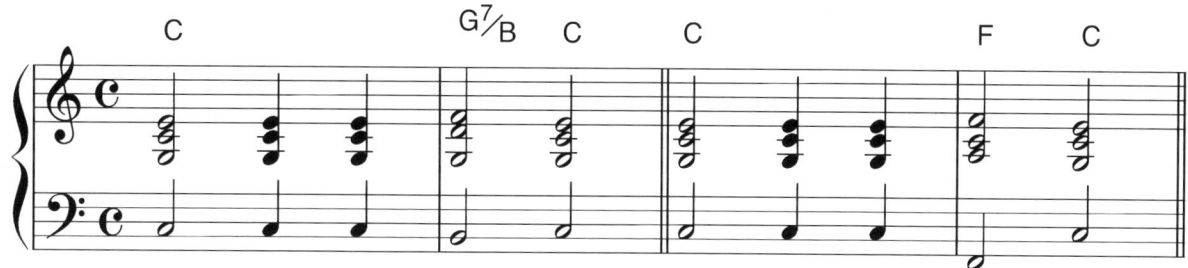

The second step involves replacing the F triad above with an F quartal (as below). Quartals with the third in the bass sound particularly good. A nice bass line (A →C) can be fashioned by restating the G7 first inversion chord (m2. above) after the quartal.

Example 5.17 Quartal Substitution (*Spirit of God Descend Upon My Heart*)

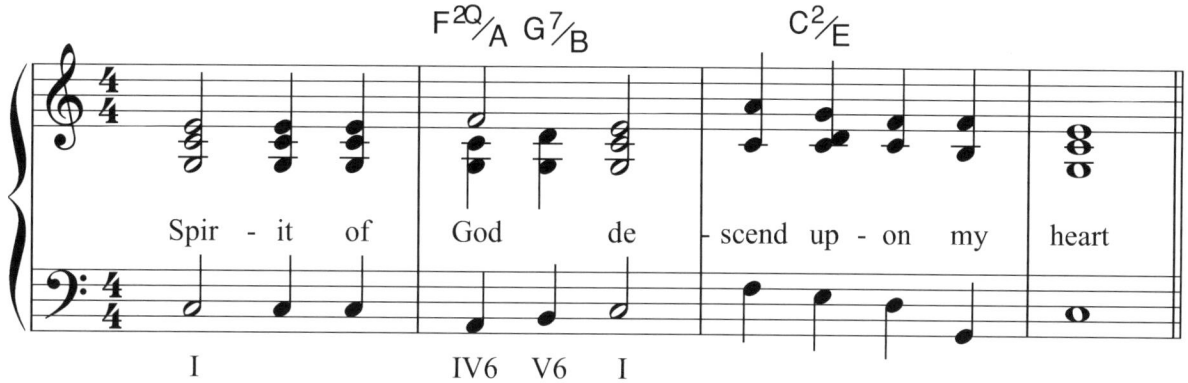

Try it! Play the excerpt above in the keys of D, E, F, G, and A.

Example 5.18 Play the Pop Symbols (*Sing Praise to God Who Reigns Above*)

Below, the Dma7 substitute for the D major chord results in more harmonic consistency with the A2Q/C# chord.

Example 5.19 *Shout to the Lord*

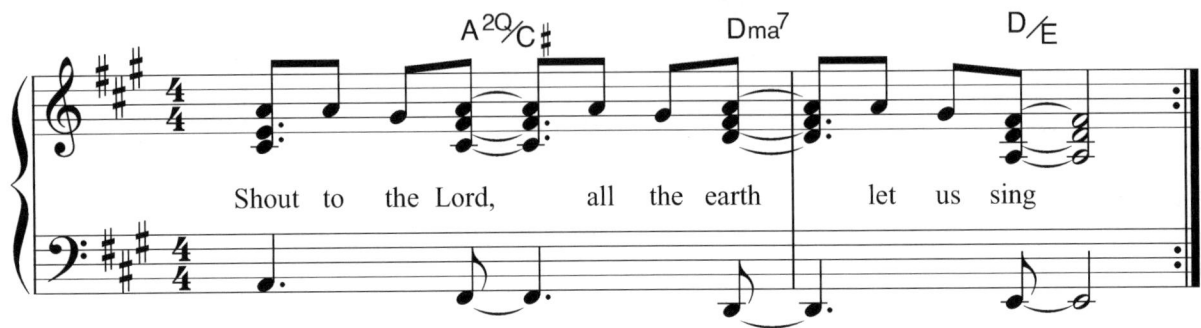

Example 5.20 *Great is thy Faithfulness.* **Play A & B in the keys of C, D, E, F, and G.**

A.

B.

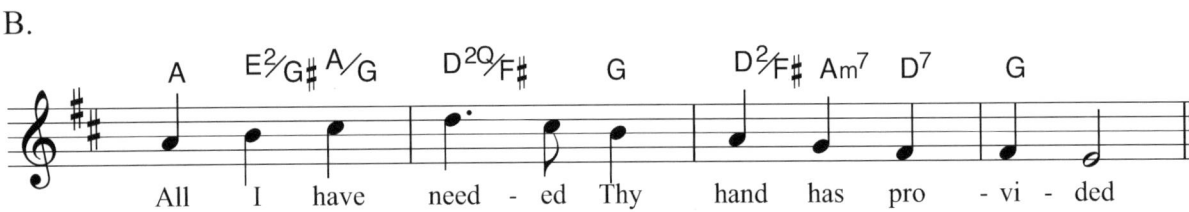

C.

Example 5.21 Solution for "C" Above

Note that D2Q/B symbol (above) is unusual. In this case the note "B" is a third below the D2Q. Below, in 5.24 (m.10) a quartal with the seventh in the bass (as in a V4/2) also works well. In 5.22, the two quartals occur respectively on scale degrees I and IV.

Example 5.22 *The Solid Rock*

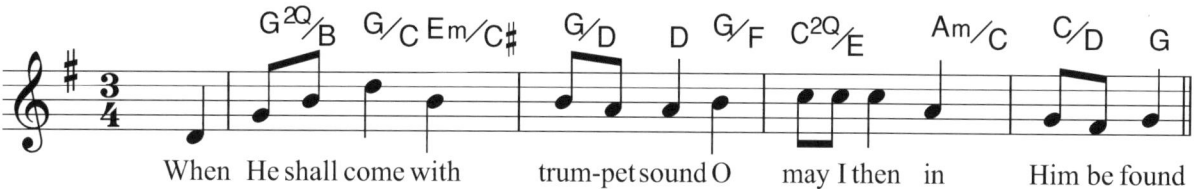

Example 5.23 Hymnbook Version of *Holy Holy Holy*

The hymnbook harmonization below has nice voice-leading qualities. Let's keep the same basic contour, but incorporate added second and quartal chords into the texture.

Do you like the quartal modification of *Holy, Holy, Holy* below?

Example 5.24 Play it! Quartal Modification of *Holy Holy Holy*

Notice (above) that in measure six a substitute quartal chord makes possible the rising bass line (E, F#, G). In measure eight the bass walks up to C, using two consecutive added second chords. In the last measure, the F in the G2Q/F symbol is the seventh of the G2Q chord (similar in function to a V4/2).

Example 5.25 Added Seconds/Quartals *(O Come All Ye Faithful)*

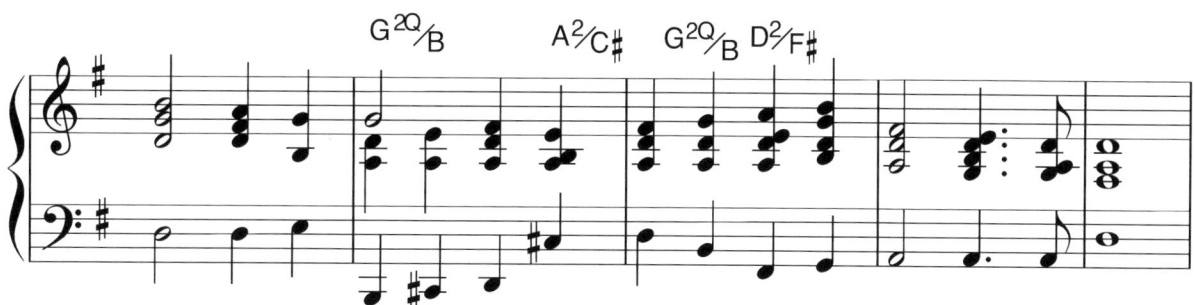

Stars or Fireworks?

Some songs may not explode or dazzle like fireworks, but like stars, their light shines. Stars, ablaze so many million miles away, pierce our atmosphere and reach us with their steady, enduring light. Similarly, classic hymns bring deep theological truth within our reach and with words and melodies we can remember.

In contrast, worship choruses
have the inflections and turns of phrases of today.
They speak engagingly to the moment. *Valuable!*
Like fireworks, they shoot up into the sky,
captivate our attention,
but all too quickly fall to the ground.

Because they are so short-lived,
and often gone after a couple of years,
and since we don't continue to sing them any more,
their long-term value is diminished, unfortunately.

Both stars and fireworks are valuable,
but they function differently.
Which is ultimately most valuable?

Seek *a* song—any spiritual song—that you can cherish
and sing when you are 20, 40, 60, or 80 years old,
and that can continue to impart deep, lasting, meaning and truth.

That song can become *your companion for life!*

It's spiritual value,
because of its longevity, is extraordinary.

Quartals II—Extending the Concept

- 10 pages
- 23 examples

OUTLINE	REPERTOIRE
Two Consecutive Quartals	Joyful, Joyful We AdoreThee Lamb of God
Walking Up the Bass	Great is Thy Faithfulness Change My Heart O God
Quartal Substitutions: Try it!	The God of Abraham Praise O Worship the King
Secondary Dominant Quartals	Spirit Song Christ the Lord is Risen Today
Answers	How Firm a Foundation Infant Holy, Infant Lowly
	Immortal Invisible Angels We Have Heard on High

In this chapter we continue to build on the previous chapter. We'll look at passages that use two consecutive quartals and secondary dominant, chromatic quartals.

Two Consecutive Quartals

Example 6.1 Consecutive Quartals That Walk Up to D Chord *(Joyful, Joyful)*

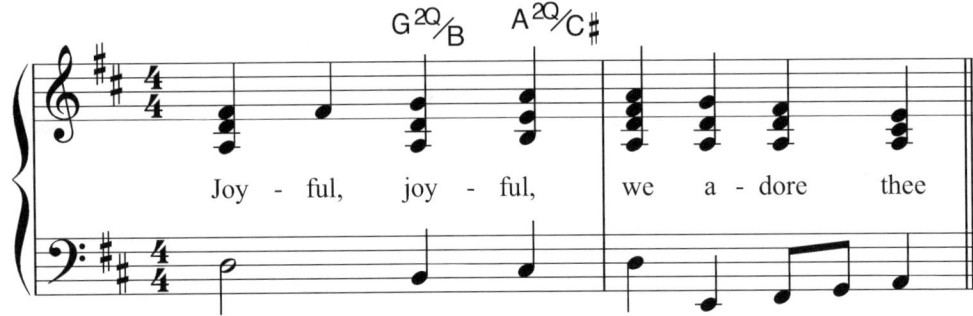

Example 6.2 Consecutive Quartals That Walk Up *(Great is Thy Faithfulness)*

Notice, above, that in walking up from A to D in the bass (m 2), the chords on beats 2 and 3 contain two consecutive quartals. The melody remains on A and acts as a pedal. The same ideas apply in measures 3 and 4.

Example 6.3 Consecutive Quartals That Walk Up *(The God of Abraham Praise)*

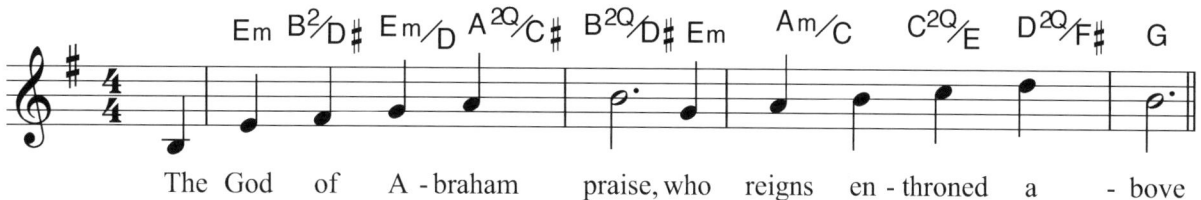

Below, look at a piece where the quartals walk up but do not sound the melody in the soprano part. Notice, the melody is embedded in an inner part.

Example 6.4 Melody in Inner Part of Quartals *(Spirit Song)*

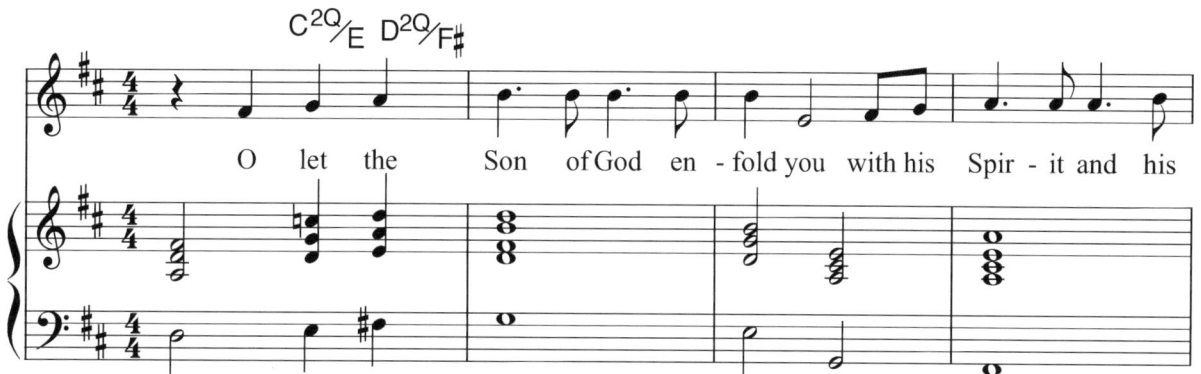

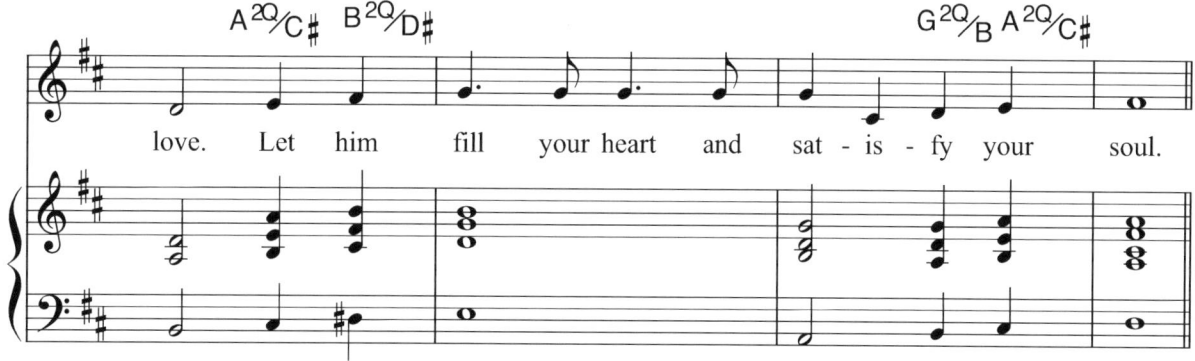

Try it! Sing and Play. Close the book and play the excerpt by memory.
Above, added second chords could have been used in walking up as well.

Example 6.5 Melody Placed in Inner Part of Quartal *(O Worship the King)*

Above, added second chords could have been used in walking up to G as well.

Example 6.6 Quartal with Third in Bass (Play through Cycle: Down 5th, Up 4th)

Example 6.7 Memorize! Play through the Cycle (Up a Fourth or Down a Fifth)

Quartal Substitutions: Try it!

Example 6.8 Create Two Quartal Substitutions *(How Firm a Foundation)*

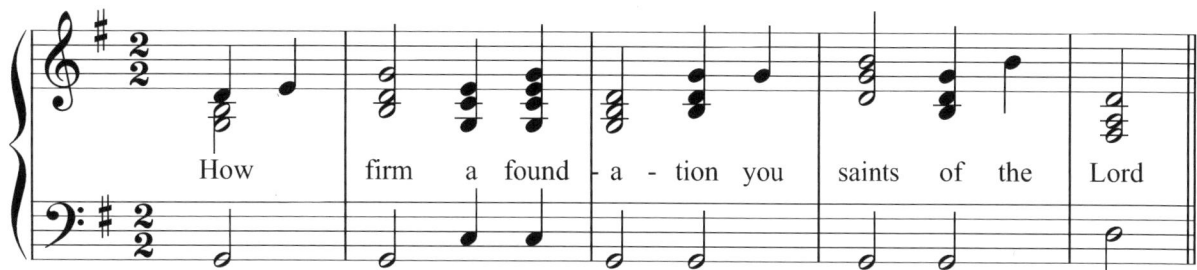

Example 6.9 Create Quartal Substitutions *(Christ the Lord is Risen Today)*

Write into the score a quartal chord substitution for measures 1, 2, and 3. Label each with pop symbols. Don't change any bass notes. Play/Compare the alternatives.

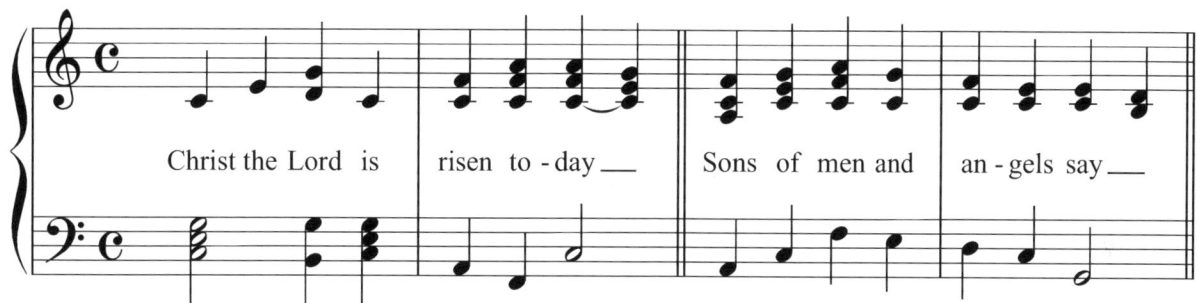

Example 6.10 Revoice, Solve, Invert (*O Come All Ye Faithful*)

See a hymn-like version of *O Come All Ye Faithful. Rewrite it.* Insert added seconds or quartal chords where asterisks occur. *Revoice* the piece so that single bass notes occur in the bass clef (left hand) and three or four note chords occur in the treble clef (right hand). Feel free to change the inversion of chords. You may need to change the chord itself.

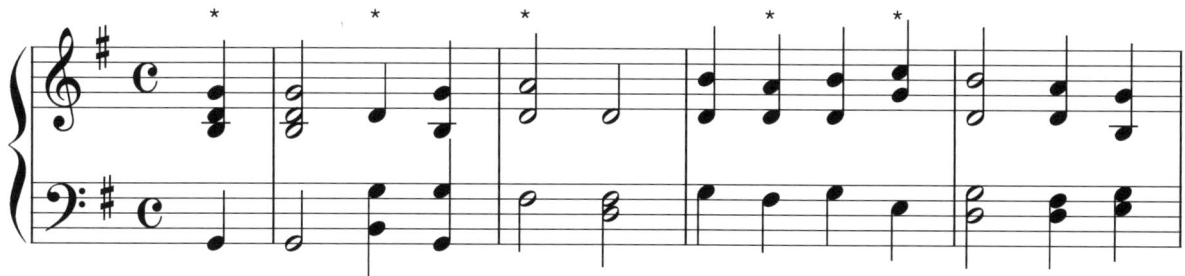

Write your solution into the score above. Maintain the melody. Play/Compare each version (traditional and revised).

Example 6.11 Create Three Alternatives (*O Worship the King*)

Below, the first line of *O Worship the King* is repeated three times. Create three versions of the excerpt, incorporating added seconds and quartals. Write into the score. Label.

Chromatic, Secondary Dominant Quartals

Example 6.12 Quartal Secondary Dominants in First Inversion (Play in All Keys)

Notice the powerful chromatic, half-step movement in the bass.

Below, write into the score the secondary dominant voicing. Use three notes in the right hand and one in the left.

Example 6.13 *Infant Holy, Infant Lowly* (Secondary Dominants)

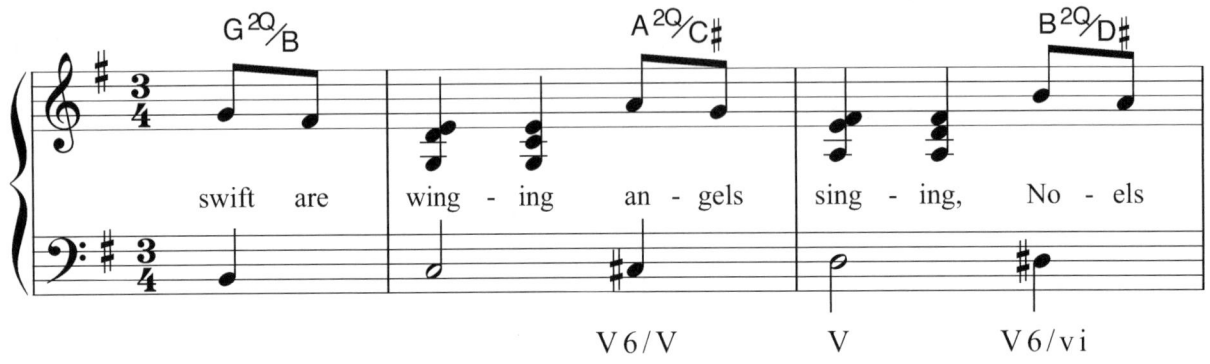

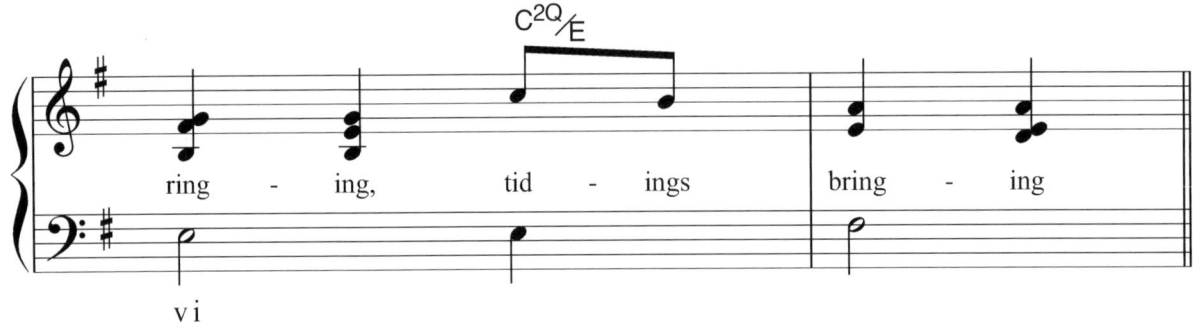

Example 6.14 Realize the Lead Sheet *(Change My Heart O God)*

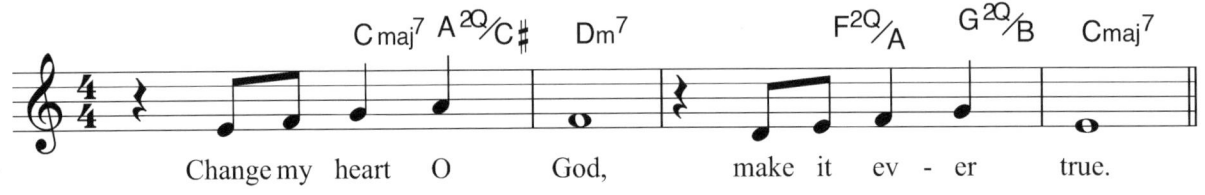

Example 6.15 Realize the Lead Sheet *(Immortal Invisible)*

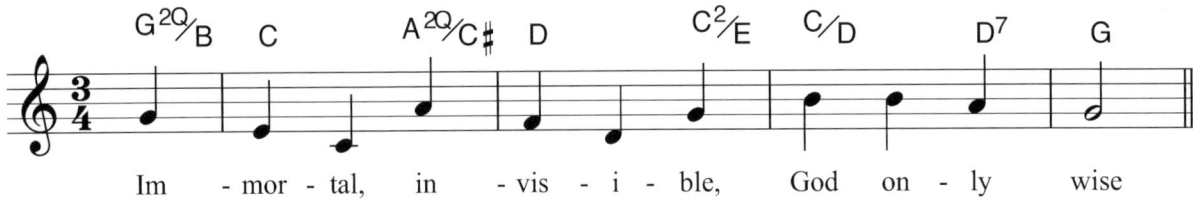

Example 6.16 Realize the Lead Sheet *(Immortal Invisible)*

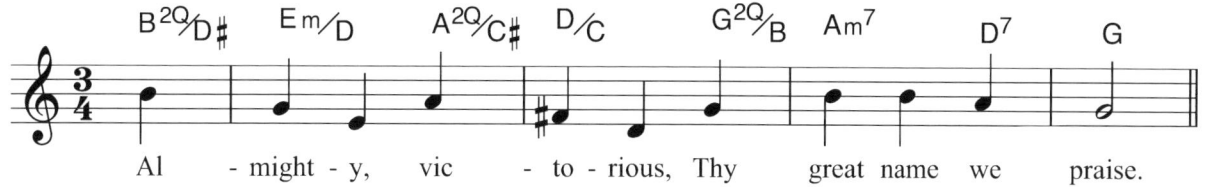

Example 6.17 *Change My Heart O God* **(Play in C, D, E, F, G, and A)**

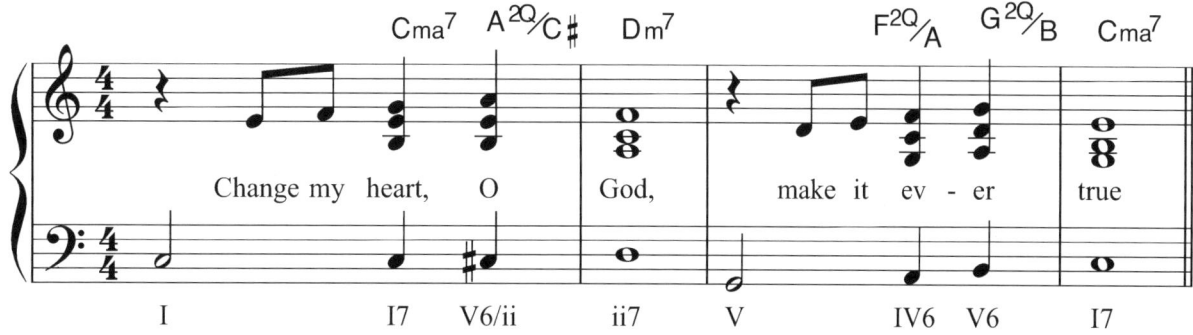

Example 6.18 *Change My Heart O God*

Play it! Play as is; then integrate quartals into the rhythmic structure above.

Example 6.19 *Immortal Invisible* **(Play in C, D, E, F, G, and A)**

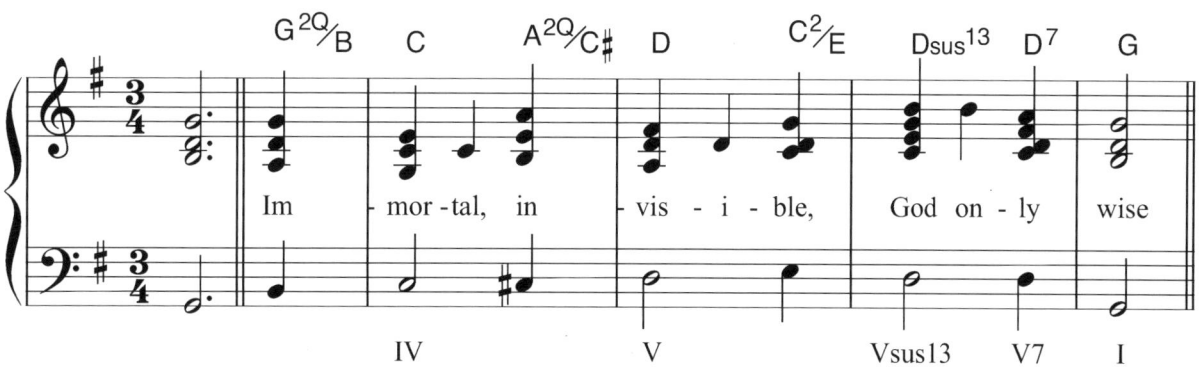

The following example can employ quartals and added seconds.

Example 6.20 Do It! Write in Quartal & Added Second Harmony *(Lamb of God)*

O Lamb of   God,   sweet Lamb   of   God,   I Love the   ho - ly Lamb of

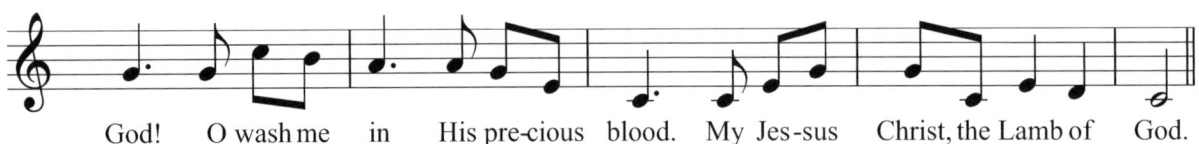

God!   O wash me   in   His pre-cious   blood.   My Jes-sus   Christ, the Lamb of   God.

Recognizing the Potential of Quartal Chords.

It is intuitively possible to stumble upon quartals, but not be able to realize their potential. Without help, musicians may not know what they can offer, how and where to employ them, and how to represent them in a chart.

I hope your understanding has increased and that this chapter has convinced you that quartals could be an effective resource. I also hope you find the quartal symbol, unique to this book, to be useable. There is one more aspect to cover.

Example 6.21 Quartal Secondary Dominants in Root Position (Play in All Keys)

RH quartal chords can function as an element in root position secondary dominants (quartal in RH, dominant 7th in LH). For sake of brevity, we're still calling these "quartal chords," though the LH notes are not perfect fourths.

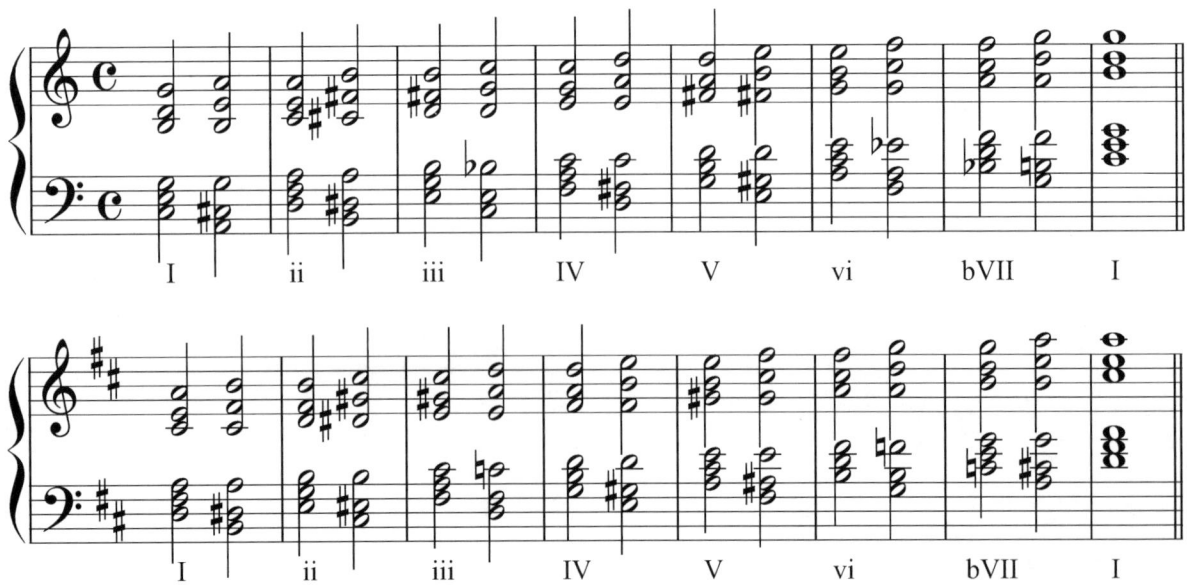

Quartals can function as secondary dominants on every degree of the scale—a powerful idea! Practice them in every key. We've given you a jump-start by writing them out in C and D. After several keys, the learning process becomes easier. Trust me.

Below, the second chord functions as a secondary dominant of scale degree ii.

Example 6.22 *Angels We Have Heard on High* **(Play in All Keys)**

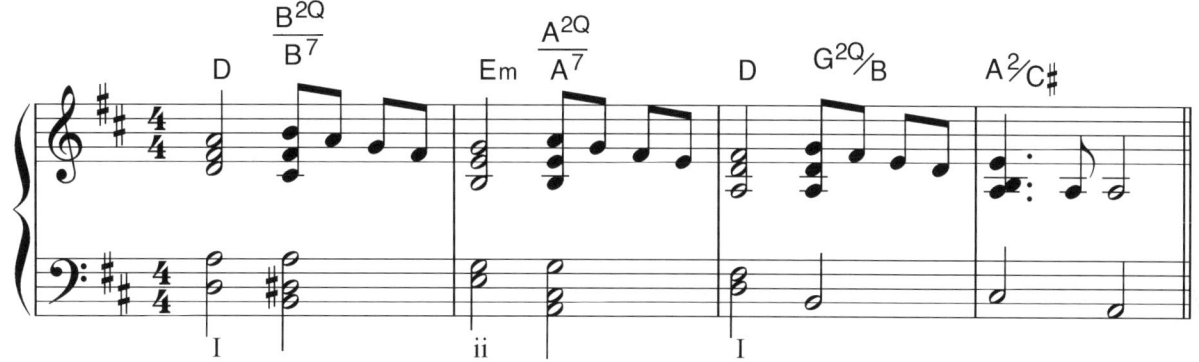

Example 6.23 Change My Heart, O God

The next chapter explores quartals comprised of three or more perfect fourths, a series of quartals based on the pentatonic scale, and an extended project on the classic hymn, *Immortal Invisible.*

Why are we working so hard?
Why we are taking so much care and expending so much effort?
We aspire to lead people into authentic worship.

There is no greater, no higher function for music!

Quartals III—Advanced Applications

• 16 pages	
• 36 examples	**For the ADVANCED KEYBOARDIST**

OUTLINE	REPERTOIRE
Five Quartal Expansions	Jesus Loves Me Great is Thy Faithfulness
The Horizontal Slash	Emmanuel I have Decided to Follow Jesus
Extensions/Drones with Quartals	Holy Holy Holy This is My Father's World
Quartals for Immortal Invisible	Mary Had a Baby As the Deer
Review of Quartal Sounds & Symbols	Silent Night Immortal Invisible

Clarification. In previous quartal chapters, when we used the term "quartal chord," the soprano part contained the root. At least two P4 intervals were not only present but *adjacent* to one another. However, we did not mean that *every* note in the chord was a P4 apart, for the bass part (with the root, third, or fifth) could be situated a long distance away. Most important, though, the distinctive quartal sound was *aurally discernable.*

In this chapter, the concept and use of quartals is expanded. The soprano part is no longer always the root. Previously we were limited to two P4s. Now three or four adjacent P4ths appear. The P4s can be situated within both hands, and in the LH itself. Furthermore, a series of quartals can arise, and quartals can function as fills.

Five Quartal Expansions

So far, we've employed two perfect fourths above the bass (C down to G and G down to D) with the root in the soprano, and the root, third, or fifth in the bass (as below). Now…

A. The soprano note could be the fifth of the chord (as below).

Example 7.1 Quartal with Root in the Soprano; then the Fifth in the Soprano

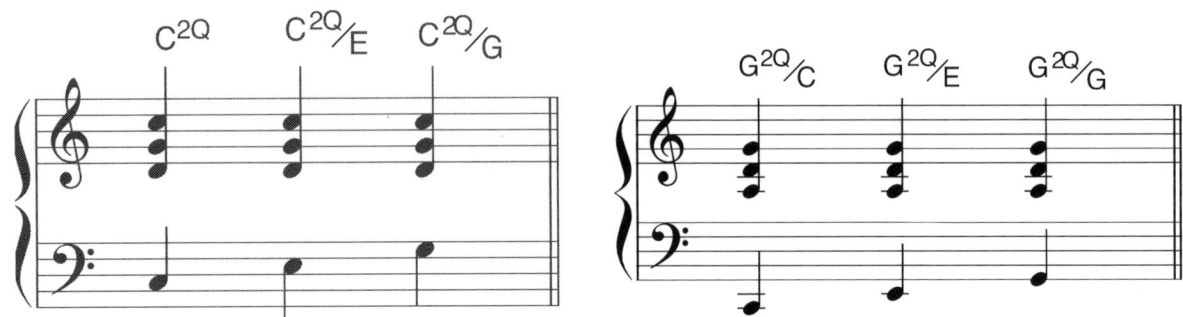

In m. 2 above, C is the root of the chord and G (in soprano) is the fifth. Yet G2Q/C seems the best symbolic alternative. The third chord could be termed a simple G2Q.

The Inadequacies of both the Q and 6/9 symbols. For measure 1 below, both pop symbols are accurate. The Jazz symbol (6/9), because it is in vogue, may seem preferable. But when a quartal chord is demanded, and no other, it is illusory. The 6/9 designation is inadequate, for it does not consistently (unambiguously) require a quartal sonority, as we shall see. Moreover, the G2Q symbol does not reflect the true root (C), a deficiency.

Example 7.2   Quartal   *(Jesus Loves Me)*

The Two problems. *Unfortunately,* (1) the G2Q symbol above does *not* indicate the true root of the chord (i.e., C). Yet, G2Q/C does unambiguously prescribe the right notes.

Example 7.3   Alternative: 6/9 Chord

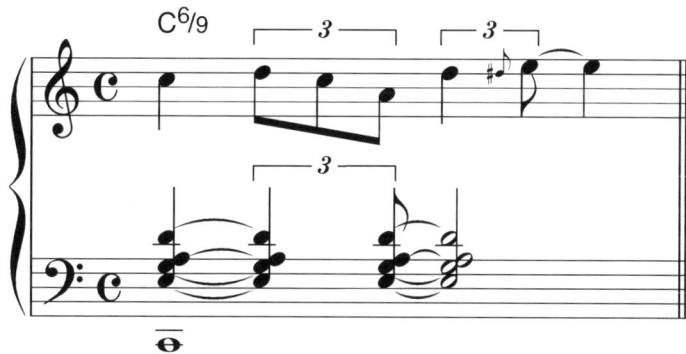

 (2) When a performer reads the 6/9 symbol above, unfortunately, there is no *necessity* to play a quartal construction. Notice, the LH plays EGAD (the 6/9 symbol) while the bass player could play the low C (the root). Clearly the symbol 6/9, though it *could* yield a quartal construction (3, 6, 9), in this case, *does not.* It's up to the player's discretion.

Without our invented sign (x2Q), there is *no unambiguous way to demand a* quartal chord when using conventional pop symbols. For this reason, a Q symbol (our own invention) is employed to satisfy unambiguously the demand for a quartal sonority.

Example 7.4 Play the Lead Sheet Containing Quartals *(Mary Had a Baby)*

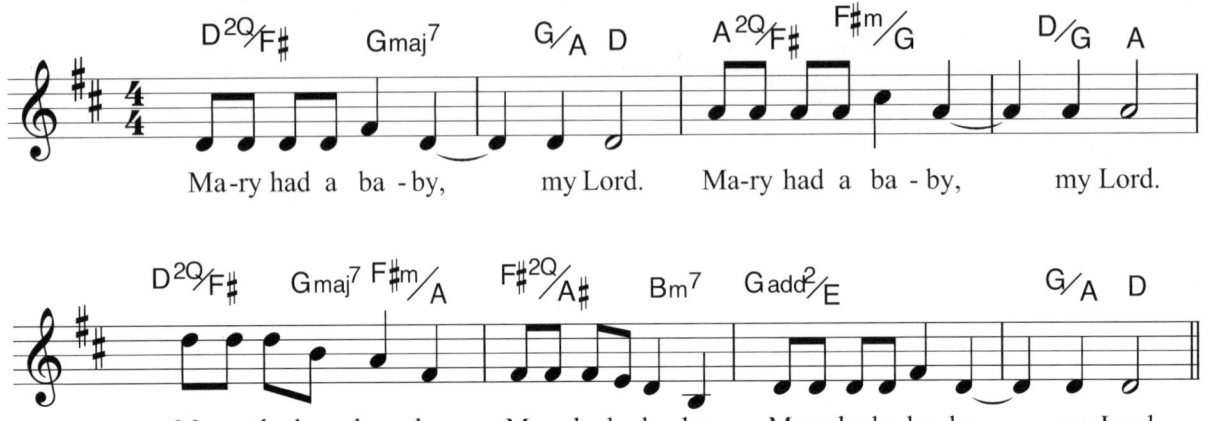

Notice, unfortunately, that in measure 3, the A2Q/F# is really a D chord, not an A chord. Also we would probably begin the excerpt with a simple D chord for stanza one, and use D2Q/F# to begin a subsequent stanza.

B. *More than two perfect fourths could occur*. Sonorities with three or four perfect fourths sound wonderful. They can occur between the LH and RH, and in the LH itself.

Example 7.5 Play it! Three or Four Perfect Fourths Included

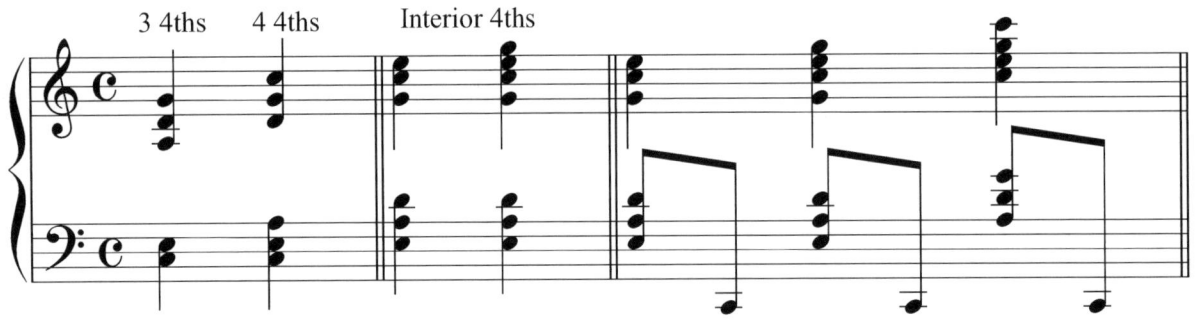

C. *Quartals could Outline 1 → 5 → 8 in the Melody*

Example 7.6 Quartals can occur with 1→ 5 → 8 in the Melody

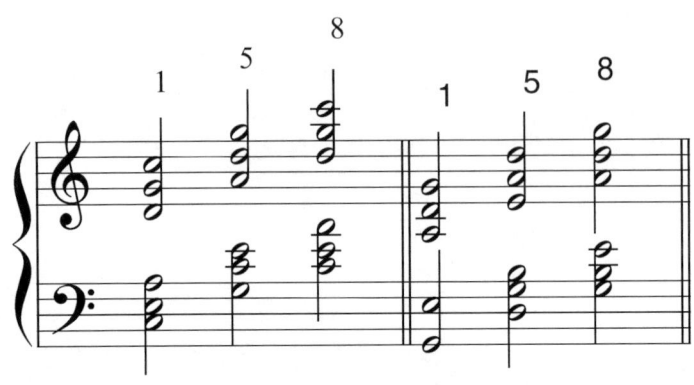

Become fluent playing them in a number of different keys. In low registers (eg, m.2), omit the third (B) above the bass (G) to avoid muddiness.

Example 7.7 Upper and Lower Helpful Guide Notes for Playing Previous Example

The above melody notes (G, C) occur often, and they occur in *Great is Thy Faithfulness.*

Example 7.8 Useful Quartals in the 8 - 5 - I Melody of *Great is Thy Faithfulness*

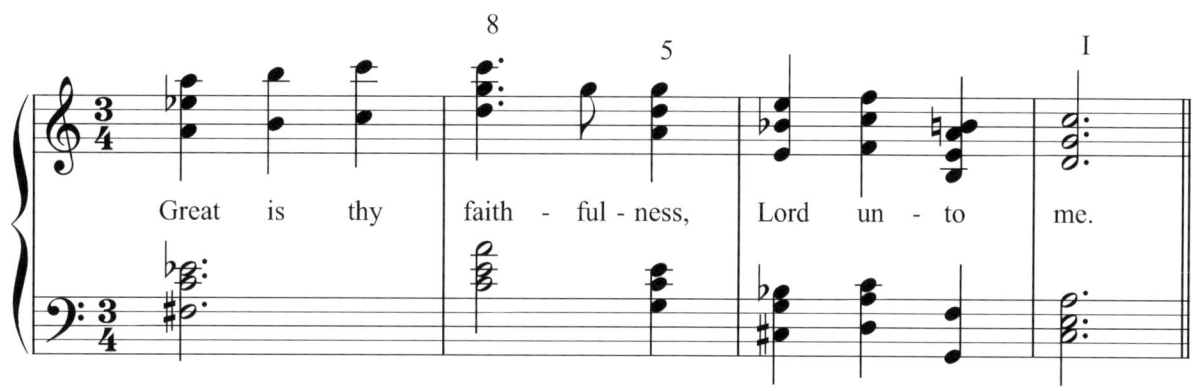

D. Quartals could Occur on 1 - 3 -5 - 8 in the Melody

Example 7.9 Quartals could Outline any Major Triad

Become fluent playing them in a number of different keys.

Example 7.10 Helpful Bass and Soprano Guide Notes.

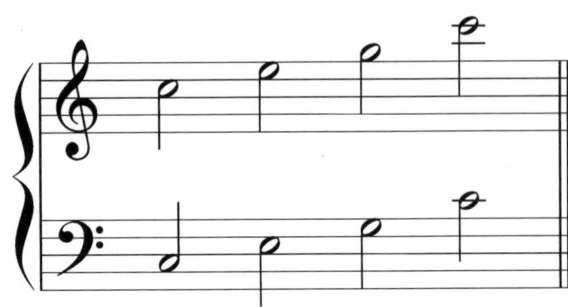

Example 7.11 C Major Chord Triad Outlined in Melody *(Great is Thy Faithfulness)*

As   thou   hast   been   thou   for   ev – er   wilt   be

E. Quartals could outline a Pentatonic Scale and function as a fill.

Example 7.12 Pentatonic Scale

Every note in the series (below) belongs to the pentatonic scale

Example 7.13 Series of RH Quartals. Play it in C, D, E, F, G.

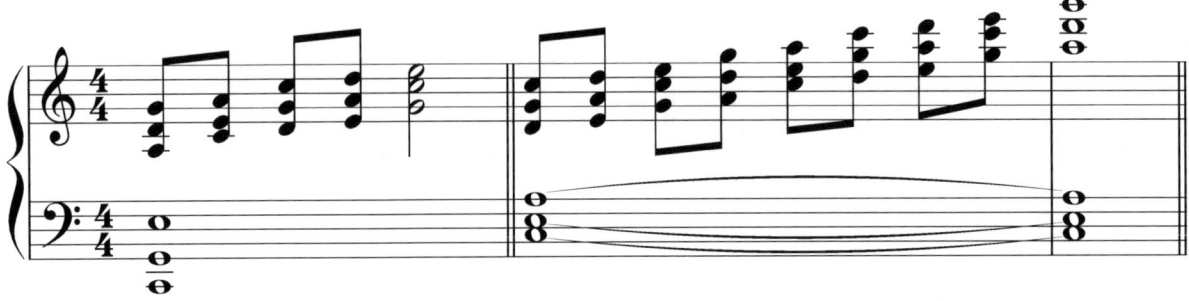

Example 7.14 Chords with Three or More P4s Employing Both Hands

Now, let's apply this basic idea to the classic hymn, *This is My Father's World.*

Example 7.15 Series of Quartals Chords Used as a Fill *(This in My Father's World)*

Take the same idea and apply it to *As the Deer.*

Example 7.16 **Try it!** Create Series of Quartals *(As the Deer)*

The Horizontal Slash

A sixth, rich-sounding possibility involves combining a C major chord in the left hand with a G2Q or a C2Q in the right hand. A *horizontal slash* indicates that *some kind of chord* should be played in the left hand, not a single note.

Example 7.17 Horizontal Slash *(Jesus Loves Me)*

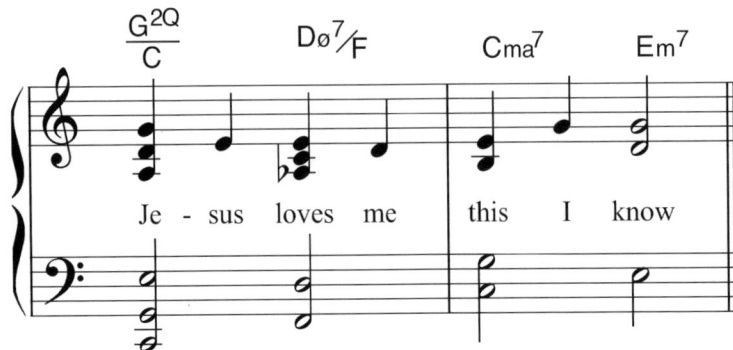

Above, when both clefs are considered in chord 1, the soprano has the fifth of a resonant C chord in root position. The triad in the LH thickens and enriches the sound.

Example 7.18 Quartals with Horizontal Slashes Work on I, IV, and V.

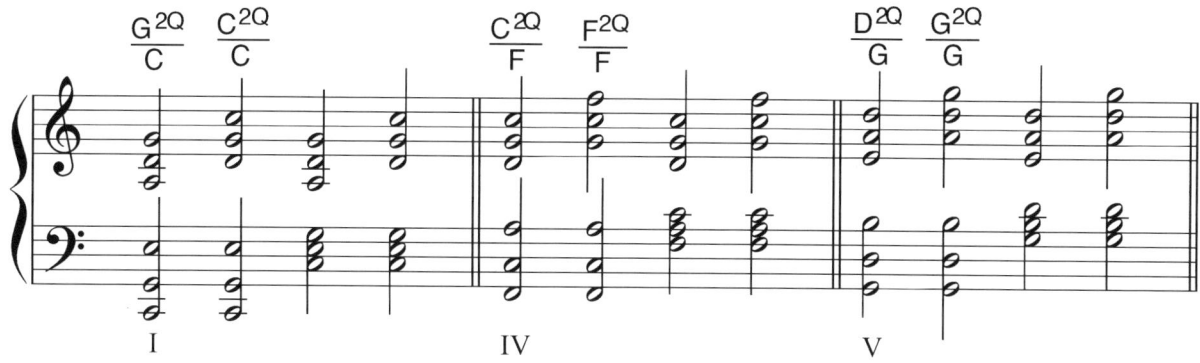

Above, the soprano has the 5th and then root of the chord, alternatively.

Example 7.19 *Holy Holy Holy* (Horizontal Slashed Quartals)

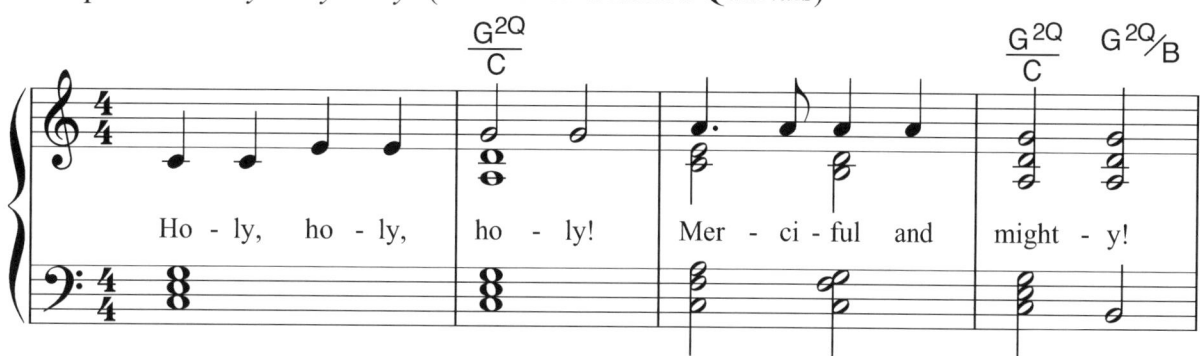

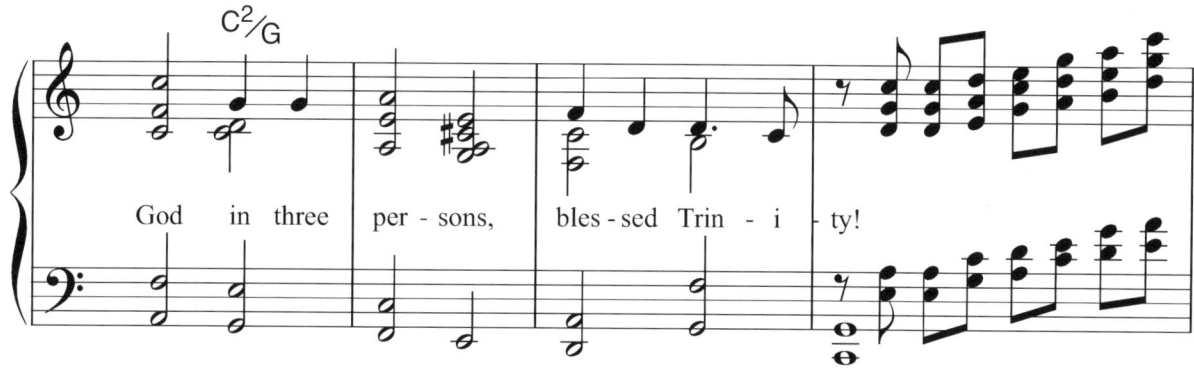

In m.4 (above), the G2Q/B quartal functions as a passing chord. In m. 8, a series of quartals (outlining a C pentatonic scale) function as a fill.

Try it! The first 7 measures also sound good an octave higher.

Below, the quartals function on scale degrees I and IV (ms. 1, 3, and 9).

Example 7.20 *Silent Night*

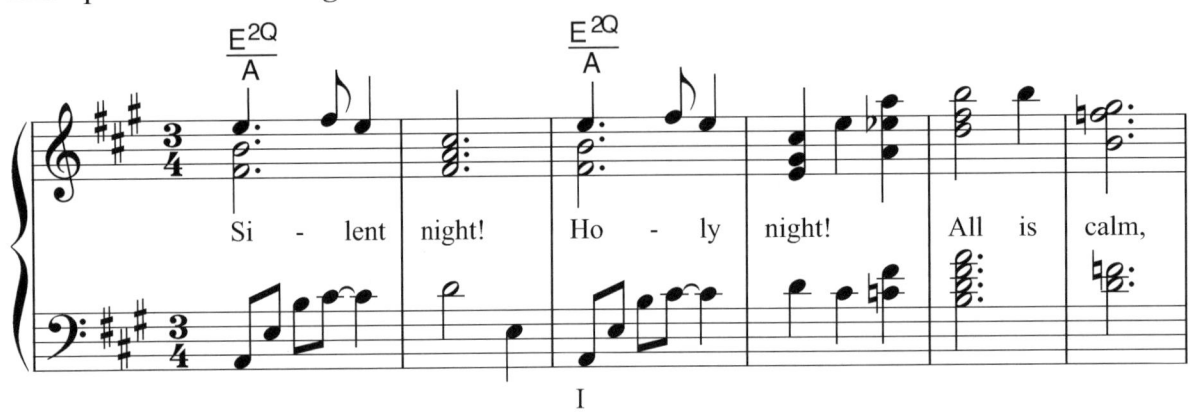

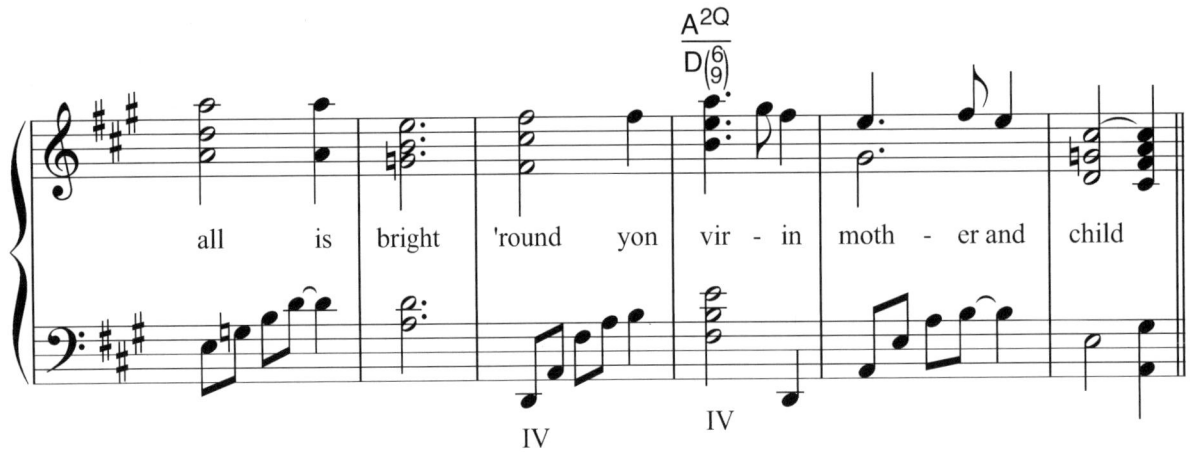

Example 7.21 **Do it!** Play the Lead Sheet *(I have Decided to Follow Jesus).*

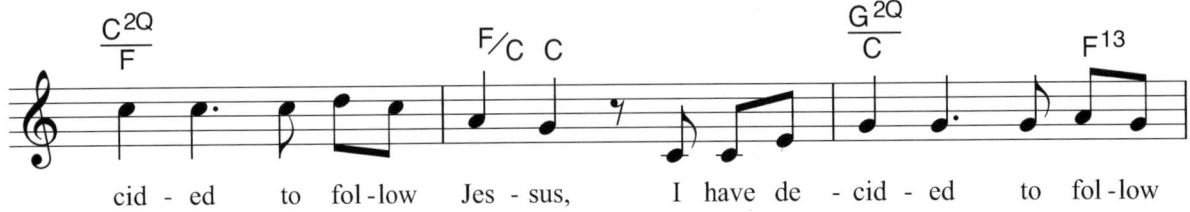

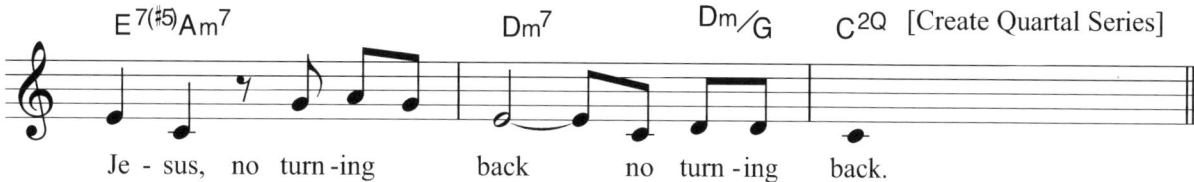

Je - sus, no turn -ing   back   no turn -ing   back.

Some Solutions. Some possible realizations are offered below of pieces above.

Example 7.22 *As the Deer* (Possible Realization)

Try it! For a more dramatic effect, the measure 2 fill (above) could be 2 measures long.

Example 7.23 *Mary Had a Baby* (Possible Realization)

Example 7.24 *I have Decided to Follow Jesus* (Possible Realization)

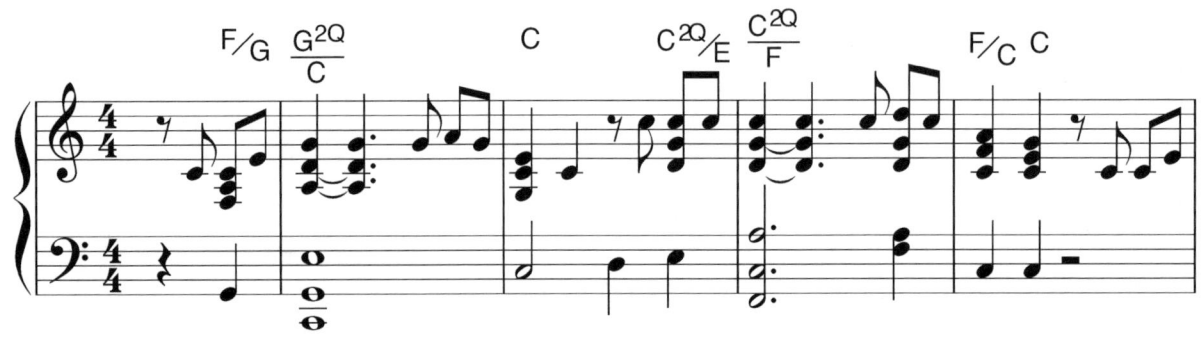

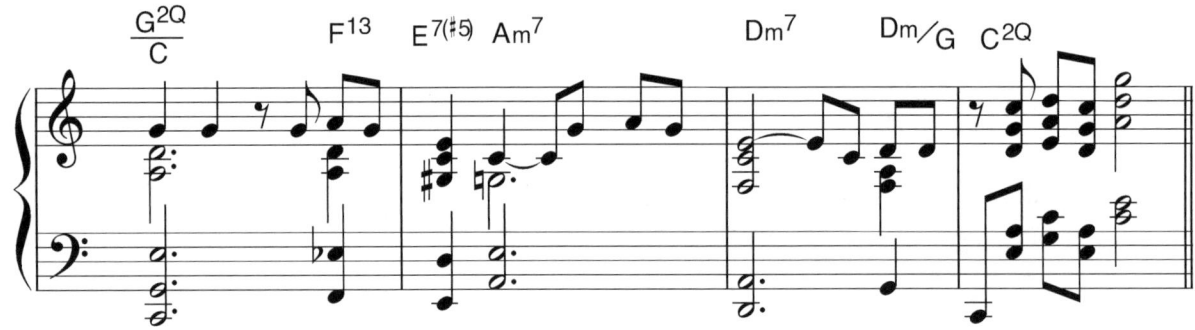

Example 7.25 Quartal Fill. *Great is Thy Faithfulness*

Extensions/Drones with Quartals

Just as we had extensions and drones with added second chords, so we have the same situation with quartal chords. Bass substitutions up or down thirds work beautifully.

Example 7.26 Added Second and Quartal Drones

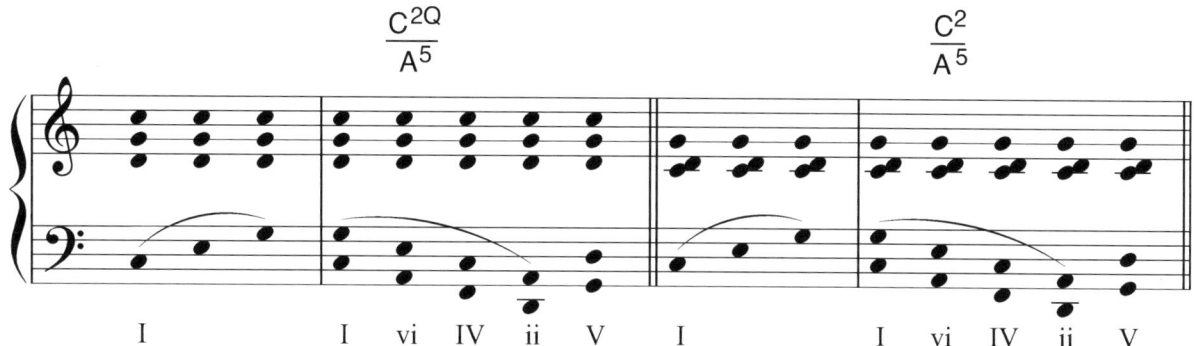

Above, in beat 2 of ms. 2 and 4 a colorful substitute for a vi chord emerges. (Here the horizontal slash indicates a fifth in the bass, not a single note.) Let's apply this chord.

Example 7.27 Holy Holy Holy

Above in ms. 2 & 6, the quartal chord could also be analyzed less elegantly as a Am7add4.

Below, a pedal quartal chord is retained while the bass moves to vi, IV, and ii.

Example 7.28 Play it! *Emmanuel* with Droning Quartals

Above, a droning F quartal (m. 1) is held over the I, vi, IV, and ii chord (ms. 1-3). A C quartal occurs over a iii chord (m. 4), and a Bb quartal is held over a ii and V (ms. 6-7).

Quartals for *Immortal Invisible*

Example 7.29 *Immortal Invisible* Line One

Example 7.30 Alternatives for Line One

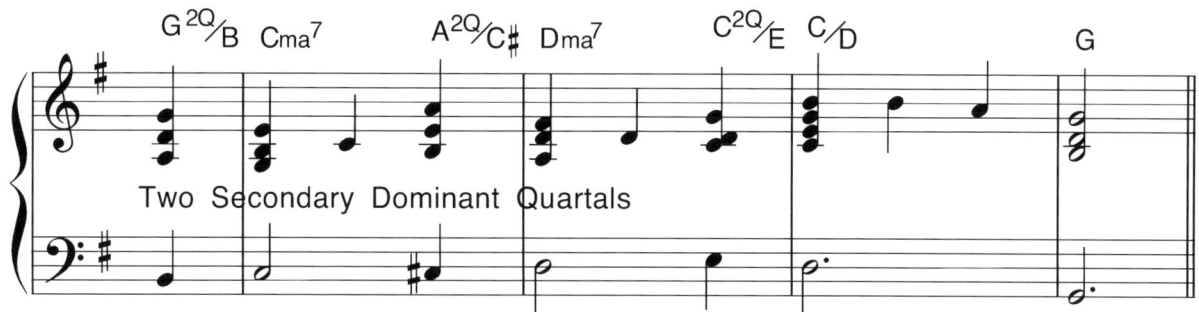

.Example 7.31 *Immortal Invisible* Line Four

Example 7.32 Two Versions for Line Four

A.

B.

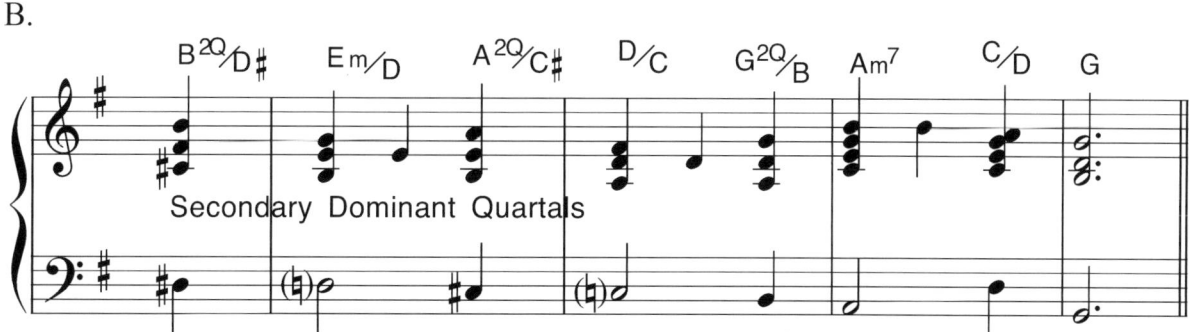

Let's provide more context. See line four combined with line three.

Example 7.33 Dissonant, Pervasively Chromatic Version of Lines Three and Four

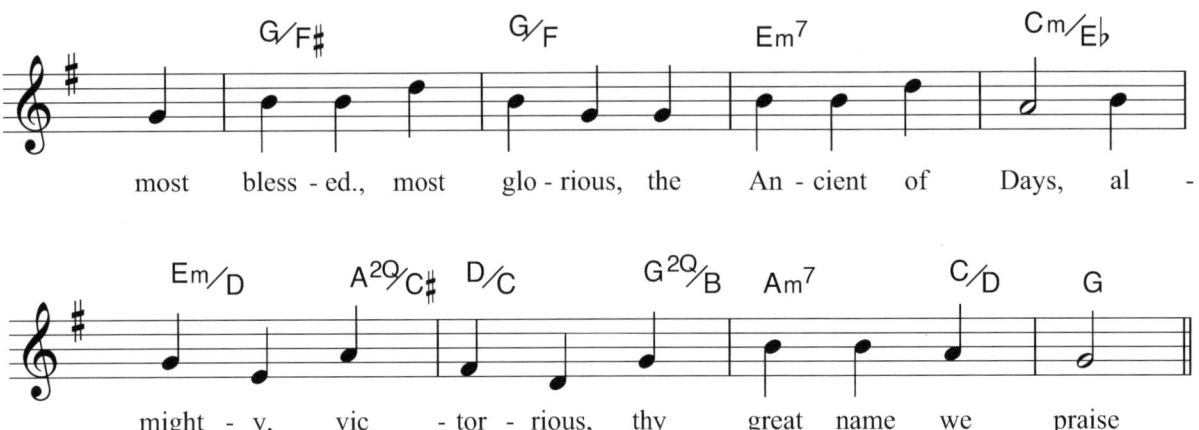

As we can see, with a little effort we can come up with a number of contrasting harmonizations that can help breath life into this great, classic hymn.

Review of Quartal Sounds and Symbols

At the beginning of the Quartals I chapter, we specified that the root, third, and fifth of the Quartal chord could be in the bass.

Example 7.34 Root, Third, and Fifth of the Quartal Chord is in the Bass

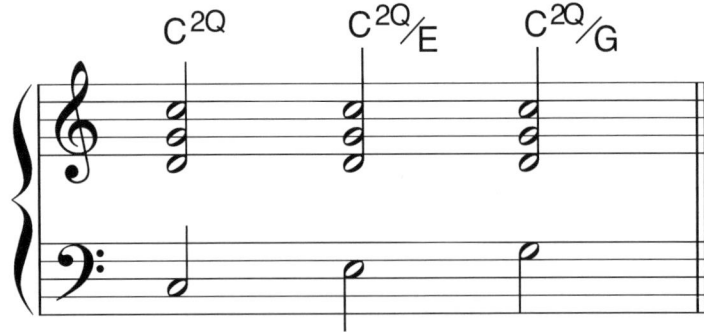

In Quartals II, (1) we placed the 7th of the chord in the bass. It functioned like a dominant seventh with the seventh in the bass (that is, like a V4/2). (2) We also placed a third below the root of the Quartal chord in the bass. (3) If a fifth is added to the bass clef, a useful sound results. See below for illustrations of the three points.

Example 7.35 Third Placed in Bass Below the Root of the Quartal Chord

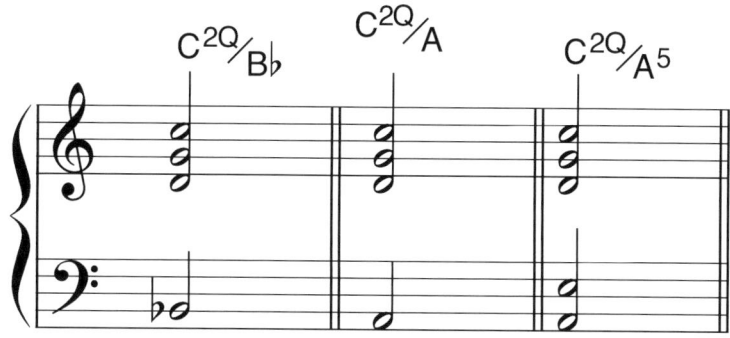

In the Quartal III chapter, (1) the soprano note was the fifth of the chord rather than the root, and we employed up to four P4ths in a quartal sonority. Illustrated below.

Example 7.36 Soprano Note is the Functional Fifth of the Quartal Chord

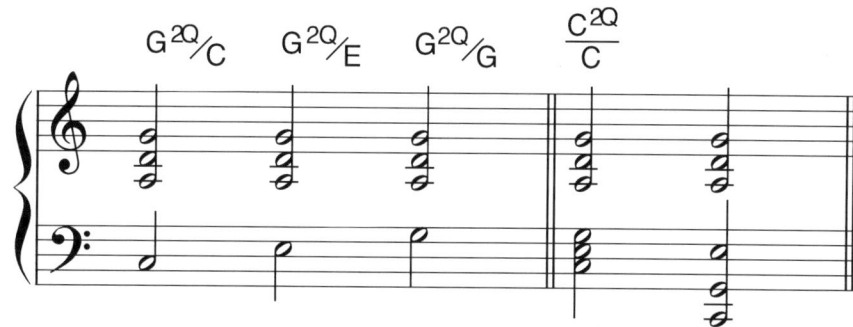

We did not employ a G2Q/E chord, yet it would seem to be a useful possibility.

This concludes our thoughts about quartal chords, and our attempt to represent them not only symbolically but functionally in ways you may be able to use them. We've presented our unique symbol (x2Q). We've demonstrated that quartals can be a valuable resource for modernizing worship choruses and hymns. Adjacent quartals were limited to perfect fourths only (no augmented fourths or diminished fifths were used).

> *And we, who with unveiled faces all reflect the Lord's glory*
> *are being transformed into his likeness with ever-increasing glory,*
> *which comes from the Lord, who is the Spirit.*
> 2 Cor 3:18

CHAPTER 8

Sus Chords I—Learning its Shapes

> • 11 pages
> • 30 examples

Why study and use sus chords? Sus chords have a broad application to both contemporary and traditional worship styles. For this reason, we need to learn sus chords both thoroughly and well, so that we can play them instantly in a variety of situations.

The standard dominant seventh often sounds "very old." Sus chords provide a more modern, colorful alternative. Since dominant sevenths occur so frequently in hymns and worship choruses, you will find many opportunities to use sus chords.

Moreover, sus chords can function as secondary dominants, further expanding their scope of usefulness. Additionally, they are invaluable in creating segues and in effecting modulations in the free-flowing praise format. We'll explore those aspects in Books 3 and 4. Besides, they are eminently playable on both guitars and keyboards.

OUTLINE	REPERTOIRE
What is a Sus Chord?	Amazing Grace Be Thou My Vision
Sus, Sus7, Sus9, Sus13 in Cadences	Great is Thy Faithfulness
The Sus9	Infant Holy, Infant Lowly
Use Wisely	O Worship the King

Below, see a phrase without sus and with sus chords that demonstrates the difference.

Example 8.1 *Amazing Grace*

A. Simple

B. Complex (This Level of Complexity is Addressed in a Later Sus Chapter)

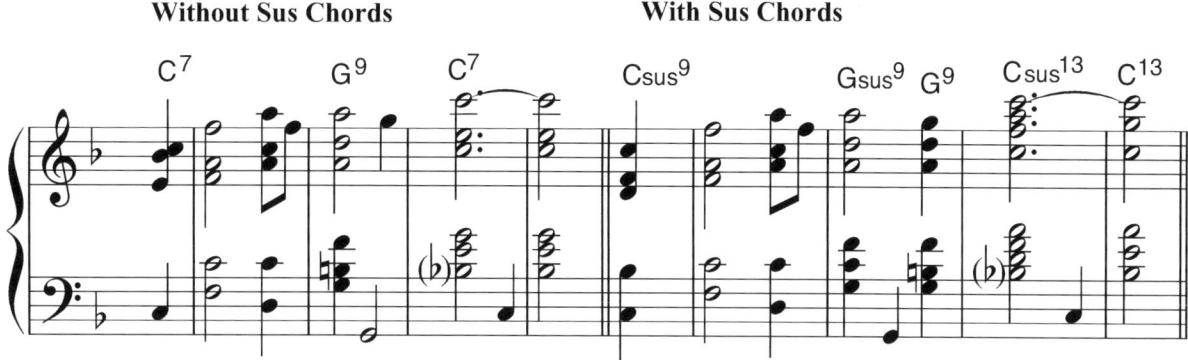

What is a Sus Chord?

What is a sus chord? It's different from a major triad. A C major triad, for example, has a root (C), a third (E), and a fifth (G).

Example 8.2

On the other hand, a sus chord has *no third*. It substitutes/replaces the third with a fourth. A Csus chord is comprised of a root (C), a fourth (F), and a fifth (G). Various sus symbols are employed.

Historically, the name "sus" is short for "suspended." In earlier classical music a sus sound was considered to be dissonant and needed resolution. In the music of J. S. Bach, for example, the F in the Csus (3rd measure above) would invariably resolve by step to the E of the C major chord. Also note, alternative symbols for the sus are also indicated above. In contemporary practice, however, the sus (4th) is not always required to resolve, nor must it be prepared (as required in "common practice").

You will encounter Csus2 terminology in chord charts.

Example 8.3 Csus2 Resolves Up to the Third of a C Chord.

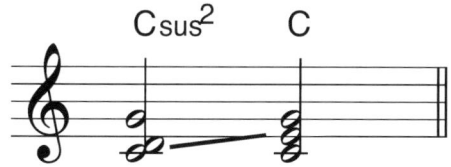

This book does *not* employ Csus2 terminology. Instead of Csus2 we will use C2. A sus chord, for us, will always means a 4th is contained in the chord.

Example 8.4 Assignment. Write the Designated Chord. Resolve the Sus.

Example 8.5 The Sus Inverted

Example 8.6 Most Likely Sus Chords

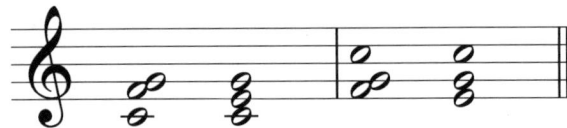

Example 8.7 Most Likely Sus Chord Embedded in *Amazing Grace*

A. Play it in E, F, G, A

B. Play it in E, F, G, A

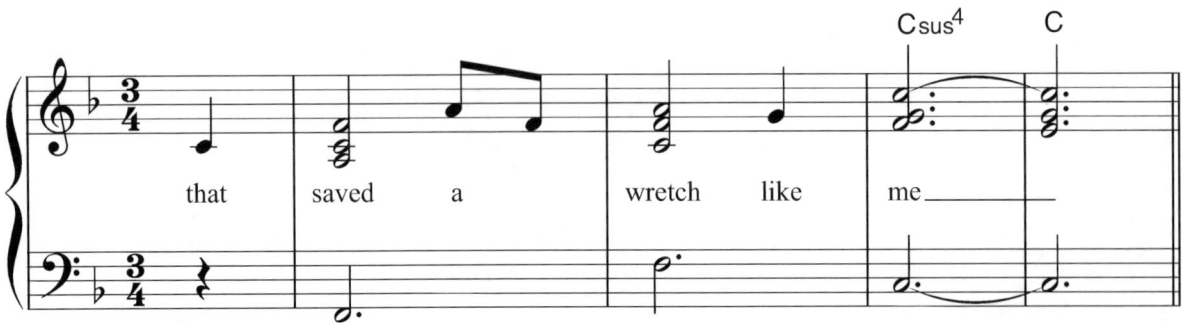

Example 8.8 ***Try it!*** Write the Sus Chord   (Great is Thy Faithfulness)

Example 8.9 ***Try it!*** Write the Sus Chord and Resolution *(Be Thou My Vision)*

Example 8.10 The Sus through the Cycle (Up a 4th, Down a 5th)

Now play the same pattern but with a 7th in the tenor part.

Example 8.11 The Sus7 through the Cycle (Up a 4th, Down a 5th)

In contemporary music the sus chord can resolve, *but often it does not.* The sus has obtained an independent status in the same sense that a C major chord is its own entity.

Sus, Sus7, Sus9, Sus 13 in Cadences

One major way sus chords function is as a **substitute** *for cadencial dominant sevenths.* Let's get a quick overview of Sus, Sus7, Sus9, and Sus13 in half cadences. Cadences occur at the end of phrases. Half cadences typically end on a V chord (the "dominant" chord), and consequently have an incomplete feeling. Below a half cadence occurs on the word "me." In hymnbooks, typically a simple G major triad is used, but instead we have substituted a Gsus below.

Example 8.12 Half Cadence Using a Gsus in *Amazing Grace.*   Play in C, D, E, F, G.

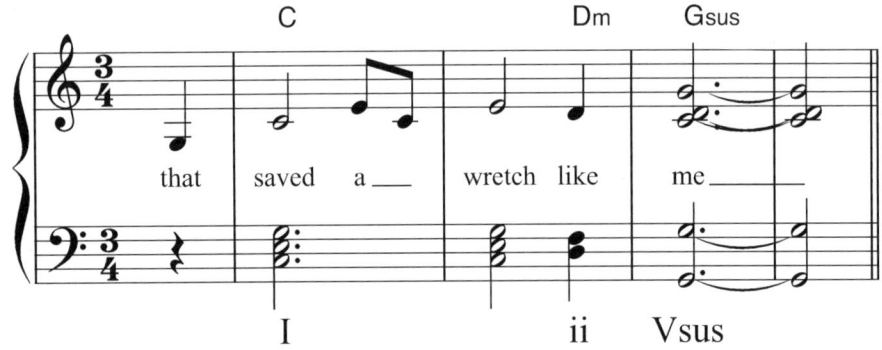

Above, the Gsus chord does not resolve (the C does not resolve to B). Sus chords at cadences can remain unresolved or resolve. Below all the sus chords resolve.

Example 8.13 Four Resolving Sus Chords used at a Half Cadence. Play in C, D, E, F, G.

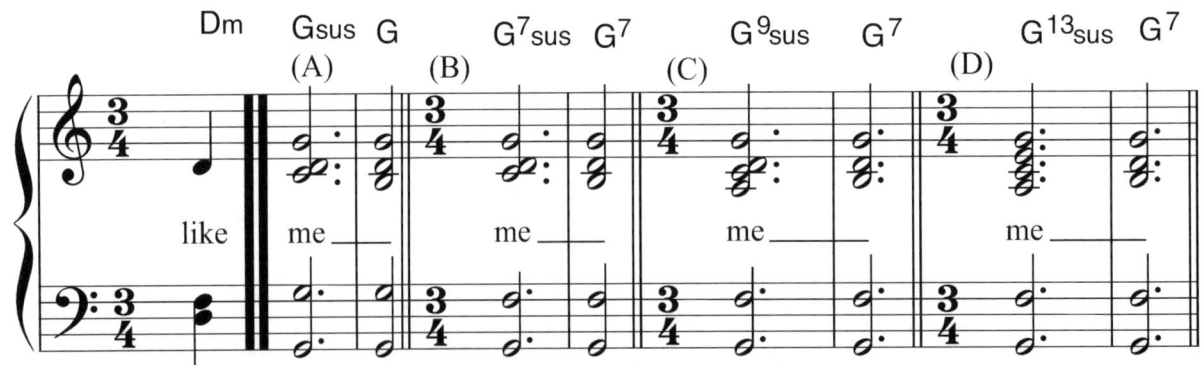

In each case above, the 4th (C) in the alto resolves to the 3rd (B) of the G or G7 chord. In examples B, C, and D, the seventh of the chord (F in LH) is situated in the tenor—a good voicing idea, if the seventh isn't so low as to sound muddy. Examples C and D, with the 9th (A), are *the crucial ones* for keyboardists. See the two different resolutions. In both cases the 4th (11th) falls to the 3rd (10th) of the next chord, whereas the 9th can rise or fall. Listen carefully to the G9sus above. It sounds more modern than a G or a G7, right?

Example 8.14 Three Sus Substitutions with a V7-I Full Cadence. Play in C, D, E.

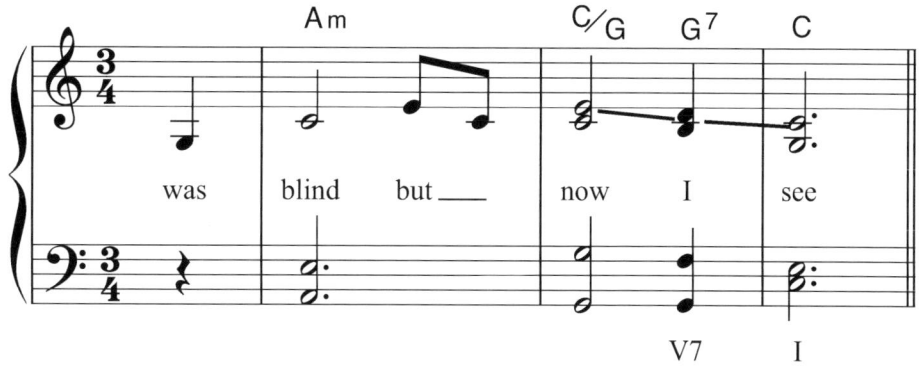

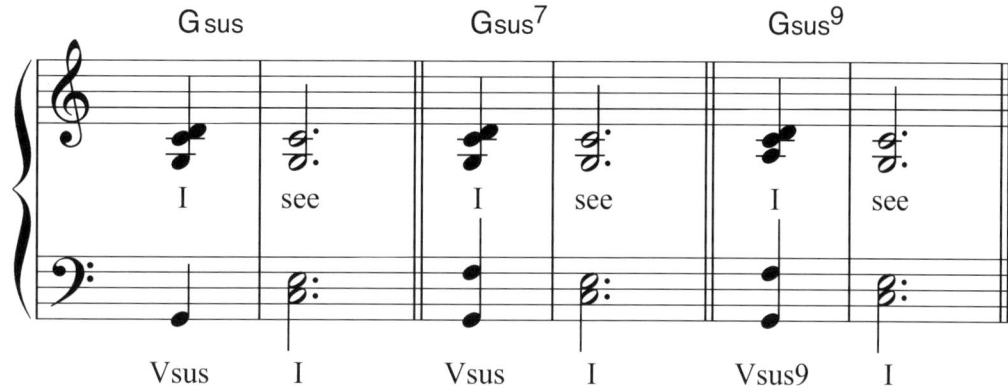

Example 8.15 Replace Asterisk with a Sus Chord *(O Worship the King) Play in G, A.*

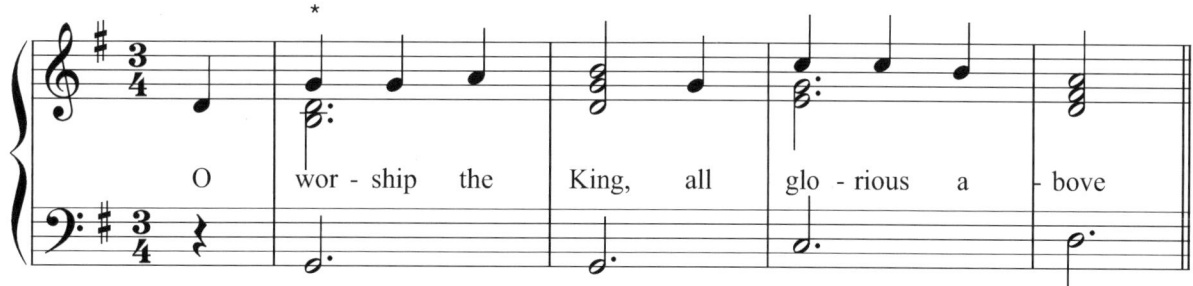

Example 8.16 Replace Asterisk with a Sus, Sus7, Sus9 Chord. Play in G, F, E.

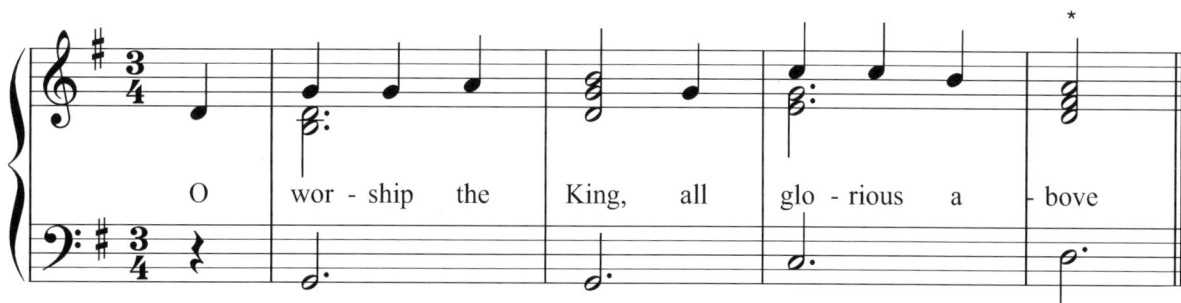

Example 8.17 Replace the Asterisks with a Sus and then a Sus7 Chord

Example 8.18 Replace Asterisk with a Sus, Sus7, and Sus9 Chord *(I Love you, Lord)*

The Sus9

The sus9 is the chord we particularly want to emphasize. It's a particularly valuable alternative to the dominant seventh because the ninth contributes a lot of color.

However, many students have trouble becoming comfortable with the sus9. Let's break it down into easy exercises. Strive to get the *sound* into your ear, and the *feel/shape* of it into your fingers. This chord needs to become "automatic." Once you have learned to play each exercise fluently, *close the book* and play! Closing the book (or your eyes) helps you concentrate on the sound, and forces you to think more independently.

We are going to look at *two fingerings* of the su9 now (and a third later), for students may be able to find the sus9 quickly with one but not the other. Both are essential.

Example 8.19 Ways to Practice the Sus9 (Fifth in the Soprano)

Below, with the minor 7th in the tenor, the fingering in the right hand (123) leaves fingers 4 and 5 free for ornamenting melodies and chords. Absorb the physical feeling of it.

Example 8.20 New Fingering in Right Hand (123)

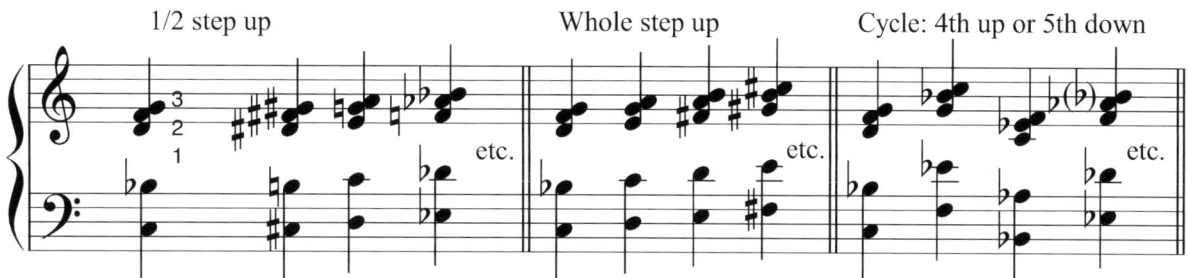

Example 8.21 Play through the Octave

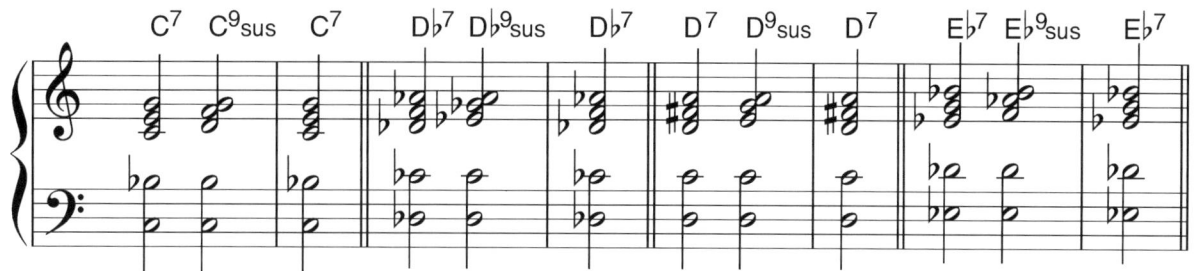

Students have found it easier to play the C9sus when it is preceded by a C7, because they are more familiar with the C7 shape. Therefore it makes sense to begin with the "known" shape and then proceed to the "unknown" one.

Example 8.22 Play through the Octave. Sus9 Compared with a simple triad.

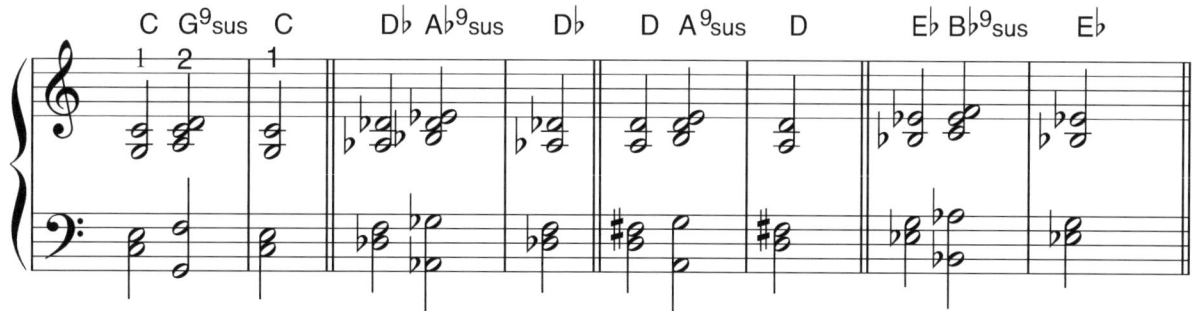

Above, start with the known chord, and then proceed to the lesser known one.

Example 8.23 C9sus (Root in the Soprano)

Work on the exercises that appear to help you the most.

Example 8.24 Two Simultaneous Spacings of the Sus9 chord. Play Through the Octave.

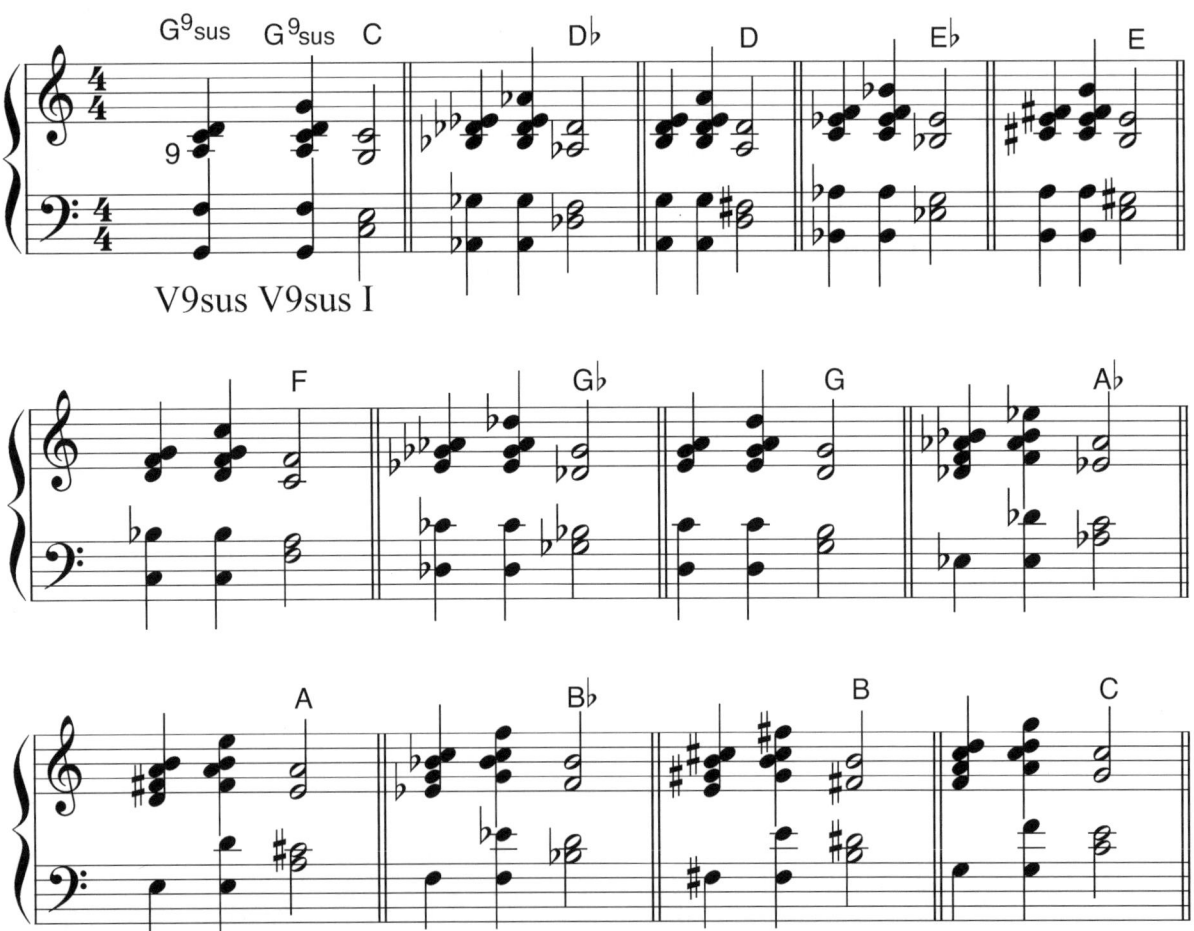

Example 8.25 Play through the Octave. The Known C7 Chord is Struck First.

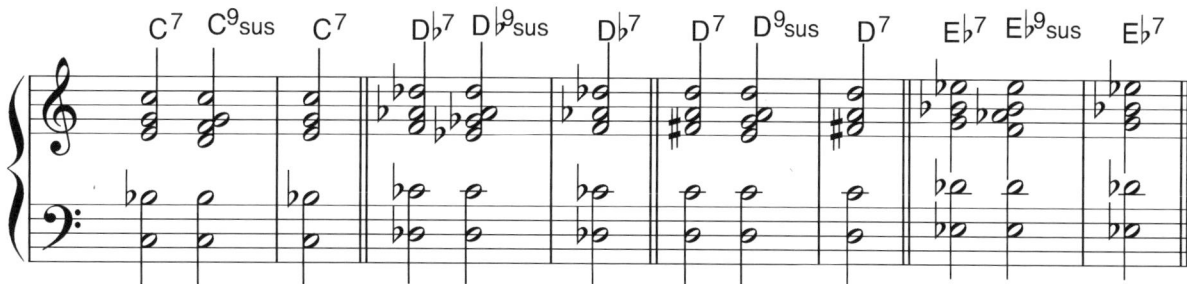

Example 8.26 Play through the Octave.

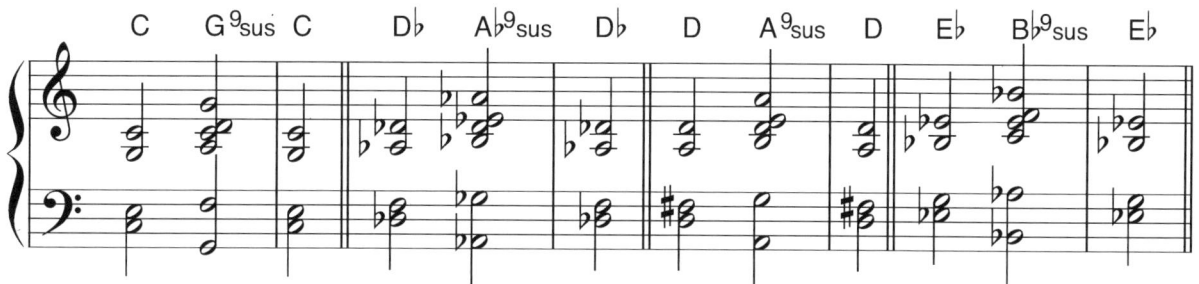

Example 8.27 Play through the Octave

This exercise is a little harder, because it starts, not with the "known" C triad, but with the more "unknown" sus9 chord.

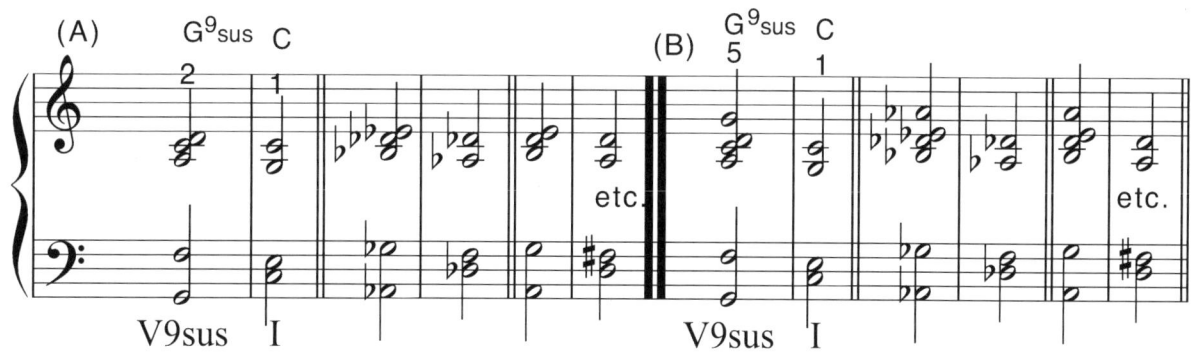

Example 8.28 Play through the Octave. Resolving the Sus9.

The plethora of exercises above is probably *"overkill."* Why do that? I want to make sure you are able to incorporate the valuable sus9 sound into your style.

Example 8.29 Hark! The Herald Angels Sing. Play in A and G.

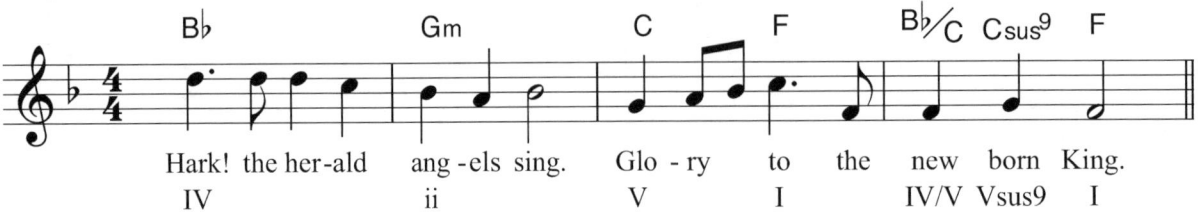

Example 8.30 *Rock of Ages.* Play in A, G, F.

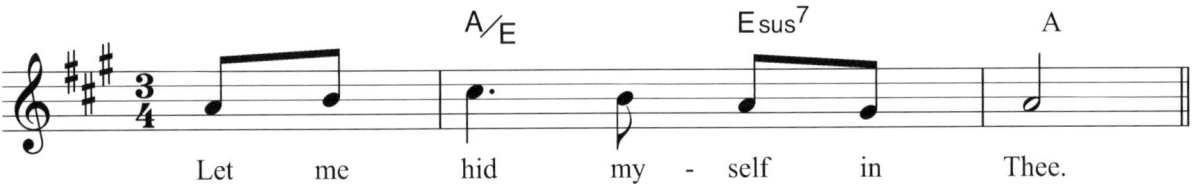

Use Wisely

Regard the sus as an *option*. Don't use it in every situation—rather, when it adds value or provides needed color or variety. Be assured, however, that you are not wasting your time! You will find many uses for the sus9. It will have an immediate, transforming effect on your improvisation. It will sound more modern than a plain V7 chord.

A Companion for Life
Which college friend would be most valuable? Someone you hung out with but didn't connect with after college? Or someone that you kept in contact with, and shared your life with for 10, 20, 50 years after college?

In the same way a song that could be your companion for life which you could sing when you are 40, 60, 80 years old, and which embodies your cherished values and life's very meaning, is of inestimable value.

Longevity serves spiritual development! Can you think of a song that could be your companion for life?

Sus Chords II—How to Incorporate

- 14 pages
- 39 examples

OUTLINE	REPERTOIRE
Sus 9 in Half Cadences	He is Lord Great is Thy Faithfulness
Sus9 in Full Cadences	Seek Ye First Let There Be Praise
Try it! Apply the Sus9	O Worship the King
Modify the Bass	Knowing You I Worship You
Voicing the Sus9	All Creatures of Our God and King
	I Surrender All Glorify Thy Name
	Crown Him with Many Crowns
	How Great Thou Art

In this chapter we will actively incorporate sus chords. We'll use sus chords in half and full cadences. In some cases, the opportunity to use a sus may not seem evident at first. We may have to change the written bass note to allow for the possibility.

Sus9 in Half Cadences

<u>Play/Write into the score a V9sus substitution</u> at the half cadences (asterisk). <u>Label,</u> using the two possible pop symbols (shown below). Indicate the Roman numeral, if you are able. Place the melody on top. Don't omit the 7th of the chord when playing a sus9.

Example 9.1 Two Possible Symbols for the Sus9

Example 9.2 *He is Lord*

Example 9.3 Shorter Excerpt of *He is Lord*   Play in D, E, F, G, A.

Example 9.4 *Seek Ye First*   Play in C, D, E, F, G

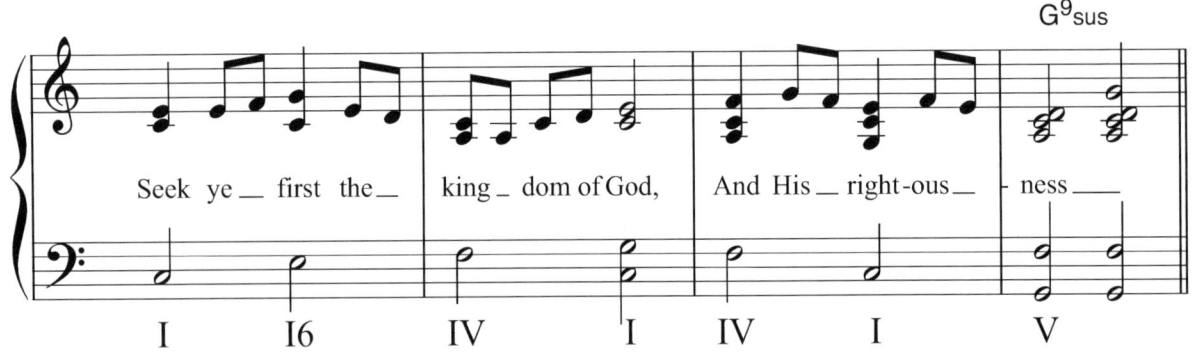

When playing in the various keys (above), play only measures 3 & 4 (shorten exercise).

Example 9.5 *Great is Thy Faithfulness*

there is no shad - ow of turn - ing with thee

Example 9.6 *Let There Be Praise*

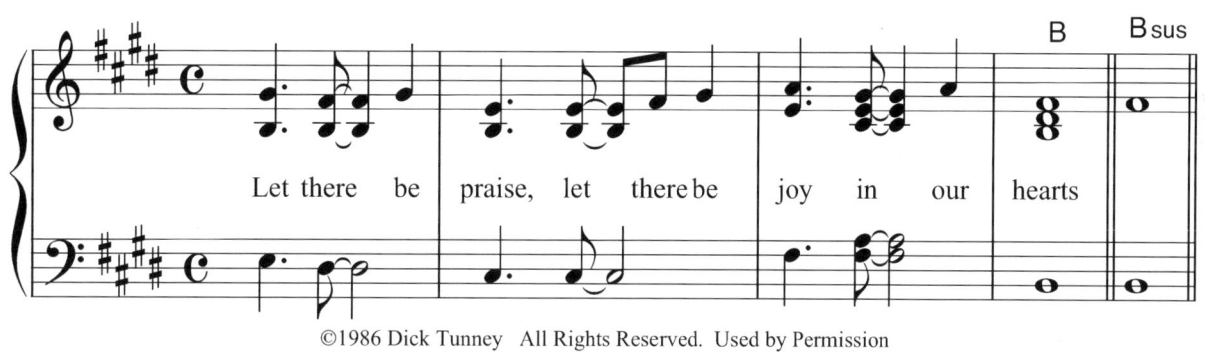

Let there be praise, let there be joy in our hearts

Can you also include a sus9 (above), and employ two different fingerings?

Sus9 in Full Cadences

Example 9.7 **Assignment: Write** the Cadential Sus9

Write the three-chord progression below. For the first chord, write a single note for the LH (bass part) and a three-note chord for the RH. For the second chord, use four notes in the RH (keep the 7th in the RH). When improvising, the 7th can be played by the LH (tenor area) or the RH (alto area).

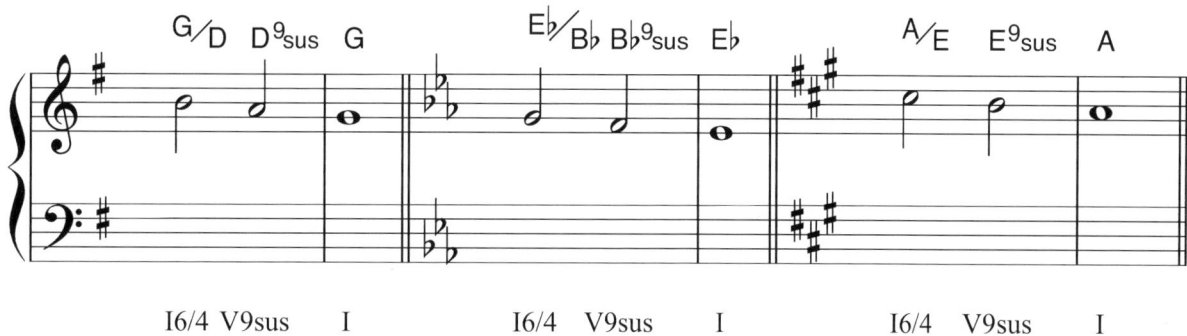

Example 9.8 *He is Lord*   Play in D, E, F, G, A.

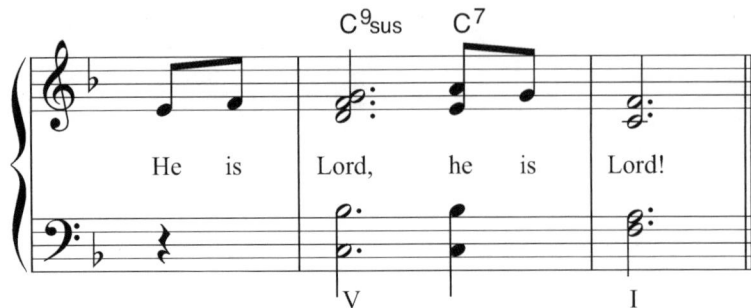

Example 9.9 *Seek Ye First*:   Sus9 in Full Cadence Play in C, D, E, F, G.

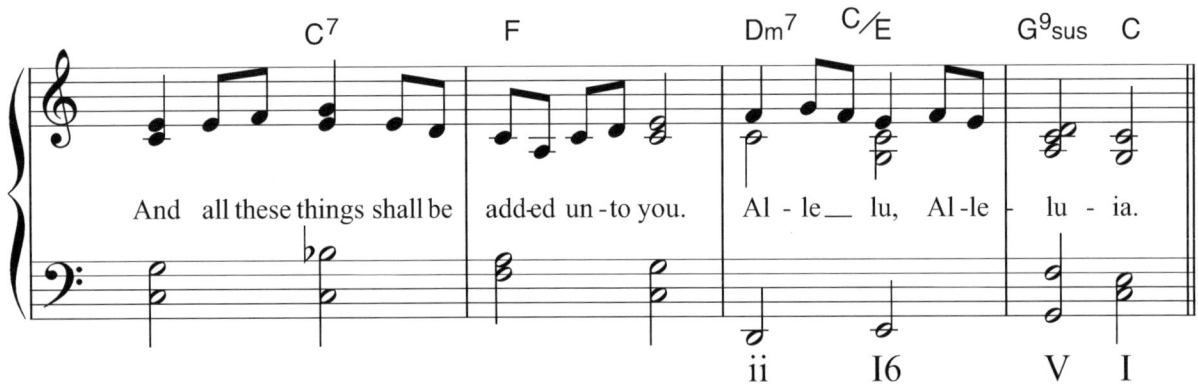

To shorten the above exercise when playing in different keys, play only measures 3 & 4.

Example 9.10 *Silent Night* Play in C, D, E, F, G

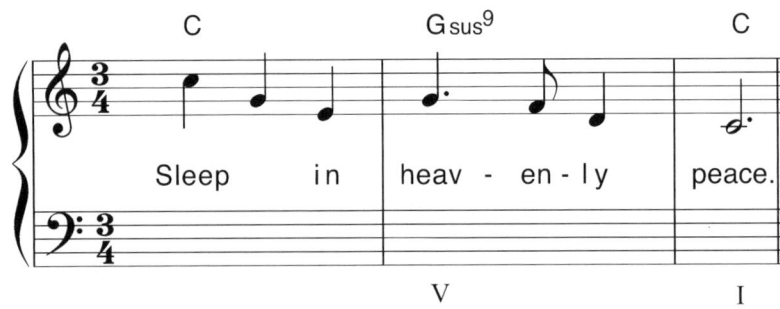

Example 9.11 *O Come All Ye Faithful* Play in F, G, A.

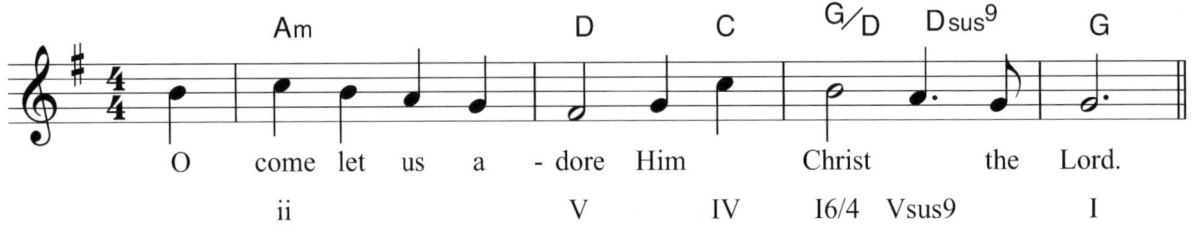

Example 9.12 *All Creatures of Our God and King.* Play a sus, sus7, sus9.

Question: Can you resolve the sus9 above?

Example 9.13 *Knowing You.* Play a sus, sus7, sus9.

Example 9.14 *Amazing Love.* Play a sus9 at the Asterisk and Resolve it

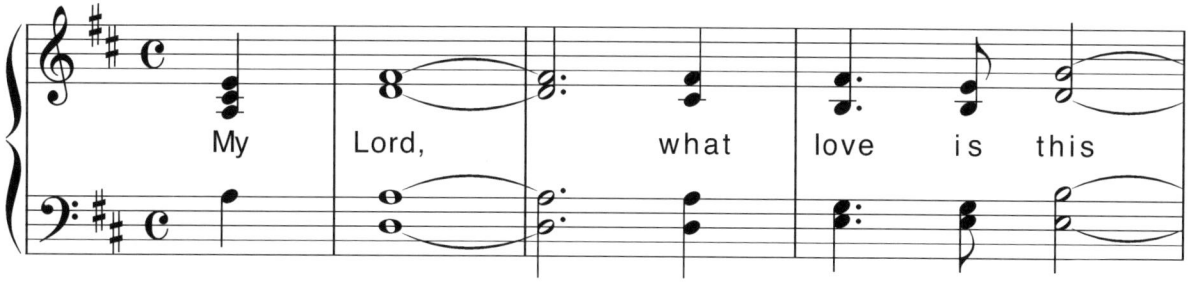

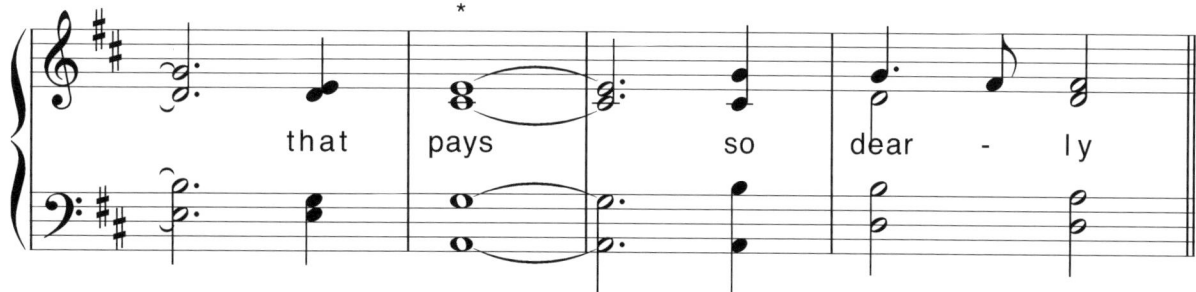

Above, can you resolve the asterisk sus chord (m.5) on measure 6?

The following exercise is difficult, but the pay-off is great. Here, the sus9 *resolves*. It requires you to play through the cycles of fifths.

Example 9.15 **Play it!** Play through the Cycle (Up 4th, Down 5th) by Memory

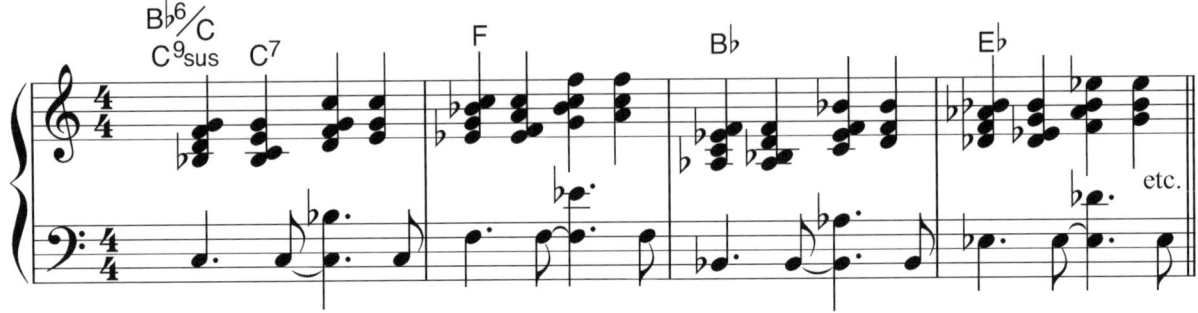

Permutation of sus9. The sus9 can also be permutated, which opens more possibilities. (We will not spend much time on these permutations.)

Example 9.16 Permutation of Sus9

Below, the two sus chords are permutations.

Example 9.17 **Try it.** Sus9 (I Worship You, Almighty God)

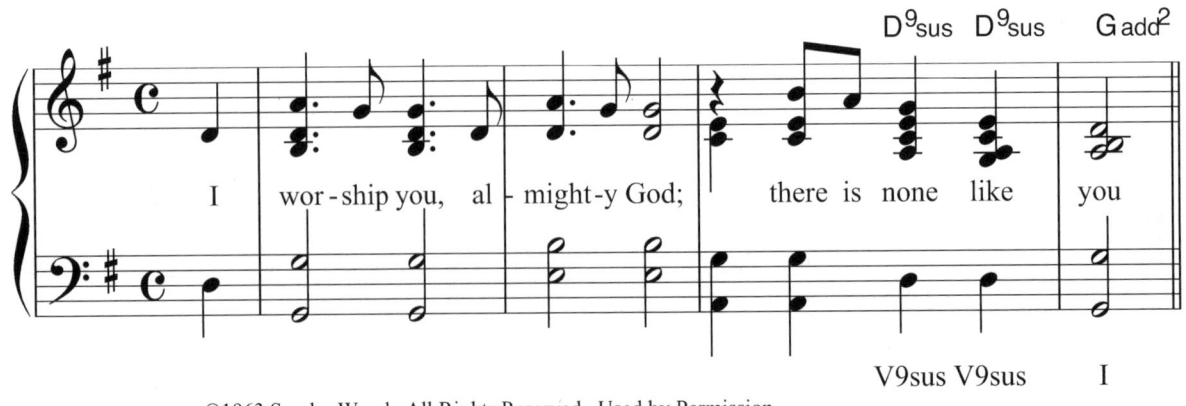

Try it! Apply the Sus9

See the hymnbook version immediately below. We'll develop this excerpt.

Example 9.18 Hymnbook Version of *I Surrender All*

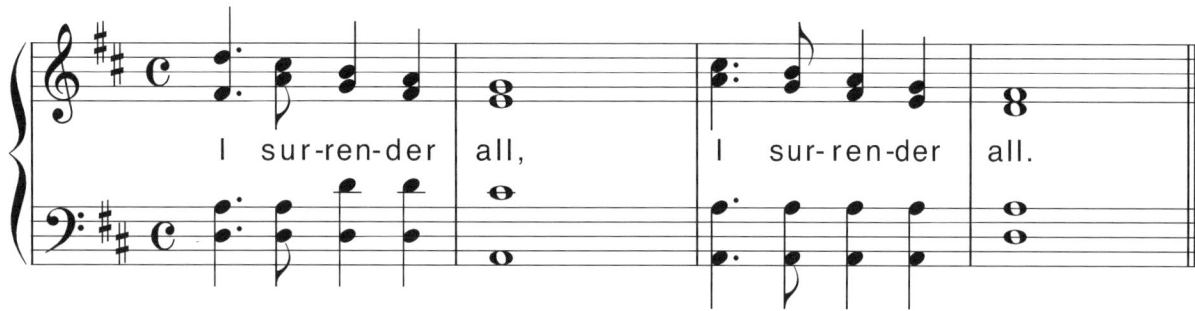

Now <u>write two sus chords</u> in the template provided below. Improvise upon your solution.

Example 9.19 *I Surrender All*

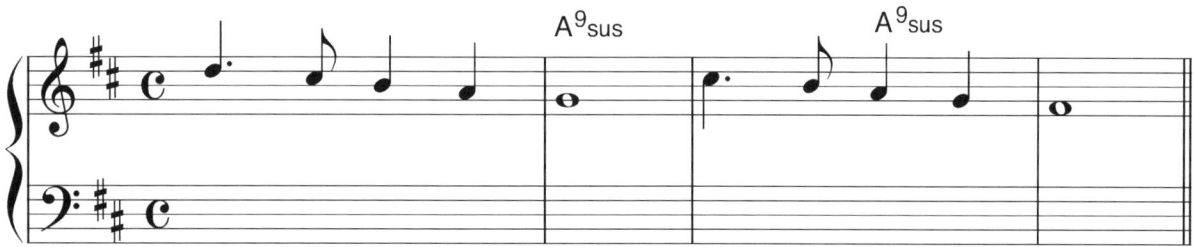

The example below is more complex but also more expressive. This time the bass note and chord of measure2 is changed. <u>Write sus chords</u> where the asterisks occur and then label.

Example 9.20 *I Surrender All*

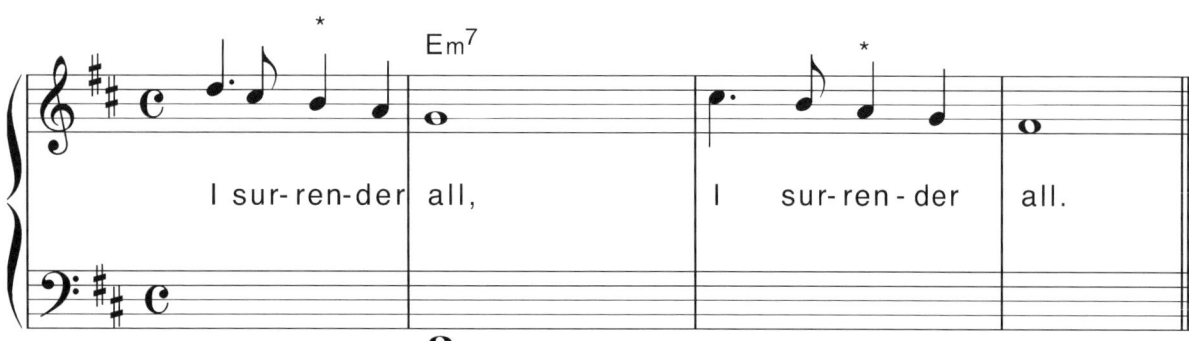

Example 9.21 *I Surrender All* (Sus9 Substitution followed by a minor ninth)

Below are some further enhancements. Diminished chords occur in the right hand on beat 4 of measures 1 and 3.

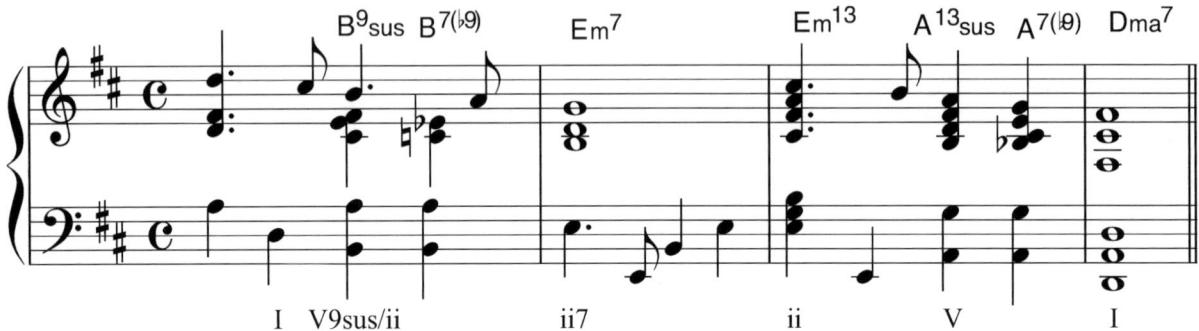

Notice the drooping, chromatic movement in the inner voice in measure 1.

Example 9.22 Chromatic Inner Voice Leading

Now, it's your turn to introduce sus9 chords into the texture.

Example 9.23 Hymnbook version of *Glorify Thy Name*

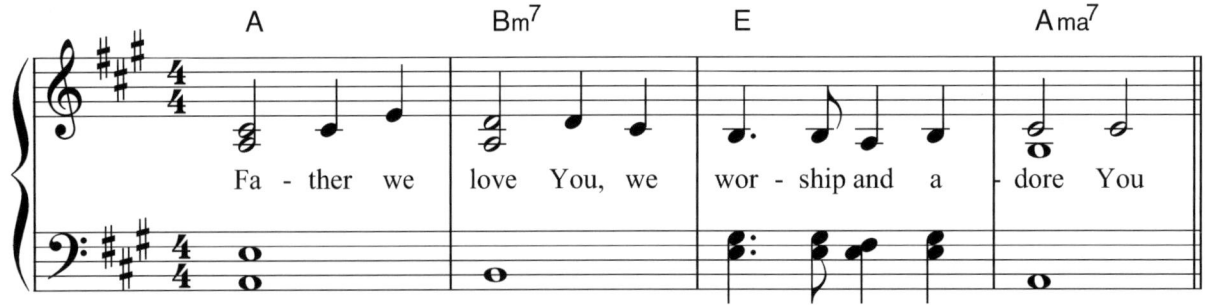

Your sus9 chord (below) can last the duration of measure 3. Improvise with your solution. Change the octave. Try different spacings.

Example 9.24

Example 9.25 *Great is Thy Faithfulness* (add sus chords at the asterisks)

Modify the Bass

Sometimes you will need to modify (alter) the bass line in order to be able to substitute a sus chord. Frequently a IV or I chord can be substituted with a Vsus. And, if you are in a worship team with guitars, you will need to slow down the harmonic rhythm (the number of chord changes per measure).

Vsus Substituted for I. A Vsus chord can often be substituted for a I chord, especially when the 5th of the I chord is in the melody (soprano part). In the example below the G9sus is the alternative for the C chord.

Example 9.26

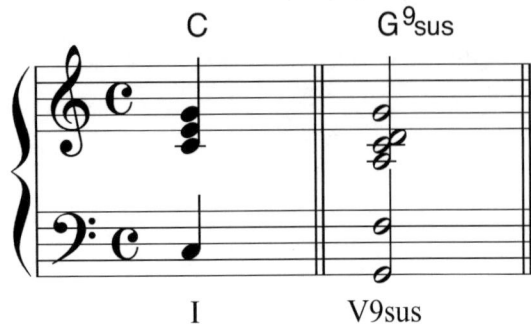

In the hymn *How Great Thou Art,* the hymnbook version begins with the melody on the fifth of the I chord, the note G. We're in the key of C. We could substitute a Gsus9 chord (as demonstrated above).

Example 9.27 Play it! *(How Great Thou Art)*

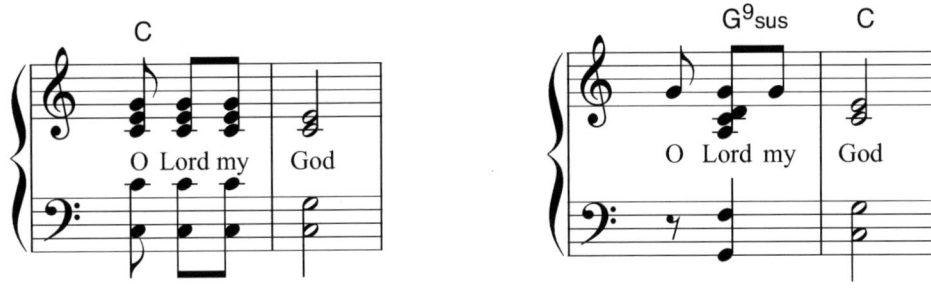

Example 9.28 Hymnbook Version

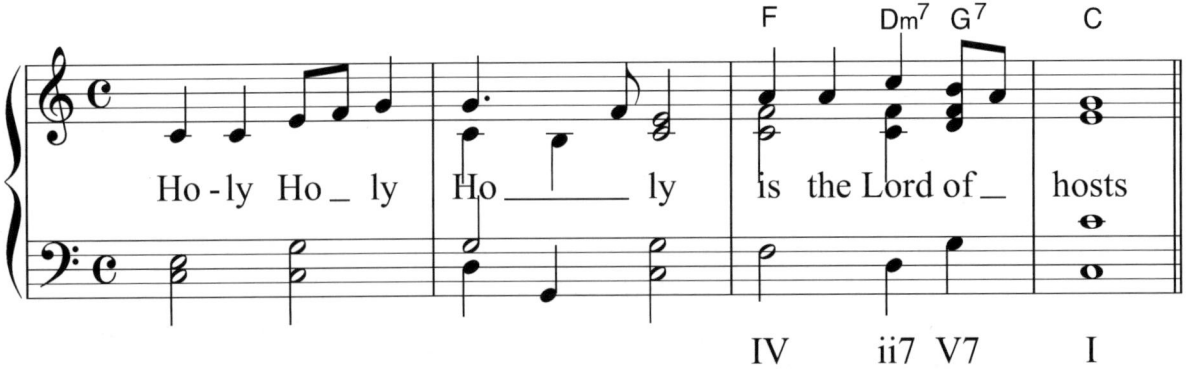

Above, we could slow up the chord changes by substituting a G for D in the bass of measure 2, and by holding the D (beat 3) of measure 3.

Also, a V9sus chord could be substituted for the I chord in measure 4, as below.

Example 9.29 V9sus Substitutions

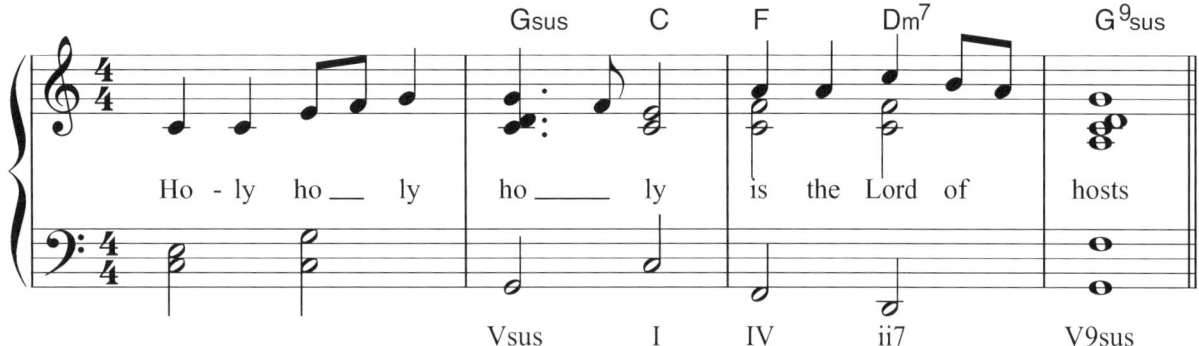

Below, a IV chord appears in measure three.

Example 9.30 *Be Thou My Vision*

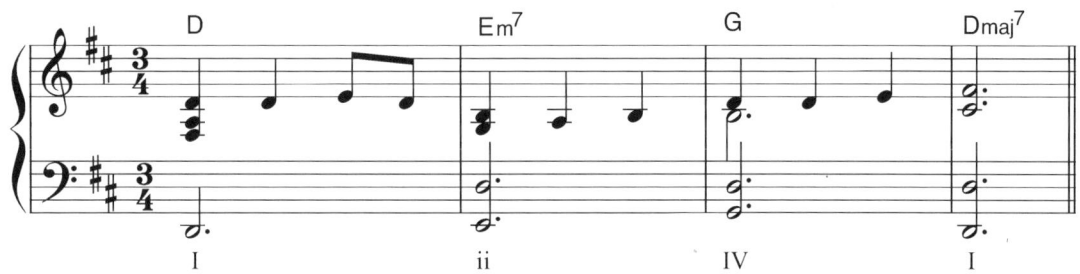

Notice (below) that the V9sus makes an excellent substitution for the IV chord above.

Example 9.31 V9sus Substitution

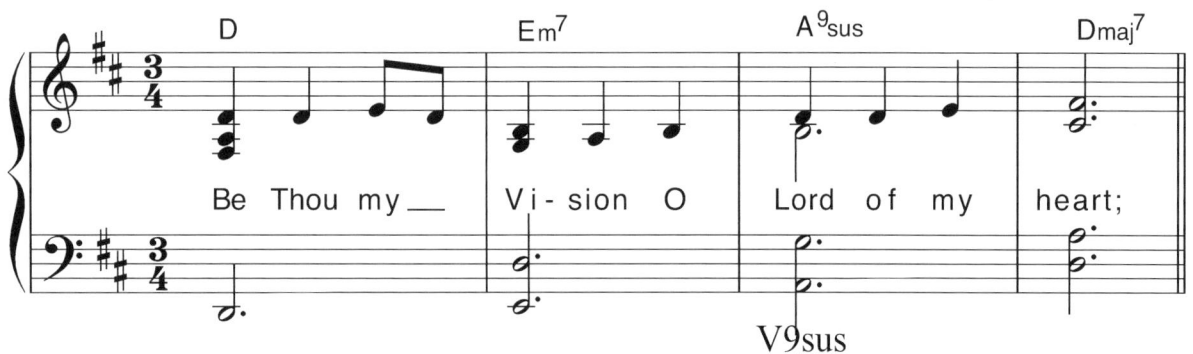

Focus on the pickup chord to measures 1 and 3 below.

Example 9.32 Hymnbook Version of *Crown Him with Many Crowns*

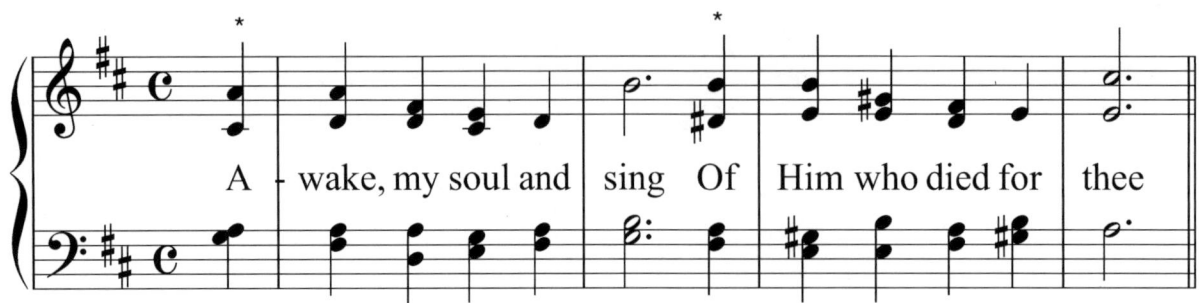

The G and F# sharp pickups in the bass (the seventh and fifth of A and B chords respectively) could remain or be changed. The next example retains those bass notes while employing a sus9 chord.

Example 9.33 Inverted Sus9 in *Crown Him with Many Crowns*

The A9sus/G is a substitute for a third inversion dominant seventh chord, whereas D9sus/F# is a second inversion dominant seventh substitute. Below the bass is changed and the sus9 chords appear in root position.

Example 9.34 Bass Modified for Sus9 Substitution (Root Position Sus9)

The example below shifts the sus9 chords to a different beat.

Example 9.35 Sus9 Shifted (*Crown Him with Many Crowns)*

Voicing the Sus9

There are many ways to voice the sus9. Below, the first chord of each measure is a sus9.

Example 9.36 Play it! Voicings of the Sus9

Sometimes an intervening chord can occur between the Vsus9 and the I chord (as below).

Listen to the progressions below carefully. Note carefully the voicing leading qualities—the inner voice D-Db-C movement, and the G-G#-A movement. In a few cases, the progression resolves somewhere other than F.

Example 9.37 Play it! Colorful Progressions using the Sus9

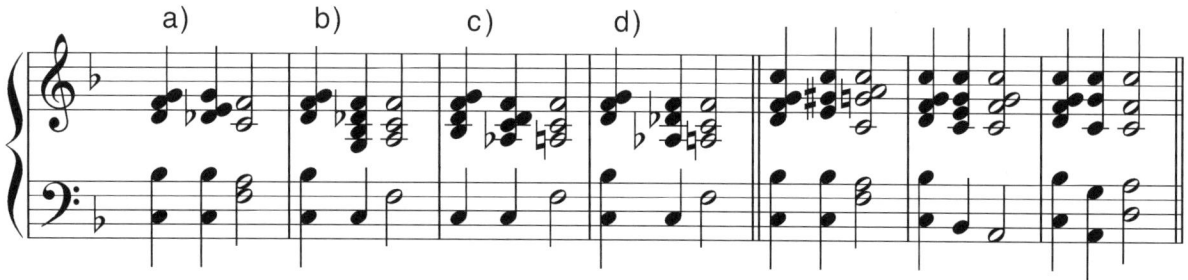

Improvise! Try out b, c, d (above) in the cadential area of the piece that follows.

Example 9.38 *Come Into My Heart*

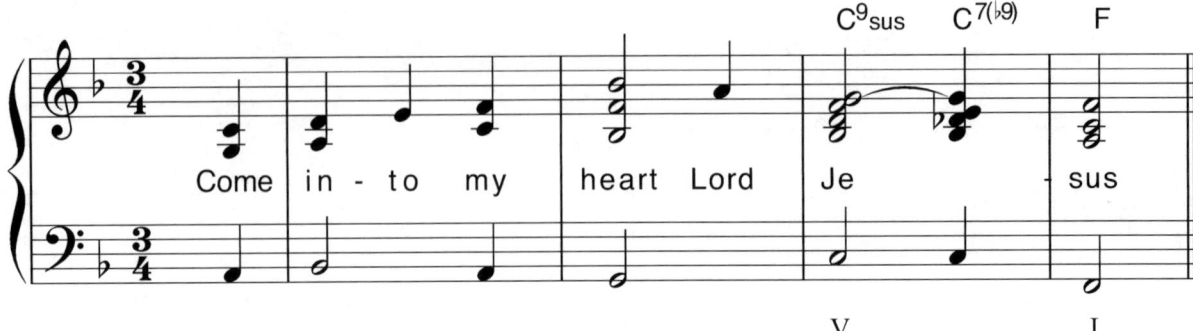

You may want to use highly colorful progressions sparingly, but when employed in the right place, they can be really effective, as with the C7(b9) above.

Example 9.39 Using Sus in Waiting or Background Situations

You may be asked to play some waiting music between pieces or underscoring, background music as someone speaks. Alternating a C chord with any sus chord is one way to provide innocuous background music.

Voice leading properties can't be stressed too strongly. Chords become striking as they relate smoothly to other chords. The interactive horizontal relationship in 9.38 (D - Db - C) is so critical. A kind of synergism results.

Regard the sus as an *option*. Don't use it in every situation—rather, when it adds value or provides needed color or variety. Be assured, however, that you are not wasting your time! You will find many uses for the sus, and particularly the sus9.   It will have an immediate, transforming effect on your improvisation.

The Magna Carta of Worship
Let the word of Christ richly dwell within [among] you,
with all wisdom
teaching and admonishing one another
with psalms, hymns, and spiritual songs,
singing with thankfulness in your hearts to God.

Paul implores us to let Christ dwell in us richly by means of songs.
Songs can have a teaching function.
In singing, we worship "to God" vertically,
and horizontally to "one another."

Sus Chords III—Fourths in Left Hand

> • 14 pages
> • 33 examples

Sus chords have a broad application to both contemporary and traditional worship styles. When the fourth of the sus chord is situated an octave lower in the left hand, it warms up the sound. It also becomes (in the following chapter) one of the primary ways to fashion rootless sus chords.

OUTLINE	REPERTOIRE
Fourth of Sus in Left Hand	Amazing Grace
Non Cadential Sus Chords on iii and vi	Great is Thy Faithfulness
Try it! Modernize the Harmonies	Holy, Holy, Holy O Worship the King
Change the Bass Note	What a Friend We Have in Jesus
Sus 11	Infant Holy, Infant Lowly
Review & Clarification	I Love You, Lord God is So Good
The Value of Transposition	Be Thou My Vision

Example 10.1 Three Fingerings for the C9sus

When the fourth is played in the left hand an octave lower (measure three, above), the resulting sound is often warmer. See if you agree (as below).

Example 10.2 Fourth Played in RH then LH

Example 10.3 4th in the Tenor Part of D9sus *(Amazing Grace)*

Example 10.4 *Amazing Grace.* Change the Asterisked Chord so Fourth is in the LH

Example 10.5 Sus9 Possibilities with the Fourth in the LH

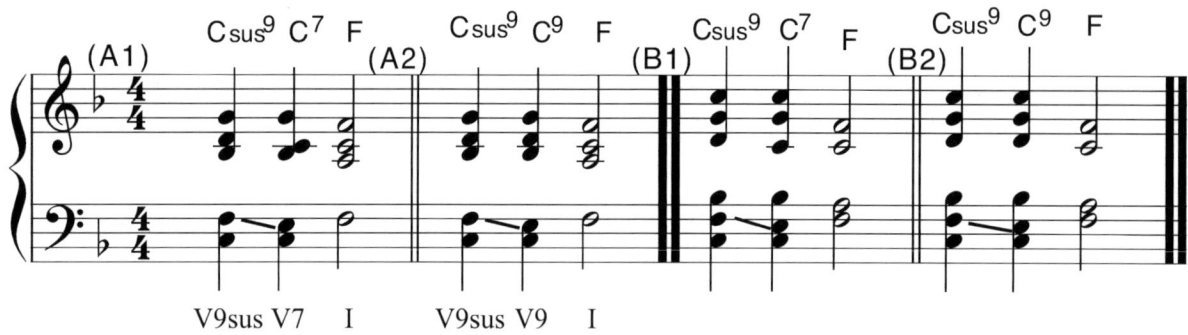

Example 10.6 Play Through the Octave

Example 10.7 Play Through the Octave

Example 10.8 *Great is Thy Faithfulness   Play in C, D, E.*

Example 10.9 *Great is Thy Faithfulness.* Rootless Sus9. Play in C, D, E.

Example 10.10 Play Through the Octave. The sus13 (or 6th) resolves.

Example 10.11 *Amazing Grace.* Supply the Dsus13 and Resolve it to Dsus9

Example 10.12 *Great is Thy Faithfulness.* Place the Fourth in the LH

Non-Cadential Sus Chords on iii and vi

So far we have only considered cadential sus chords on the fifth degree of the scale.
Sus chords, however, can be formed on every degree of the major scale including the
bVII, and they can be left unresolved. Resolved (or unresolved) sus chords can appear on
scale degrees 1-6.

Example 10.13 Resolved Sus Chords on Scale Degrees 1-6

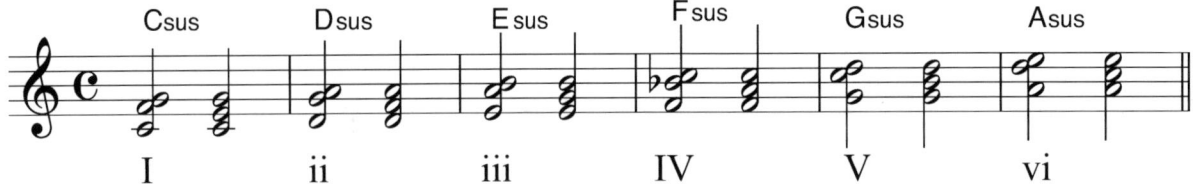

In hymns and choruses, the most frequent use of the sus will be on scale degree V (by
far), followed by scale degree I, and then more infrequently on vi, and even more rarely
on ii. A sus on V or I is your most typical opportunity.

Below, in addition to a iiisus, see the sus (V of IV) that resolves. It functions like a secondary dominant.

Example 10.14 Play it! *Holy Holy Holy:*

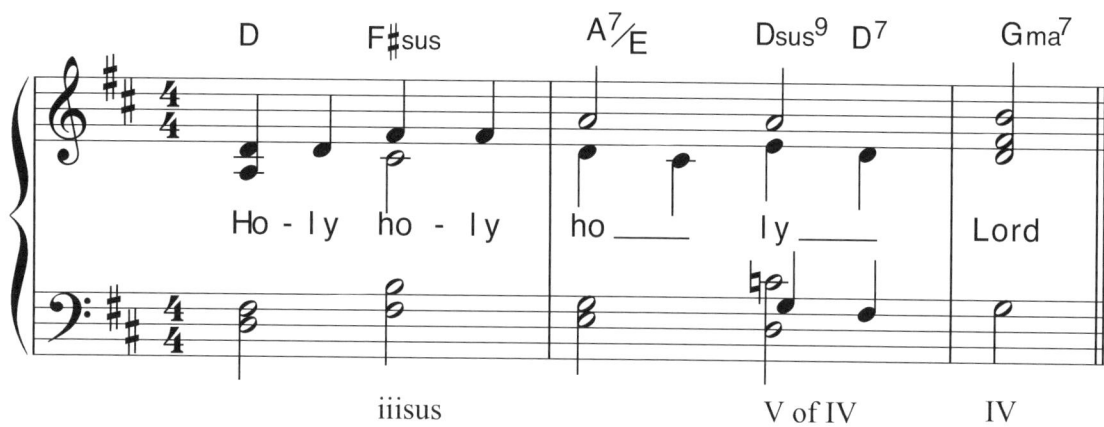

Below, the sus on scale degree six (V of ii) resolves to a dominant seventh with a minor ninth.

Example 10.15 Play it! *Holy Holy Holy:* iiisus (unresolved)

Try it! Modernize the Harmonies

Let's confirm if you're getting the idea. Modernize the harmony. *Include pop symbols and a Roman numeral analysis* at the strategic places and *write in the notes below the melody*. In general, use one chord per measure. For the sus9 chords, don't forget the 7th. Play your solutions.

Example 10.16 **Assignment One:** *I Love You Lord* Play in D and C.

Write one cadential and one non-cadential sus chord for *God is So Good*. Play it.

Example 10.17   **Assignment Two:** *God is So Good*

Do it! Play the first line of *God is so Good* in the keys of C, D, E, F, G, and A with the book closed. This will help you think in music.

Below is a hymnbook version of the carol *Infant Holy, Infant Lowly* to guide you.

Example 10.18   Hymnbook Version: *Infant Holy, Infant Lowly*

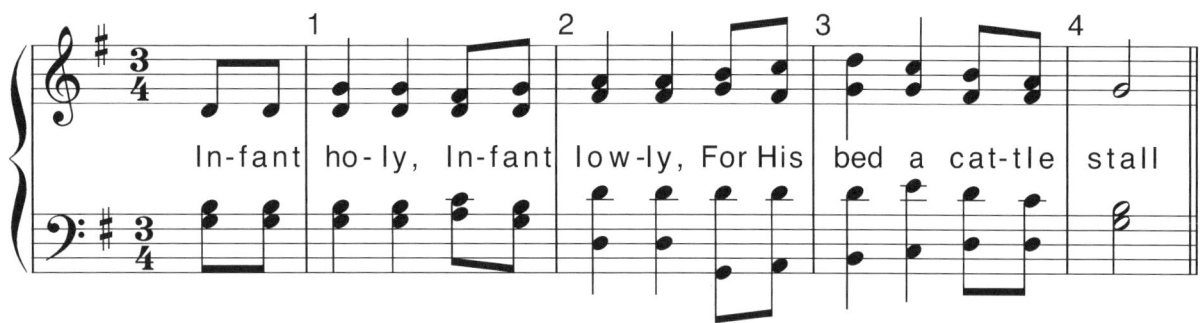

In the template of the same piece below, write only one chord for measures 1, 2, and 4 and two for measure 3. That is, slow down the harmonic rhythm so that guitars could comfortably join you. Write sus chords.

Example 10.19   **Assignment Three:** *Infant Holy, Infant Lowly*

For the next example, use chords in the right hand and a single bass note in the left. Improvise with your solution.

It's more difficult. No pop symbols are given, so you have to discover the harmonies by yourself. Write in three sus chords. Label. Sus chords work well at half and full cadence points. Improvise with your solution.

Example 10.20 **Assignment Four:** *O Worship the King*

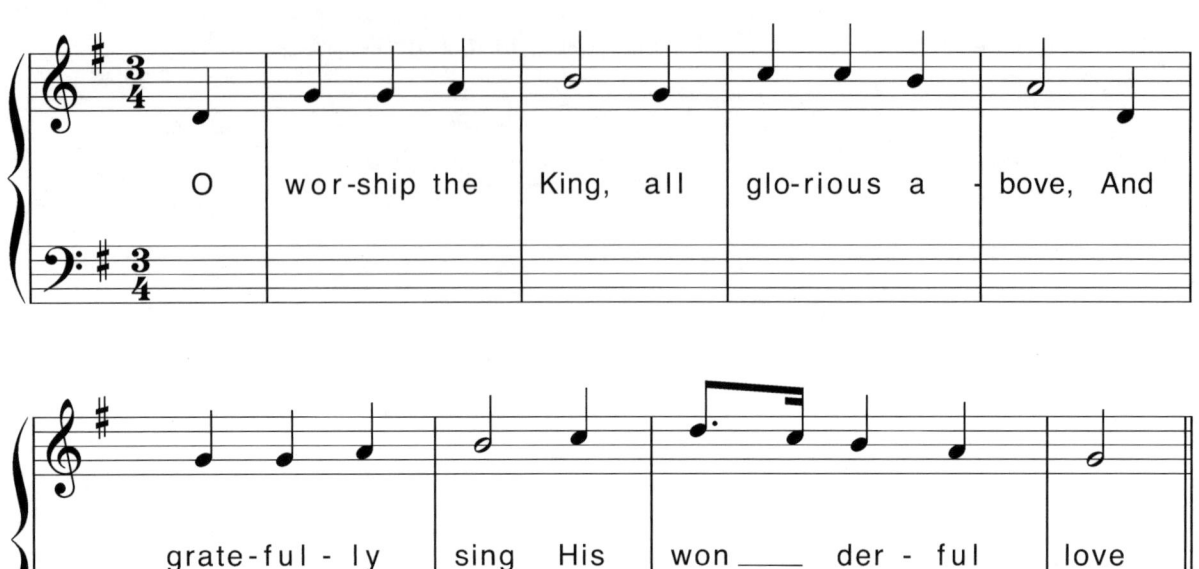

Example 10.21 **Assignment Five:** *Praise the Savior, Ye who Know Him*

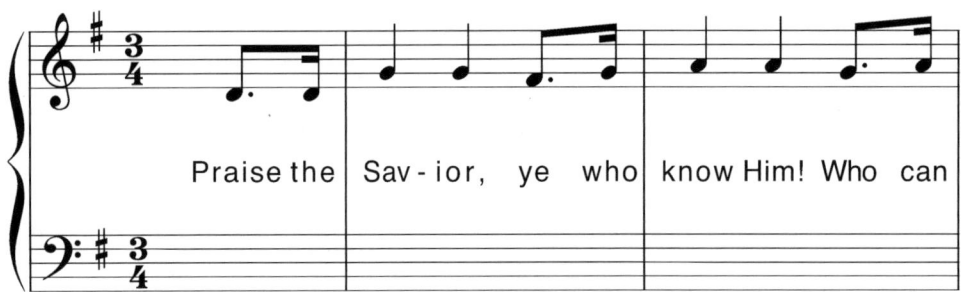

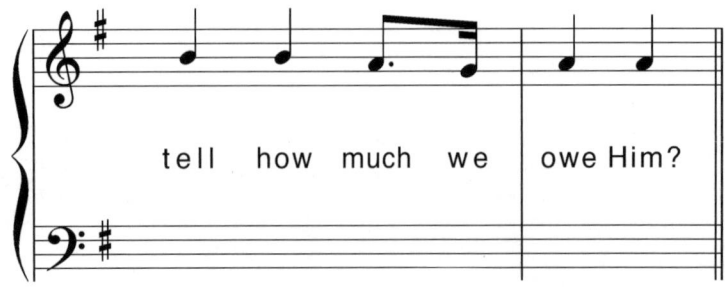

Change the Bass Note

In order to insert a sus9 chord, sometimes you will need to change the bass note. The next exercise requires that you change or add a bass note so as to create a Vsus9 - I full cadence. Write a V9sus-I cadence into the score. Label.

Example 10.22 Change the Bass *(Shine Jesus Shine)*

send   forth your Word,   Lord,   and   let   there   be   light.

The bass notes in the next to last measure should be D then E.

Non-Cadential Sus9 and IV/5

We've had examples where the sus is not cadential. Let's explore this more.

Example 10.23 Hymnbook Harmonization *(O Worship the King)*

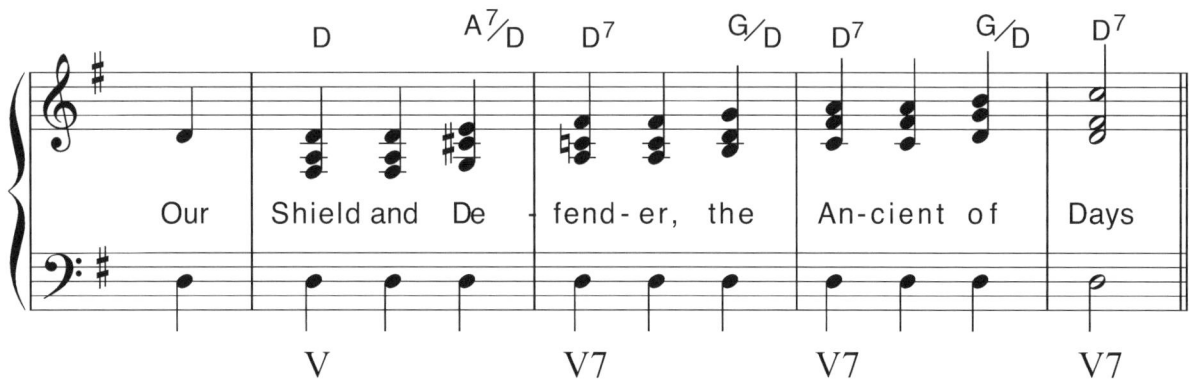

The key is G major. Notice, a V or V7 chord occurs on the first beat of every measure and that we have a D pedal in the bass throughout. Each V chord has a different spacing. The tune is by Joseph Haydn, a famous composer who lived in Austria around the year 1775, and the music style faithfully reflects the music of that period. Notice all the D7 and A7 chords, and the G/D chords. There is nothing wrong with what is written above, but we could modernize the sound by substituting some "four over five" chords. Where could the "four over five" chords occur?

Example 10.24 Play it! "Four over Five Substitutions *(O Worship the King)*

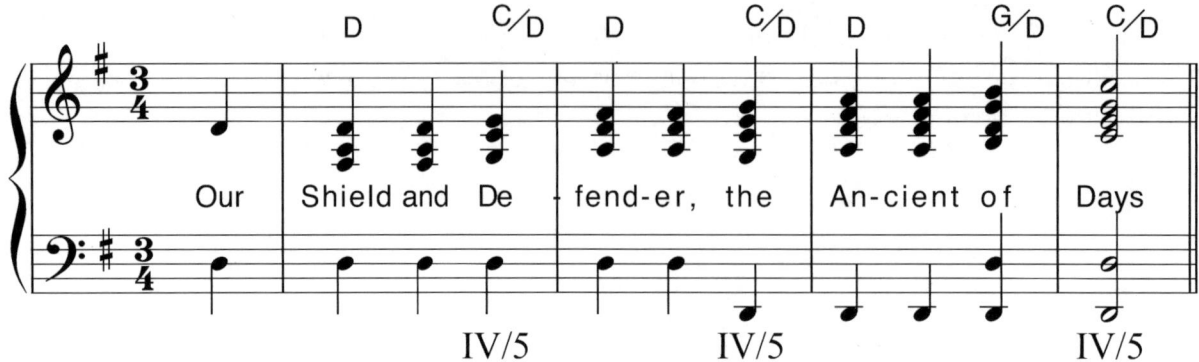

Note. We will look at the IV/5 construction in more detail in a later chapter shortly. Now let's substitute some sus chords.

Example 10.25 Play it! Sus9 Substitutions *(O Worship the King)*

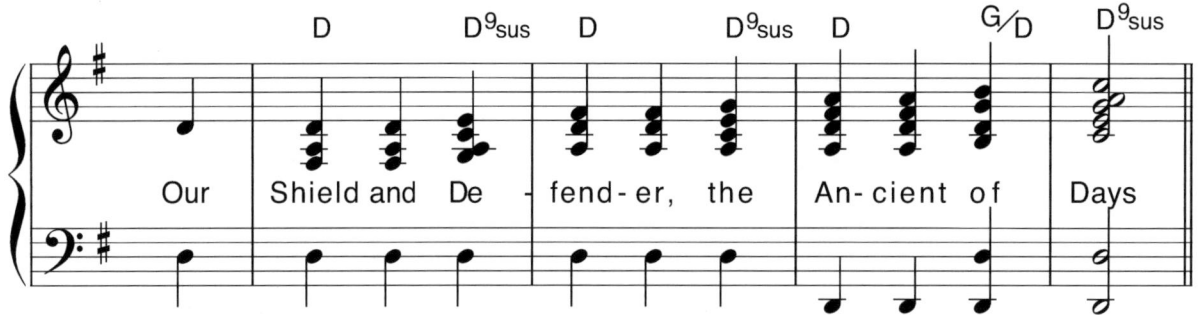

Yes, we could alternate the D chords with a sus9. And we could obtain a greater projection of power by dropping and doubling the D bass note (m.3 above).

Below, another example contains a couple of new wrinkles. Notice a non-cadential sus9 on scale degree one is followed by a 13th, and at the cadence a iisus is followed by a V—another way of handling a half cadence.

Example 10.26 Play it! Non-cadential sus9 *(What a Friend We have in Jesus)*

Sus11

Here's a primary point regarding the sus11: the sus11 sounds pleasing and is usable, whereas a dominant 11th sounds harsh and is therefore less usable.
Why? An intervallic clash exists within the dominant 11th. Below both chords appear, as they typically do, with the bass on the fifth degree of the scale (V).

Example 10.27 V11sus & V11 Compared

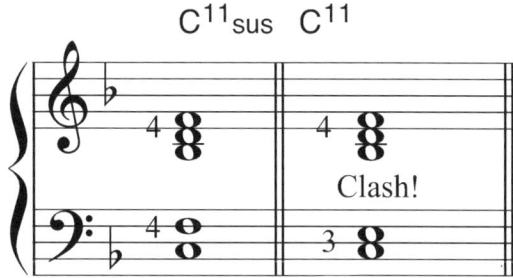

Notice above in measure one that the 11th (soprano F) doubles the 4th (tenor F)— there is no clash. In measure two, however, the F (11th) in the soprano clashes with the E (3rd) in the tenor.   Below, the sus11 is effective in *Be Thou My Vision*.

Example 10.28 Sus11 in *Be Thou My Vision*   Play in F, G, A.

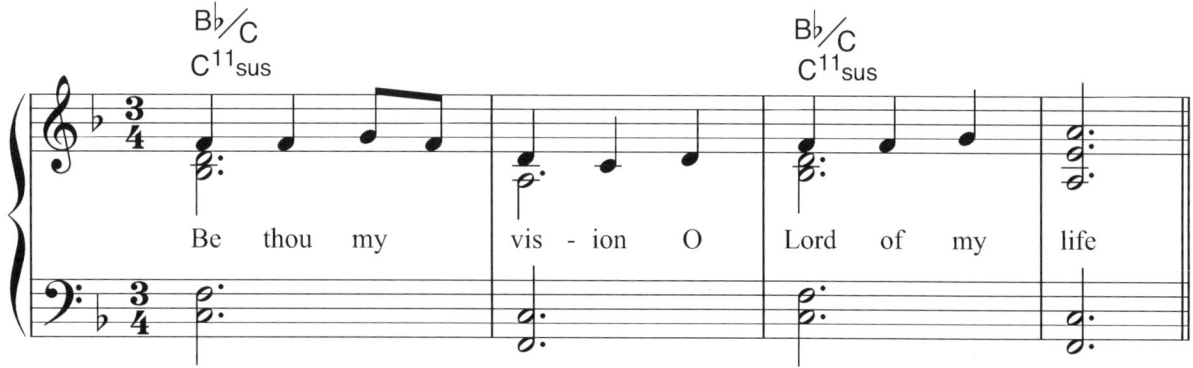

Note the C11sus could also be analyzed as the Bb/C. More on that chord later.

Note: strictly speaking, we might term the C11sus a C9sus, because the F on top is not really a new note—it merely doubles the 4th. We're designating it a sus11, nevertheless, because we want you to realize that thirds can be stacked above the sus chord (all the way to sus17) without any clashes. Note also that the Bb/C symbol works satisfactorily here because the 11th is in the melody.

In the pickup to the refrain of *O Come All Ye Faithful*, a V11sus is employed (below). Notice, it evokes a mellow feeling.

Example 10.29 V11sus in *O Come All Ye Faithful*   Play in F, G, A.

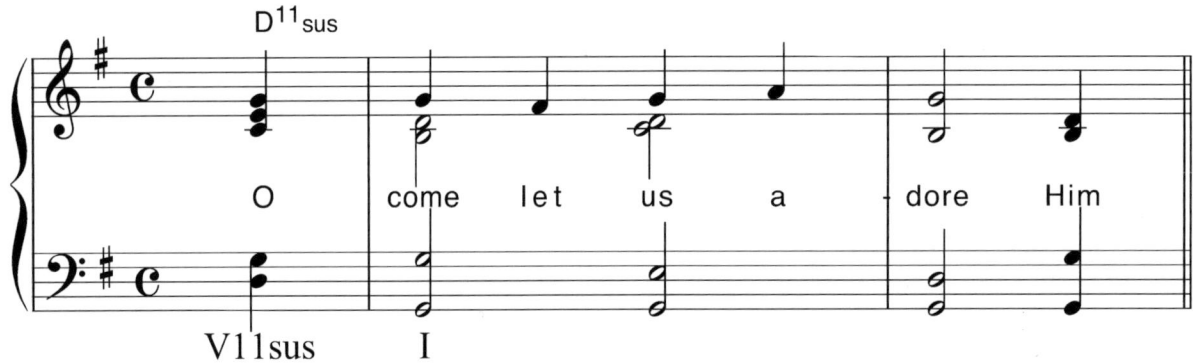

In *Come Thou Long Expected Jesus* (below), a V11sus is substituted in measure 8. Normally a V chord occurs on measure 7 and a I on measure 8, creating a full cadence. The substitution of the V11sus results in a less final sounding half cadence (rather than full cadence on I), and a nice change of harmony. The V11sus can be employed this way rather frequently.

Example 10.30 *Come Thou Long Expected Jesus*

Often a V11sus can be used when the soprano note occurs on scale degree one. This is the case in the above examples as well as below.

Write in the designated chords below.

Example 10.31 **Improvise!** *Infant Holy, Infant Lowly*

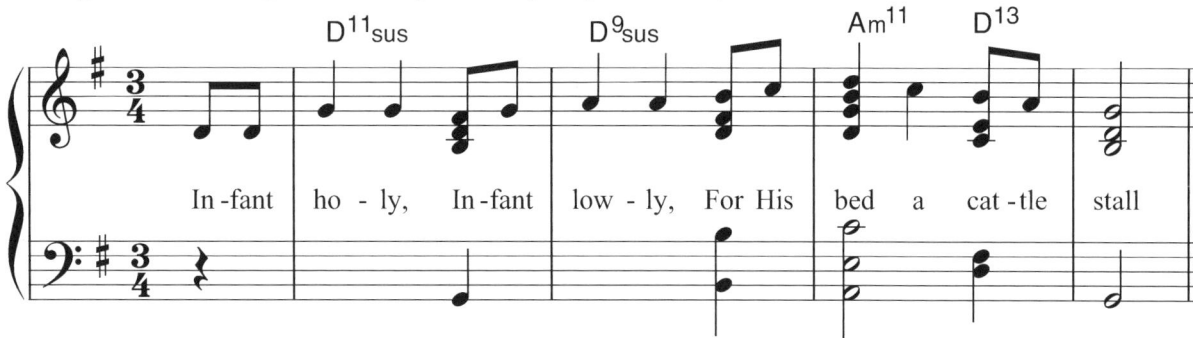

In -fant ho - ly, In -fant low - ly, For His bed a cat -tle stall

Review & Clarification

Example 10.32 Review of Likely Sus4, Sus7, and Sus9 Voicings

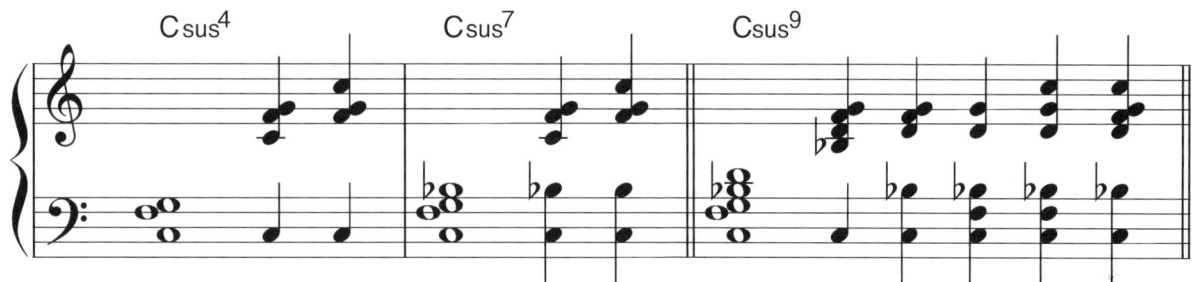

What is a Sus2 Chord? We have been defining a sus chord as 145 (e.g., C, F, G) or Sus4. You may come across situations where a chart or individual uses the term "sus 2" (125). In this case, the term "sus2' is clear. I believe, however that the term sus is better reserved for 145, especially when no number (no 4 or 2) is associated with the symbol.

Question. Have you been experiencing the sound of the examples in this chapter? Don't cheat yourself! Eyeballing it is not sufficient. You need to hear these sounds and take the time to get the feel of sus chords into your fingers.

Example 10.33 Thirds could even extend to the Sus17

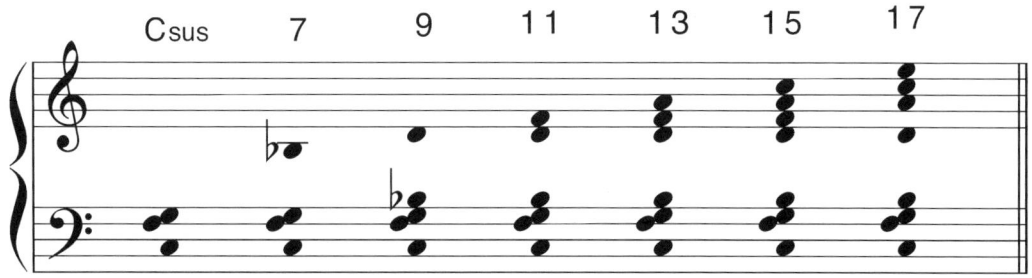

The 11th and 15th double the 4th and root. The 17th (E) clashes with the 4th (F) in the left hand. Since these notes are far apart, the harsh dissonance is mitigated.

(The designations "sus 15 & 17" are not practical terms. They're used merely for explanatory convenience.)

The Value of Transposition

A great way to gain fluency and understanding is to transpose examples. Play the examples in different keys as much as possible in every chapter. Until you transpose a song or example you may not really understand it. You may just be reading the notes.

Transposition will keep you mentally active. It will sharpen you awareness of (1) the scale degree of the first note in the melody, (2) the bass line movement and function, (3) the relationship of bass to melody, (4) chord outlines, (5) intervallic relationships, and (6) scale fragments. You'll gain much more than just an understanding of sus chords.

Do we need to think again?

Consider a statement by Paul, displayed structurally, that pertains to Christian worship. Clearly, our songs can have a teaching and admonishing function.

Colossians 3:16
Let the word of Christ richly dwell within you,
        with all wisdom
                teaching and admonishing one another
                        with psalms, and hymns, and spiritual songs,
        with thankfulness
                singing in your hearts to God. (NASB, 1995)

Below, the same functions that apply to the ministry of song, teaching and admonishing, appear to apply to Paul's own preaching ministry as an apostle. Virtually the same, exact phrases occur in close proximity in chapters one and three of the same book.

Paul in Colossians 1:28   [preaching ministry]
And we proclaim him
        admonishing every man and
        teaching every man with all wisdom (NASB, 1995)

Paul in Colossians 3:16   [worship ministry]
Let the word of Christ richly dwell within you
        with all wisdom
        teaching and admonishing one another
                with psalms, and hymns, and spiritual songs (NASB, 1995)

We often think of the sermon as the teaching part of the service, and the music as worship, but not as having a teaching function. Does this comport with Paul's emphasis?

CHAPTER 11

Sus Chords IV—Advanced Extensions

- 16 pages
- 43 examples

Our goal in this chapter is to develop more subtlety of sound and greater shading and resonance. To accomplish this we'll explore sus chords that function as secondary dominants. As well, we will look at extended *sus extensions*—especially the sus 13, and rootless sus chords. When you are a keyboardist reading a praise chart that calls for a simple sus chord, often you can include a more colorful sus extension (a sus9, or sus13, for example) without clashing with the other players—at your discretion.

OUTLINE	REPERTOIRE
Sus Functioning as Secondary Dominant	Change My Heart O God Emmanuel
Overview of Sus7, 9, 11, 13, & 17	It is Well Be Thou My Vision
Sus13	What a Friend we Have in Jesus
More Extreme Voicings for Sus13	Jesus at the Center Silent Night
Try it! Apply the Sus13	How Great Thou Art Doxology
Sus17	Jesus Paid it All
Rootless Sus Chords	Amazing Grace Great is Thy Faithfulness

Sus Functioning as Secondary Dominant

Secondary dominants can apply to ii, iii, IV, V, and vi chords.

Example 11.1 *Change My Heart O God.*   Secondary Dominant Pattern.

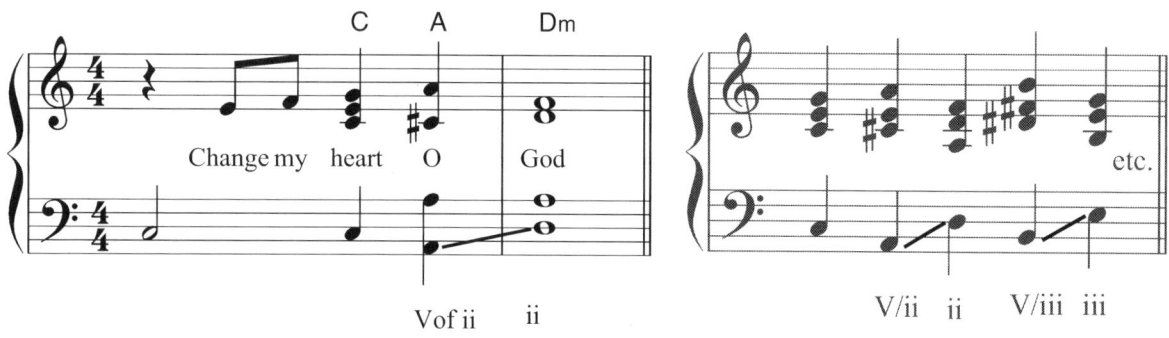

Example 11.2 Secondary Sus Dominant Demonstrated *(Change My Heart O God)*

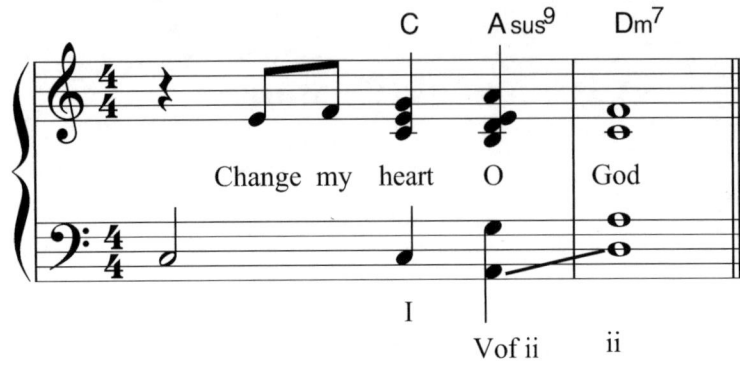

Example 11.3 Secondary Sus Dominant Pattern

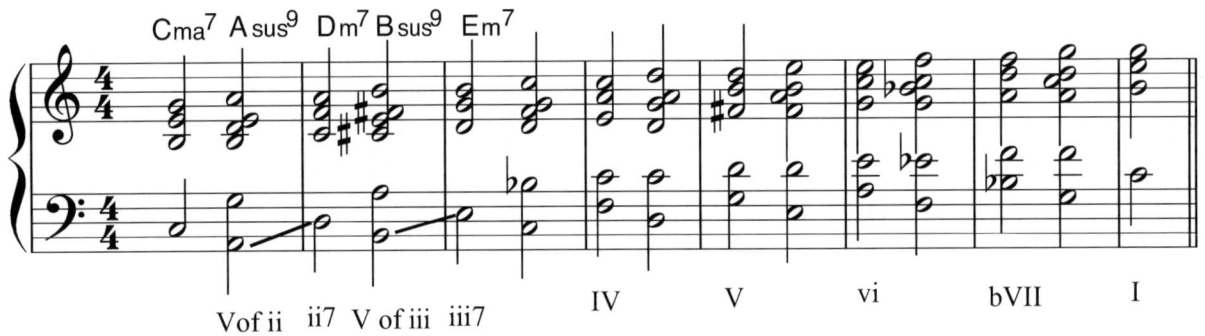

Example 11.4 Sus V of iii and ii Demonstrated *(Emmanuel)*

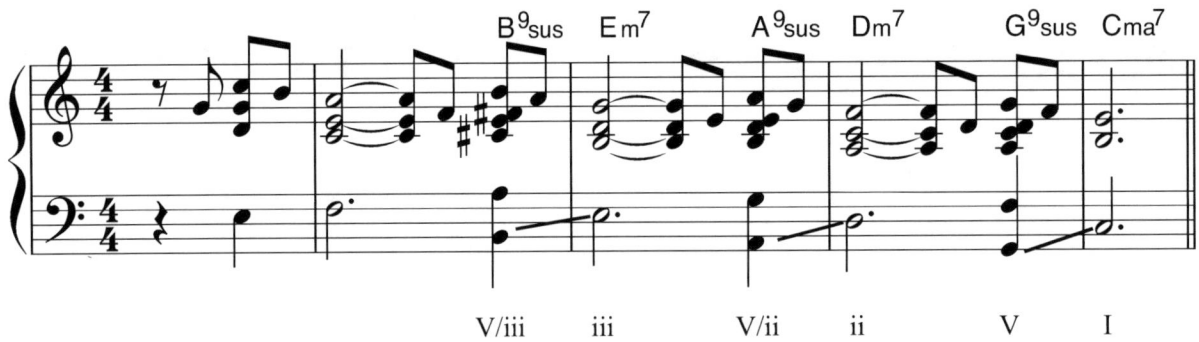

Example 11.5 Sus V of IV Demonstrated *(Jesus Loves Me)*

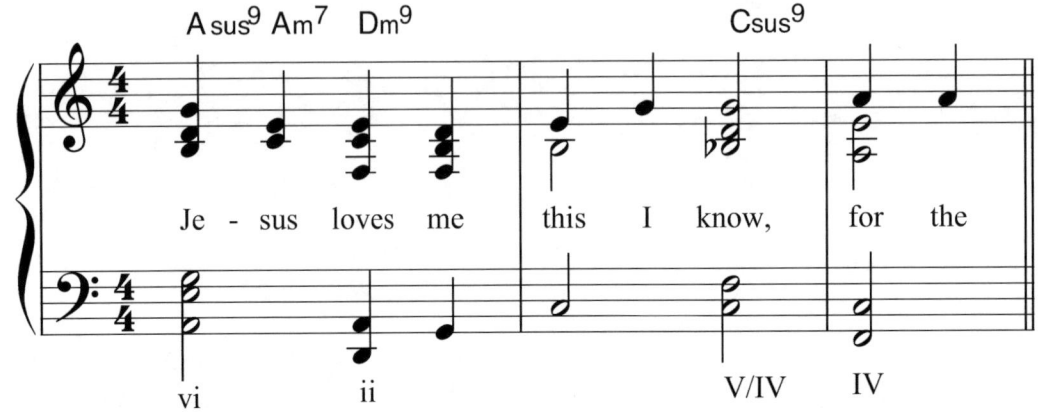

Example 11.6 Vsus of ii followed by V7(b9)   *(Fairest Lord Jesus)*

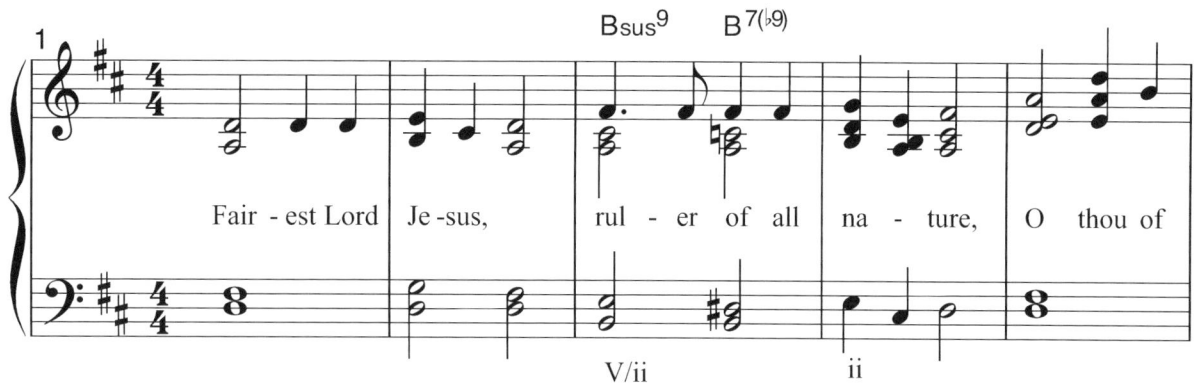

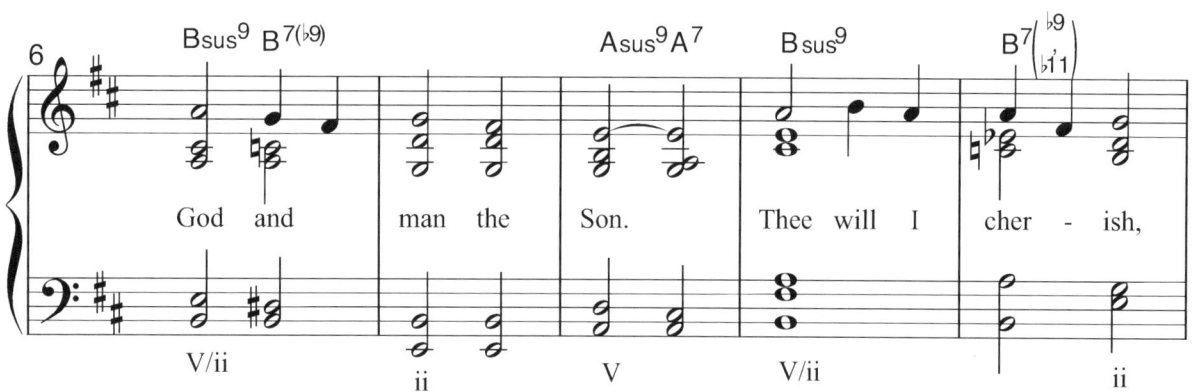

Example 11.7 Write in the Chords. Play it! *(Amazing Grace)*

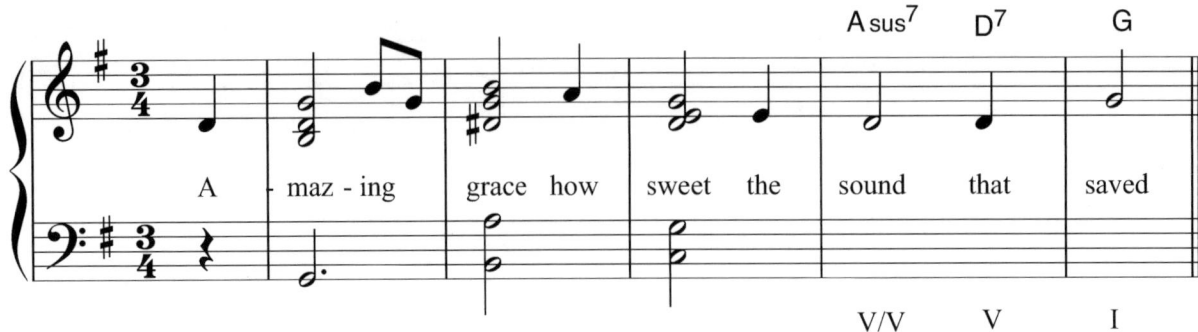

Overview of Sus7, Sus9, Sus 11, Sus13, Sus17

Remember, the difference between sus extensions and dominant seventh extensions is that the sus has a fourth while the dominant seventh has a third. (Incidentally, we are not suggesting that you learn the designation "sus17." Sus17 is used merely to indicate that multiple thirds can be piled on top of the simple sus chord.)

Example 11.8 Play it!

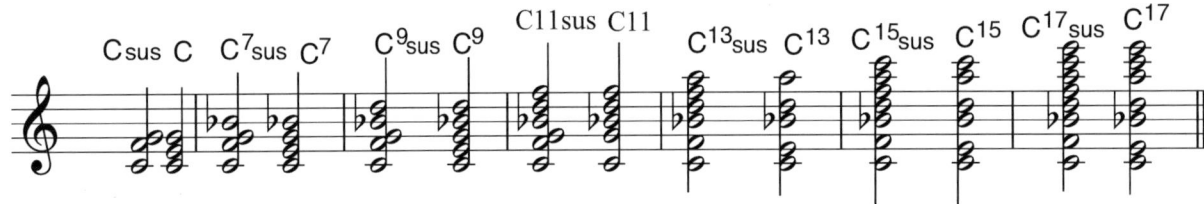

Notice that the third in the C11 (measure four) has been omitted in order to avoid a clash with the soprano (E<->F). The high F of the C13, C15, and C17 has been omitted to avoid a clash with the low third (E) of the chord. The fifth of the C13 has been omitted.

Now let's use both the bass and treble clefs and open up more resonance by offering a few additional voicings.

Example 11.9 Play it!

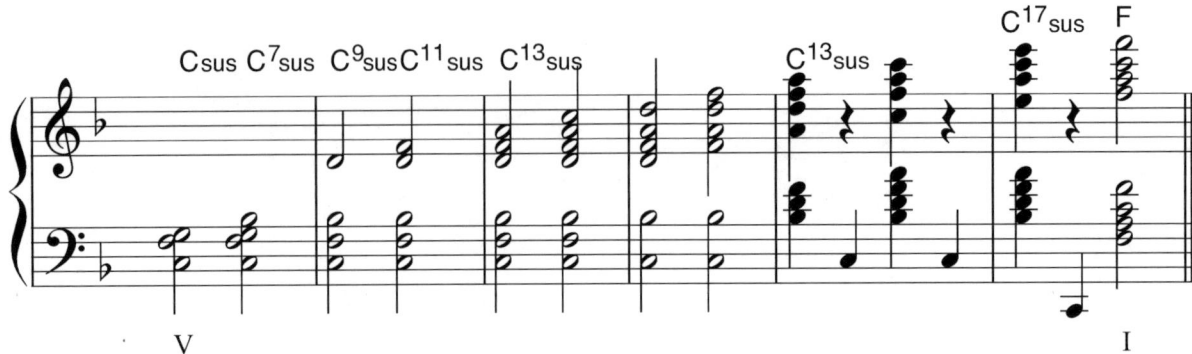

Example 11.10 Play it!

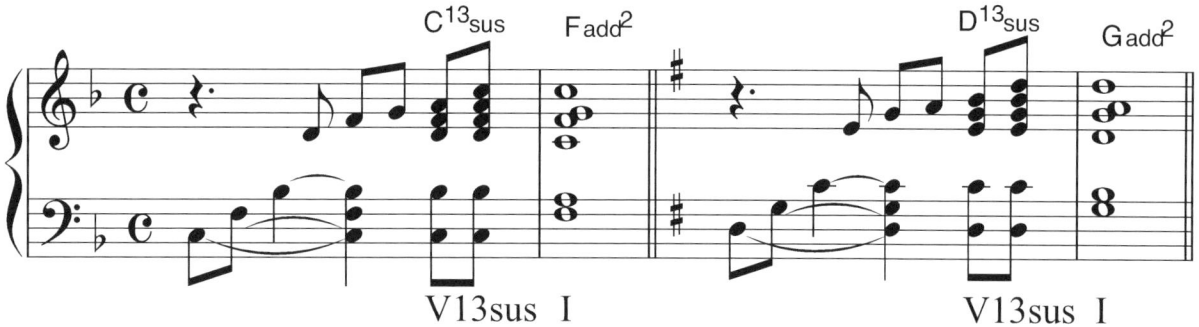

Do it! Practice playing this in four keys.

Sus13

We want to underscore that the extensions *are* useable when playing with a band or worship team—but even more so when you are leading worship from the piano alone, soloing, or when you are accompanying a singer or instrumentalist. They can have a telling effect. The sus13 is particularly useful.

Example 11.11 Sus 13 Resolves *(Amazing Grace)* Play in E, F, G, A.

Example 11.12 Sus13 Resolves *(Great is Thy Faithfulness)*

Now play the sus13 through the cycle of fifths (Up a 4th or Down a 5th)

Example 11.13 Sus13   Up Chromatic Scale

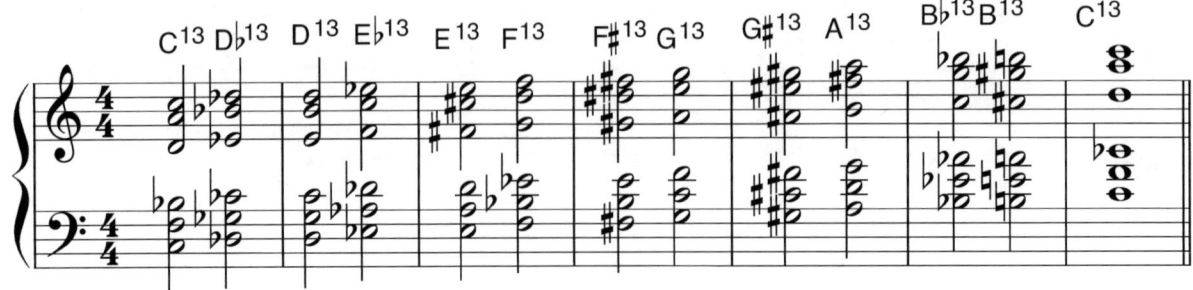

Example 11.14 Root Position Sus13. Play the Cycle (Up a 4th, Down a 5th)

Example 11.15. Supply the Dsus13. Resolve it to D9. *(Amazing Grace)* Play in F, G, A.

Example 11.16 Play it! Sus13 in *It is Well*

The G9sus (m.4) works because the third (10th) in the soprano is distant from the bass.

Example 11.17 Sus13 *(Be Thou My Vision)*. Play in E and F Major.

Example 11.18 Thirteenth in Melody *(What a Friend We Have in Jesus)*

Example 11.19 Sus13 Root Position Exercise (Descending M2 Pattern)

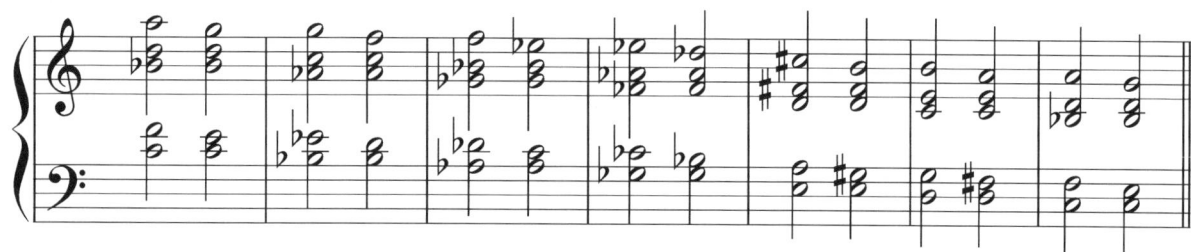

Example 11.20 Fourth Placed in Left Hand. Various Spacings.

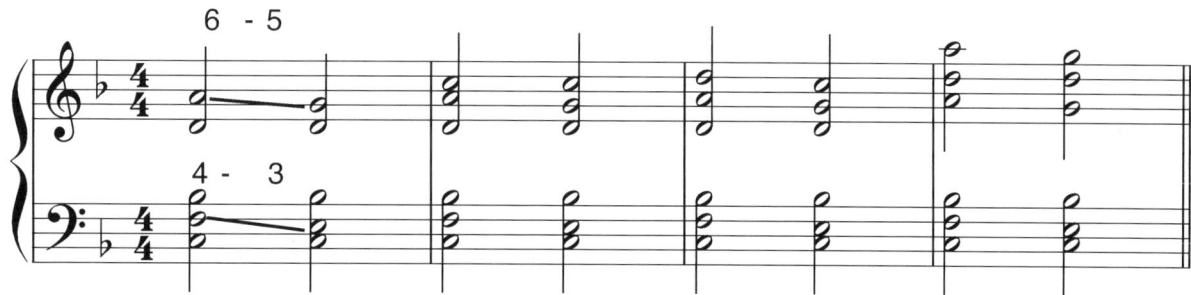

More Extreme Voicings for Sus13

Example 11.21 Some Voicings of V13sus - I

Below are more exotic progressions using the C13 with A as the top note.

Example 11.22 Play it! Colorful Progressions using C13sus (A, top note)

C13sus chords are below, but now with a higher top note. Open fifths (e,f, i, j)) are used.

Example 11.23 Play it! Wider Spaced C13sus Progressions.

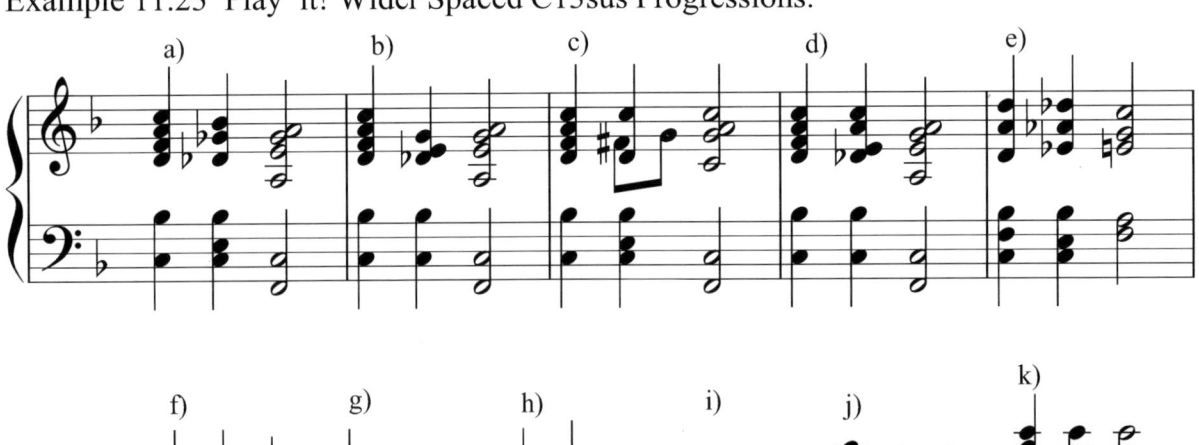

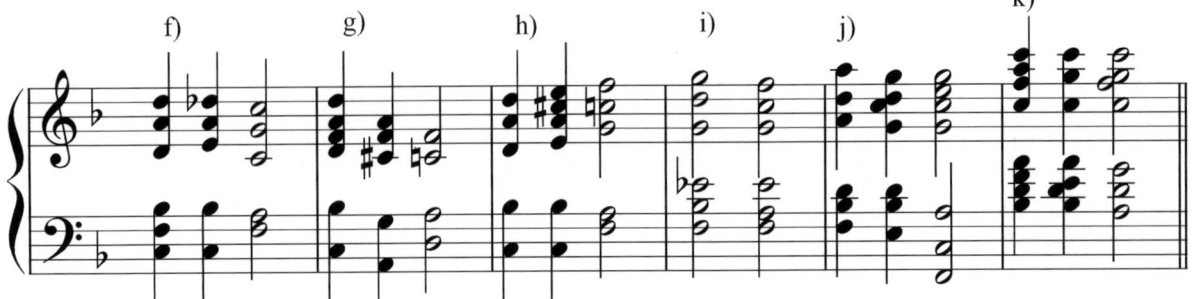

Notice, above, that "j" and "k" have rootless chords (C is the root).

Example 11.24 Play it! *Great is Thy Faithfulness* (Based on "a")

Example 11.25 Write/Improvise *Great is Thy Faithfulness* (Based on "b")

As closely as possible, duplicate the chord structures of ms. 1 & 2 in ms. 3 & 4.

Example 11.26 Improvise/Write. *Great is Thy Faithfulness* (based on "c")

As closely as possible, duplicate measures 1 & 2 in measures 3 & 4.

Example 11.27 Improvise! *Great is Thy Faithfulness* (based on "d")

As closely as possible, duplicate ms. 1 & 2 in ms. 3 & 4. Fill out the accompaniment where there are pop symbols. Notice that measure five uses material from "h."

The next exercise is designed to get sus13's into your fingers and head.

Example 11.28 Sus13 through the Cycle of Fourths

Try it! Apply the Sus13

<u>Fill in</u> <u>and label</u> a V13sus chord on beat one of measure two. Don't forget the 7th.

Example 11.29 *Silent Night*

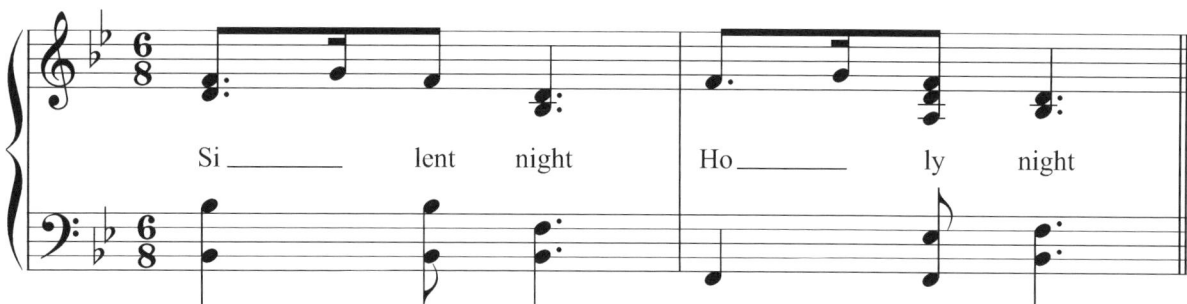

Fill in and label a V13sus chord on beat one of measure four (below).

Example 11.30   *Be Thou My Vision*

Sus 17

You might think, "There's no practical use for a sus17." Think again! Though more rare, here is an example. However, we would never use the designation "sus17" in a practical situation. The idea to grasp is that many thirds can be piled onto a sus chord.

Example 11.31 How Great Thou Art

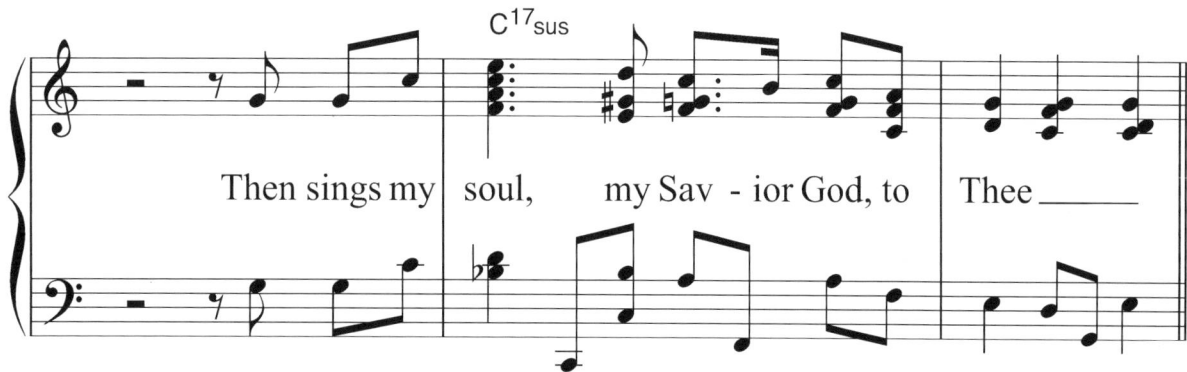

For the C17sus, the dissonant third (10th) on top works because it is distant from the bass.

Rootless Sus Chords

Students sometimes ask, "Why are they important?" Answer: (1) They are a means of avoiding stepping on (and unnecessarily doubling) the bassist's part in a band. (2) Sometimes they sound more interesting than sus chords with roots.

Let's look at how they could evolve from a simple hymnbook harmonization.

Example 11.32 Hymnbook Version *(What a Friend We Have in Jesus)*

Example 11.33 Sus9 Version *(What a Friend We Have in Jesus)*

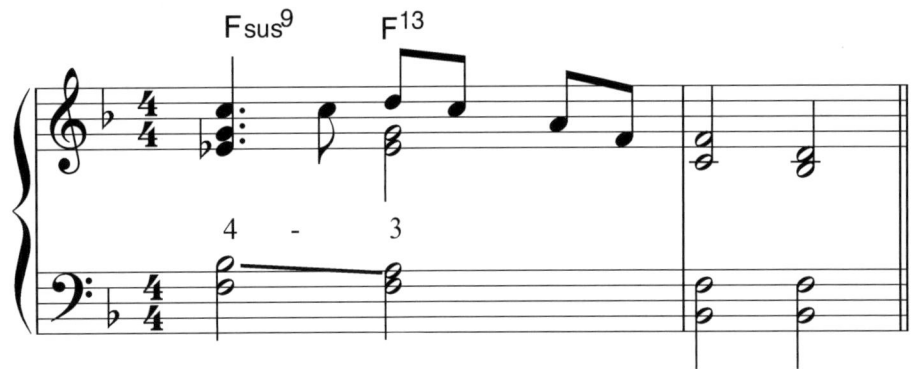

Example 11.34 Rootless Sus9 *(What a Friend We Have in Jesus)*

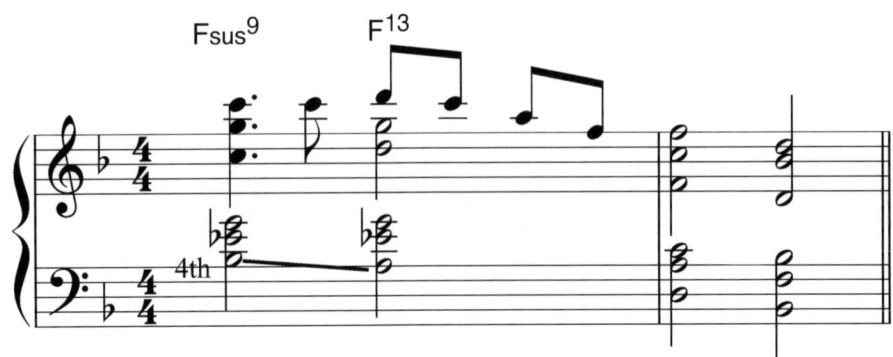

Example 11.35 Rootless Sus, with 4th as Lowest Bass Note. C is the Root.

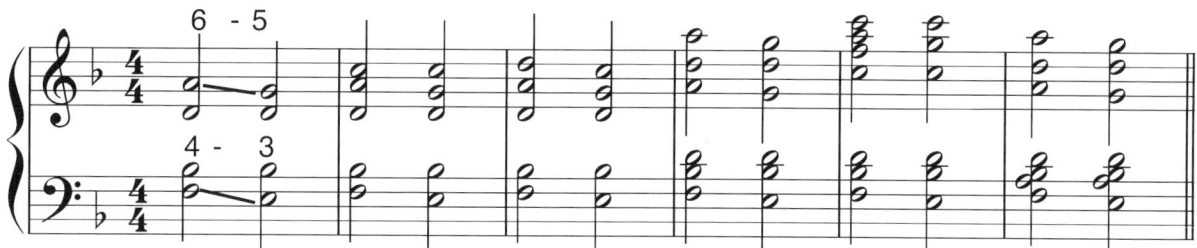

Example 11.36 Rootless Sus, with 7th as Lowest Bass Note. C is the Root.

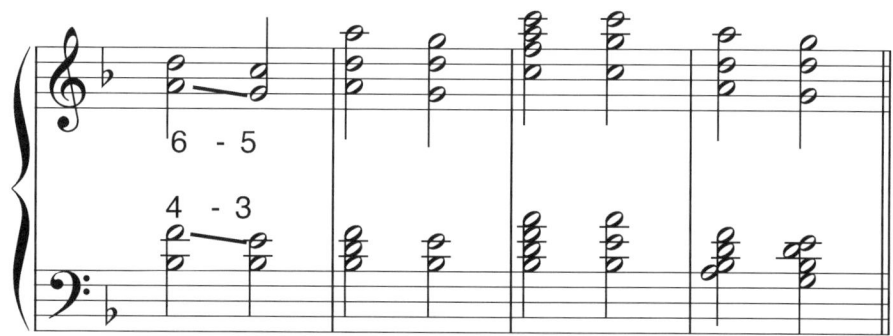

The last measure above has the 13th of the chord as the lowest note. The A-Bb dissonance has a powerful effect!

In the examples below, you will see adaptations of these voicings. Let's apply it directly to *Jesus at the Center*. First with basic chords, then with sus extensions.

Example 11.37 *Jesus at the Center* (Basic Chords)

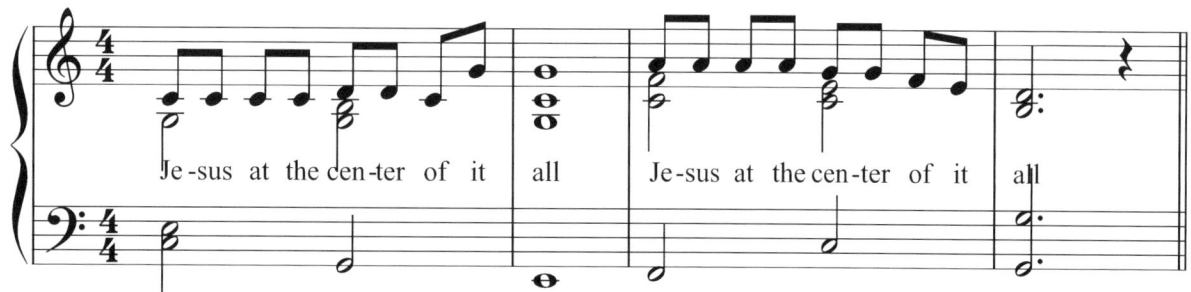

Example 11.38 *Jesus at the Center* (Sus Extensions)

In measures 3 to 6, see four ways of playing the "echo" beats 3 and 4 of measure 2 .

Measures 5 & 6 contain rootless chords (C is the root).

Example 11.39 Left Hand Resolves (4-3) Play Up/Down Through the Octave

Above, the low C and Db in the bass notes could have been omitted.
Below, the low C in the bass could have been omitted.

Example 11.40 Sus13: the 4th Resolves to 3rd in Left Hand. *(Amazing Grace)*

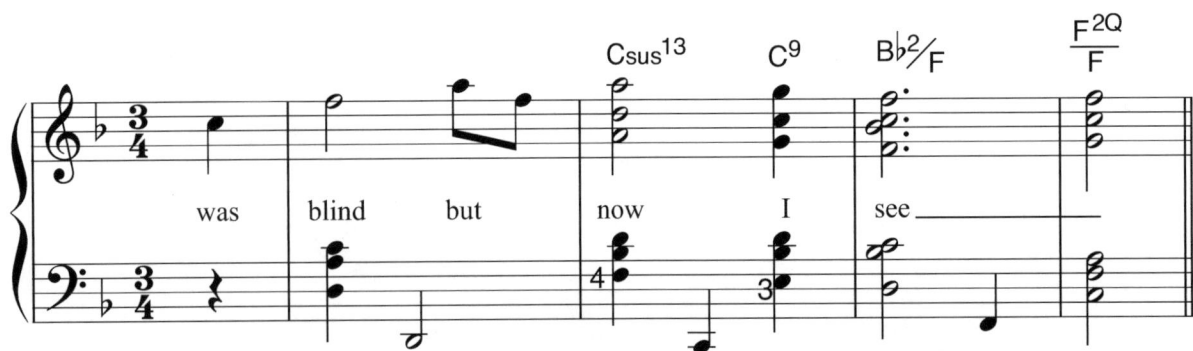

Try it! Play the above example in the keys of E and G.

Below, the roots in the bass (the low C, B and Db) could have been omitted.

Example 11.41 Sus13 Exercise: 7th in LH. Play Up & Down the Chromatic Scale

Below, the C in the Csus13 and C9 could have been omitted.

Example 11.42 Wider Sus13: 7th in LH. (Amazing *Grace)*

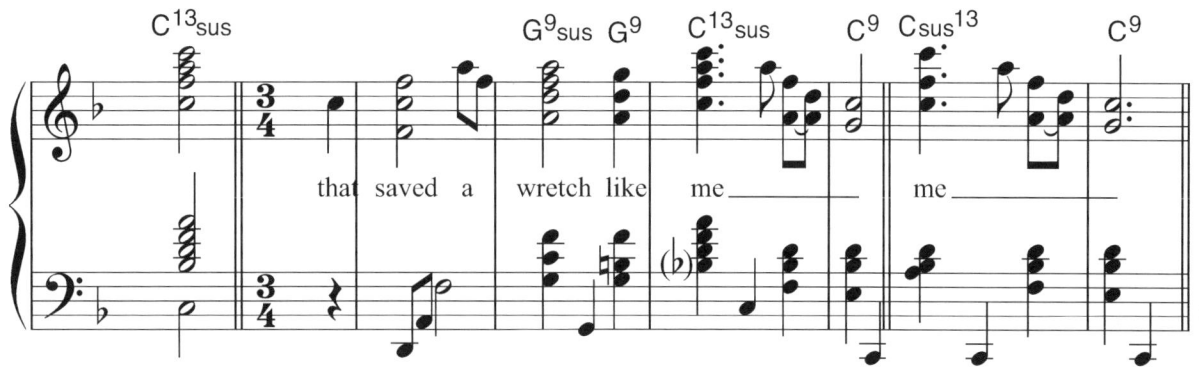

A poignant dissonance occurs in the left hand (A to Bb) on the second "me" above.
The same wide voicing works well in *Great is Thy Faithfulness* (key of C), measure 4.

Example 11.43 Play it! Unresolved Sus13 in Great *is Thy Faithfulness*

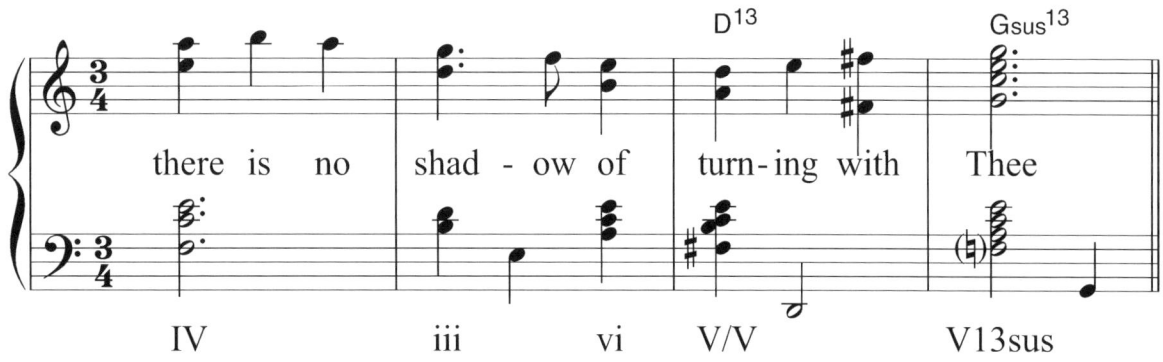

In order to get the sus13th sound into your ear and fingers (remember the 9th is included), practice the three exercises above in all keys.

Some of the things in this chapter will take time (months) for them to become truly "yours," and to become fully integrated into your style. That's the way it was with me. They won't become second nature without effort. Keep at it. Be patient. Be determined. You'll like the result!

Worthy Worship

"Worthy" worship is a magnificent concept
that we need to proclaim repeatedly, persistently.
It appears for the first time in the book of Revelation
and makes total sense. Christ has completed his mission,
and is now seated at the right hand of the Father.
He is worthy!

Consider the greatest, theological song in the book of Revelation.
And they sang a new song:
You are worthy to take the scroll and to open its seals,
because you were slain, and with your blood
you purchased men for God from every tribe
and language, and people and nation.

You have made them to become a kingdom
and priests to serve our God,
and they will reign on the earth.
Rev 5:9-10

CHAPTER 12

A Simpler Way—Four Over Five (IV/5)

> - 12 pages
> - 26 examples

"Four over Five" (IV/5) is a much simpler concept for worship bands and keyboardists to grasp and perform than sus9, yet it results in a similar, modern sound. It can be used as a substitute for sus chords or V chords at cadences. It can avoid harsh clashes at cadences. It can "resolve" like a sus chord. "Four over Five" is valuable in effecting modulations and in creating segues in the free-flowing praise format. For these reasons alone, and other reasons below, we must not fail to integrate IV/5 into our bag of musical tools.

OUTLINE	REPERTOIRE
Functions of the IV/5 Chord	Amazing Grace Be Thou My Vision
Try it!	Blessed Assurance
Avoiding Dissonance Using Four Over Five	Christ the Lord is Risen Today
Chord Reduction Using Four Over Five	The Power of Your Love Be Glorified
IV/5 as a Secondary Dominant Preparation	My Jesus I Love Thee
Bara Creativity	Rock of Ages Change My Heart O God
	I Stand in Awe of You Refiner's Fire

The "Four Over Five" can be expressed as a pop symbol (e.g., Bb/C) which is then applicable to *one* key. That construction is easy to understand. In a band, typically the guitarist plays a Bb chord while the bassist plays the note C. But more importantly and powerfully, the concept can be expressed by the generic *IV/5 symbol* which is applicable to *any key*.

For the IV/5 symbol, the Roman Numeral (IV) indicates a triad on a scale degree IV, whereas the Arabic number (5) indicates a single bass note on scale degree 5. Any inversion of the IV chord may be useful.

Example 12.1 IV/5 with Inversions

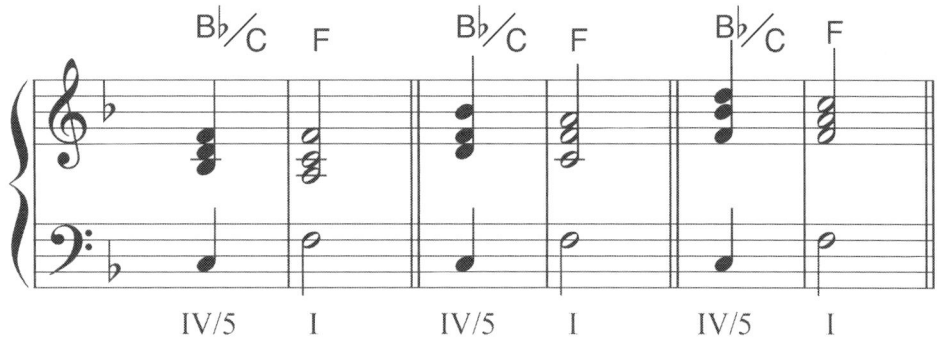

Functions of the IV/5 Chord

Eight aspects of the "Four Over Five" will be demonstrated using the following phrase of *Amazing Grace* in various ways.

(1) The IV/5 symbol can function as a *substitute* for the V chord at half cadences.

(2) The "Four over Five" chord doesn't necessarily have to include the melody note for it to function adequately (the note C in the piano part is missing at the Half Cadence).

Example 12.2 Unresolved IV/5 Substitutes for a V at the Half Cadence *(Amazing Grace)*

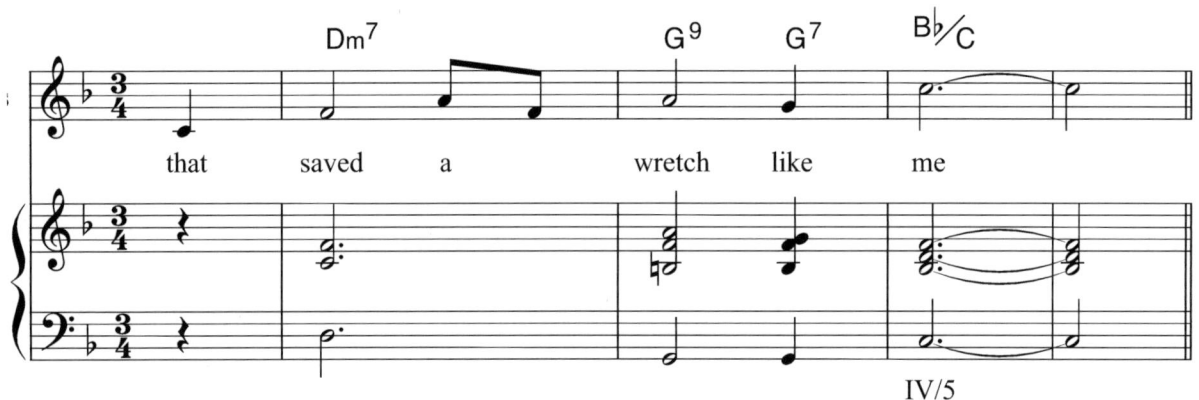

(3) The IV/5 (below) resolves to the V7 chord like a sus (the note F [4th] resolves to E).

(4) The IV/5 (below) contains a fourth, seventh and ninth above the bass. Similarly, a Csus9 would contain a fourth, seventh, and ninth. The result? Because of these common tones, the Bb/C (below) and a C9sus have a similar, modern sound.

Example 12.3 IV/5 Resolves to a the V

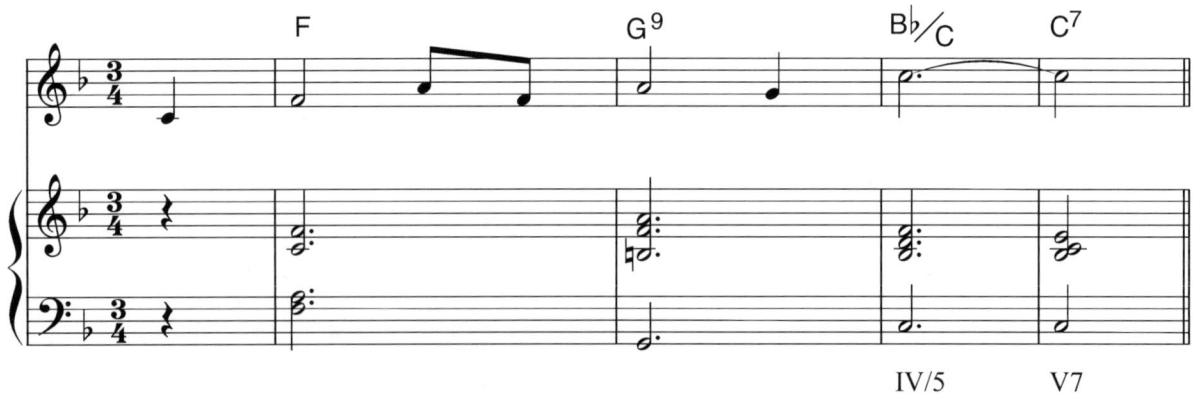

Similarly, the Csus9 (following) resolves to a C7 chord.

Example 12.4 The C9sus Resolves to C7

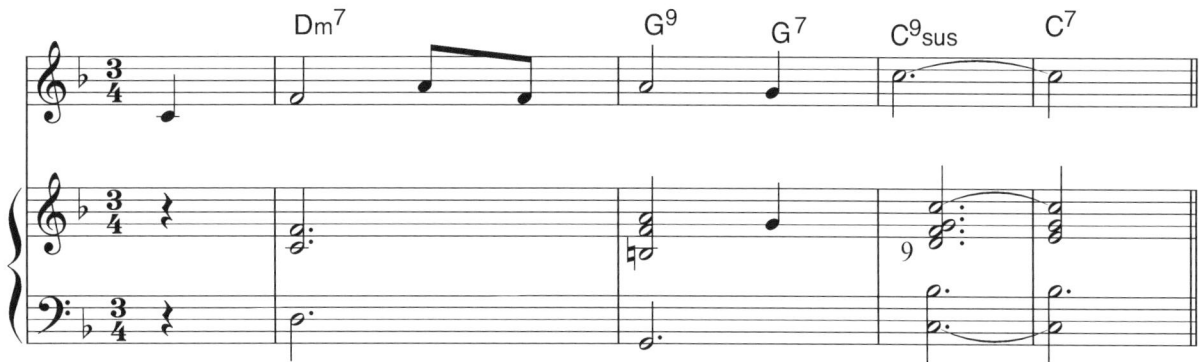

(5) Below, like the G7 chord, the F/G can function as a secondary dominant.

Example 12.5 The IV/5 functions as a Secondary Dominant

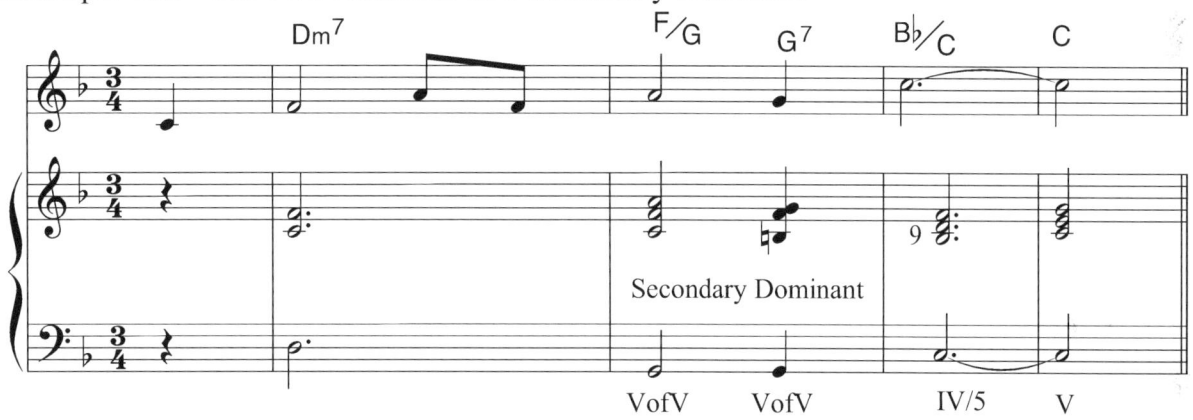

(6) Below, the IV/5 functions as a non-cadential chord (see pick up). (7) The sus quality of the IV/5 occurs in the secondary dominant and the dominant areas (ms. 3, 4).
(8) The IV/5 can resolve to a V9 extension (m.3), not just a simple V or V7 chord.

Example 12.6 The IV/5 functions as a Non-cadential Chord.

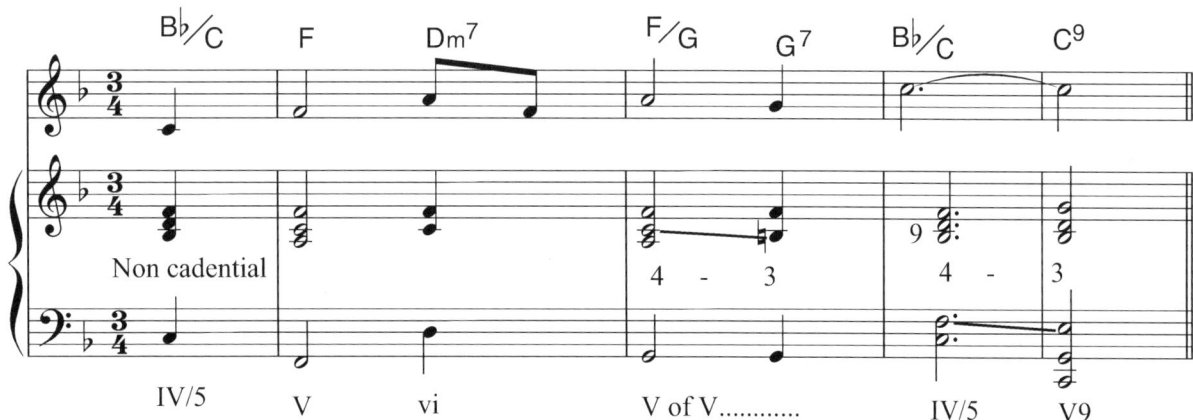

We have proved that IV/5 shares many of the same qualities/functions as the sus chord.

Avoiding Dissonance using Four over Five

Below, do you see the harsh dissonance that results? Students, unthinkingly, often use a V chord before the I here.

Example 12.7 V Chord Results in Harsh Dissonance at Cadence *(Be Thou My Vision)*

Below, the E in the C chord (m.1) clashes with the F in the soprano! Both the Csus chord (m.3) and the IV/5 chord (m.5), however, *avoid the harsh dissonance* at the full cadence.

Example 12.8 IV/5 Avoids a Harsh Dissonance at the Cadence

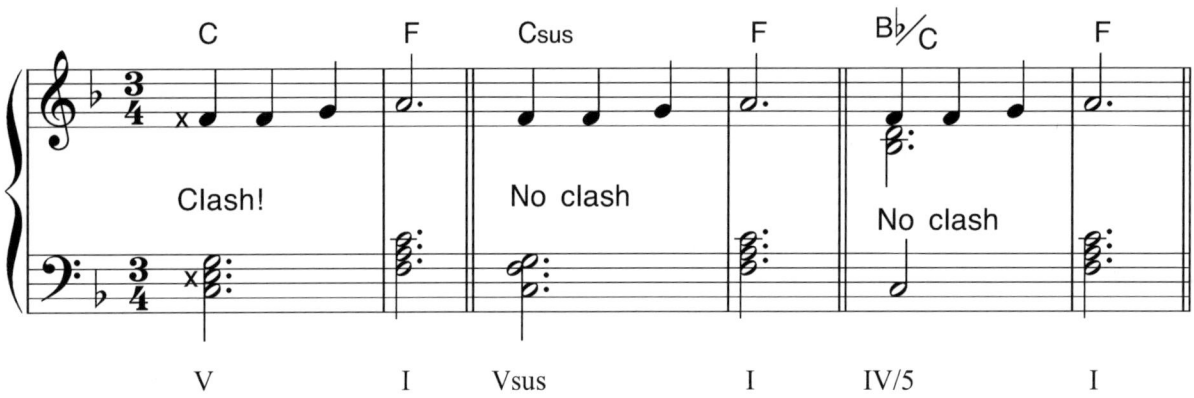

Below, the clashing issue is addressed. The D (on "all") in the IV/5 chord doubles the melody (no clash). The week beat (9) on the word "day" mitigates its harshness.

Example 12.9 *Blessed Assurance*

A. With a IV/5 Chord

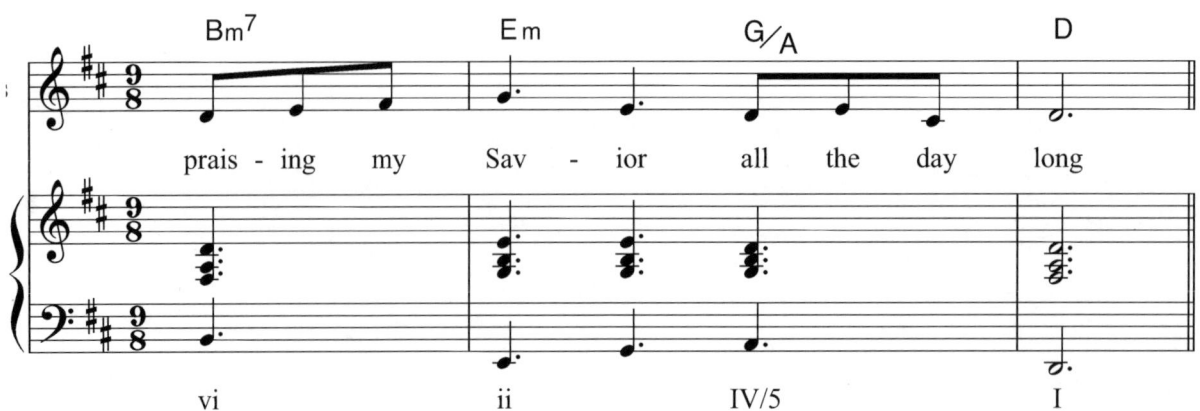

Below, the V chord results in a harsh clash with the A major chord on a strong beat (7). The D in the melody clashes against C# in the A chord. Therefore, IV/5 is a better choice than V. It demonstrates the value of the IV/5 in avoiding clashes.

B. With a V Chord

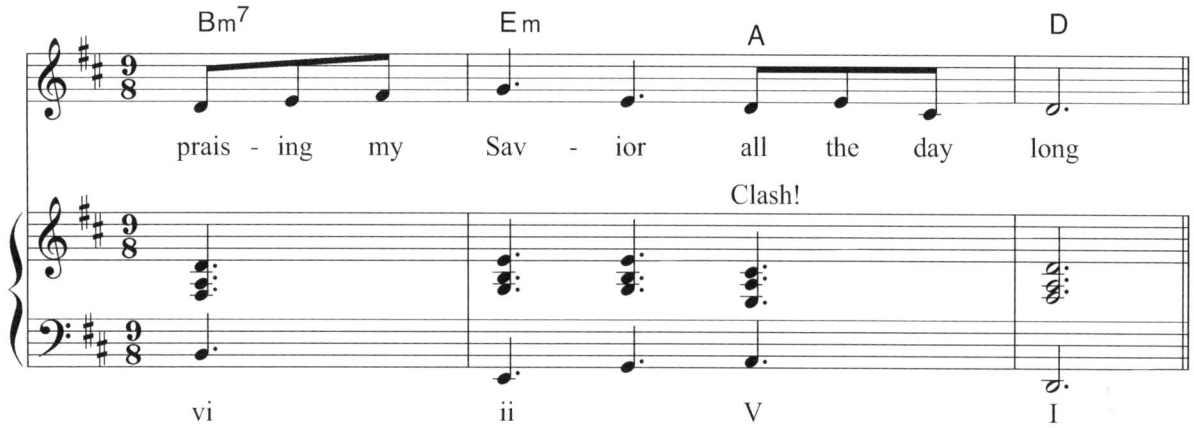

Chord Reduction using Four Over Five

The IV/5 structure can reduce the number of chords in a passage. Below, three chords are employed at the cadence. The three chords (m.4) do result in a strong finish to the stanza.

Example 12.10 Three Chords at the Cadence *(Christ the Lord is Risen Today)*

Again, the I6/4 –V-I progression is excellent, strong.

Below, the use of a IV/5, though not quite as strong, does reduce the number of chords at the cadence to two instead of three. In some situations this can be an advantage.

Example 12.11 Two Chords at Cadence *(Christ the Lord is Risen Today)* Play in D, E.

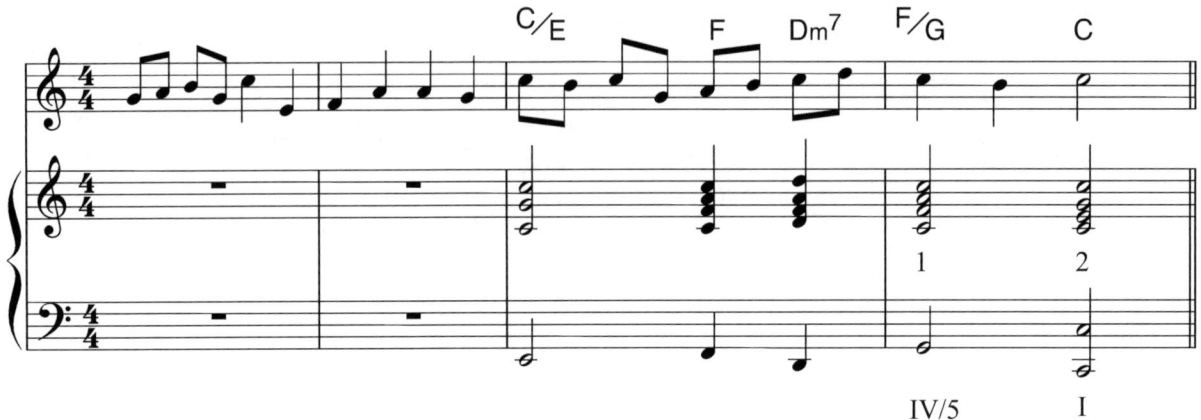

Only two chords are employed at the cadence (m.4). This can be important. Guitarists prefer fewer chords per measure than keyboardists— allowing a more flowing performance. The two-chord finish is almost as strong as the three-chord finish.

Finally, "Four Over Five" chords are valuable in crafting modulations and segues between pieces in different keys. We will explore that function in detail in Book 4.

Try it!

Example 12.12 Play it! *(Be Thou My Vision)* Play in E, F, G, A.

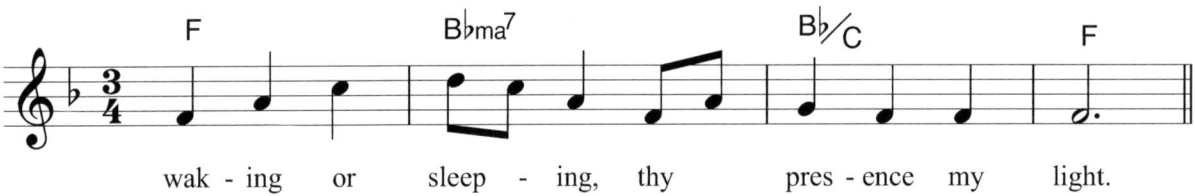

Though the Bb/C chord is not part of the melody, still it sounds good. Below, the asterisk demonstrates how close a Bb/C chord is to the C9sus. Only the G would be missing.

Example 12.13 Substitute a IV/5 at the Asterisk *(Amazing Grace)* Play in C, D, E, F.

Example 12.14 Substitute a IV/5 at the Asterisks   *(Lord, Be Glorified)*

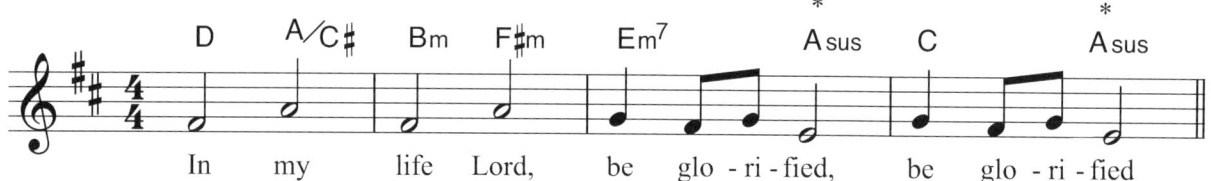

Example 12.15 Substitute a IV/5 at the Asterisk *(My Jesus I Love Thee)*

Example 12.16 *Rock of Ages* (Provide a IV/5 at the Asterisk)

Example 12.17 "Four over Five" Exercise. Continue though the Octave

The exercise above begins with the well-known major triad.

The next exercise begins with the lesser-known Bb/C chord. Students tell me this makes the exercise slightly more difficult.

Example 12.18 "Four over Five" Exercise. Continue through the Octave

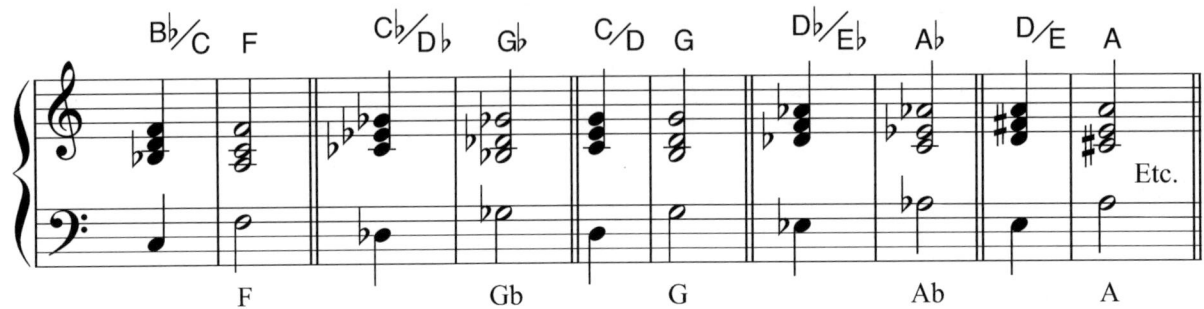

Example 12.19 "Four over Five" Exercise. Continue through the Cycle

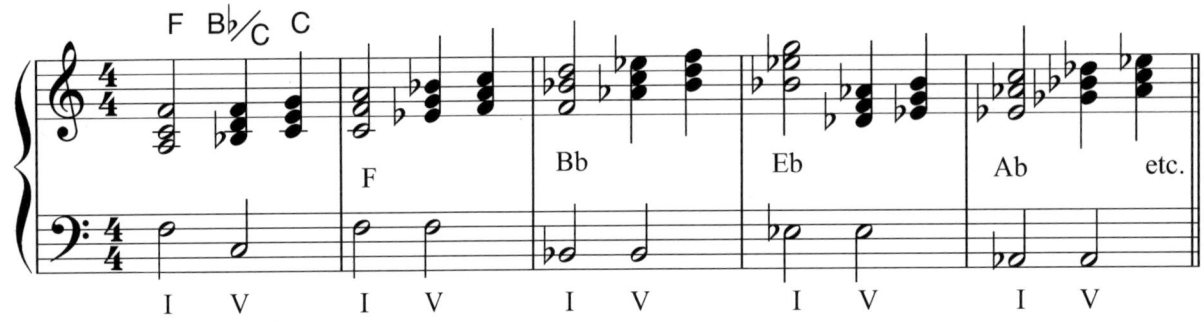

The pattern above can be employed in measure 6 below.

Example 12.20 Substitute a IV/5 at the Asterisk *(The Power of Your Love)*

Lord, I come to you   let my heart be   changed, re-newed

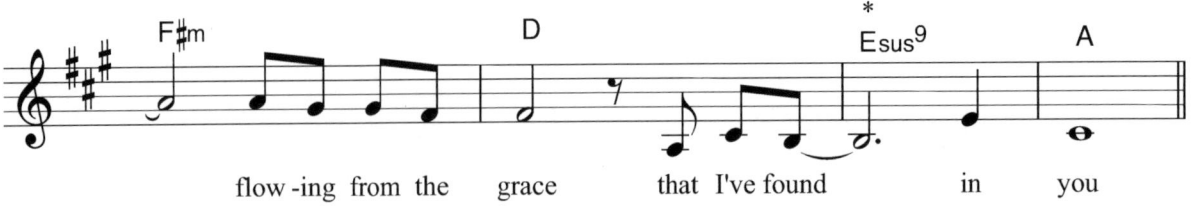

flow-ing from the   grace   that I've found   in   you

Below, experiment. Insert some IV/5 chords.

Example 12.21   *I Stand in Awe of You*

Hint: IV/5 will work in ms. 3, 6, 8, 13, 16.

The example below is more difficult for no chords are given. A challenge!

Example 12.22 Harmonize! Include some IV/5 Chords. *(Refiner's Fire)*

IV/5 as a Secondary Dominant Preparation

Example 12.23 **Play by Memory.** IV/5 Can Be Applied to Each Scale Degree

Here the IV/5 acts as a preparation to the V chord in secondary dominants.

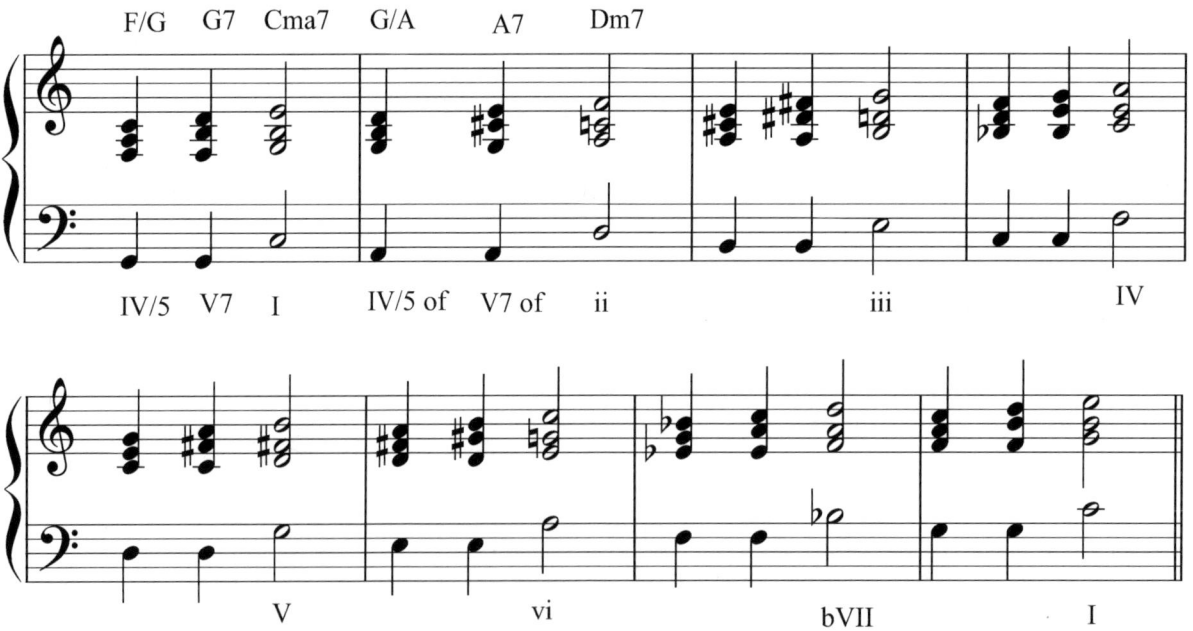

Let's apply the same idea to *Angels We Have Heard on High*.

Example 12.24 *Angels We Have Heard on High*   Play in D, E, F, G.

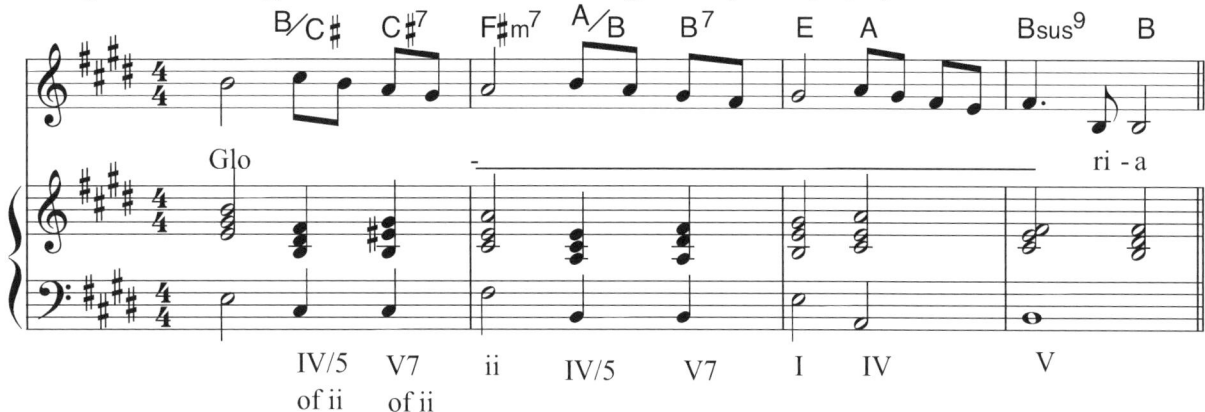

Below, see a similar IV/5 secondary dominant exercise, but using a different inversion.

Example 12.25 **Play by Memory**

Example 12.26 *Change My Heart O God*   Play in C, D, E, F.

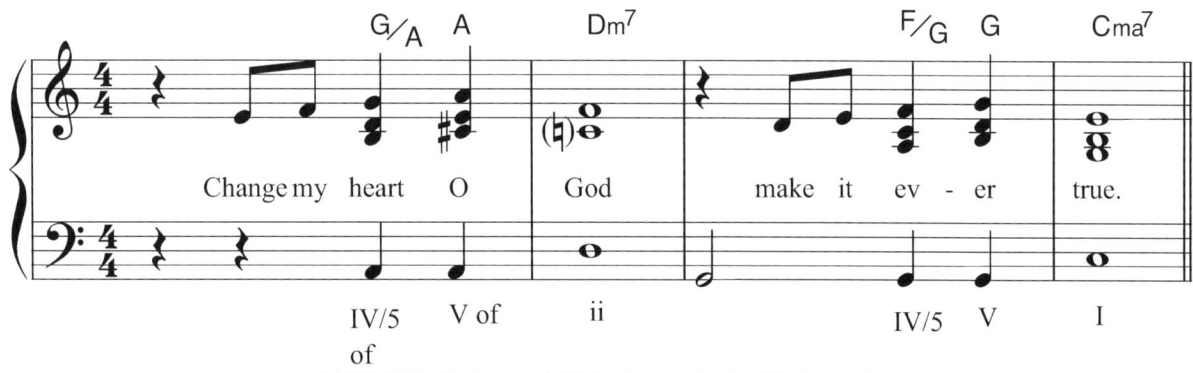

For more material on secondary dominants, see Book 3. It contains an entire chapter on secondary dominants. Secondary dominants are a major musical idea. The concept is capable of significant development and has considerable expressive potential.

Bara Creativity

Creativity has become a buzz word in our society. Everything from a child's scribble to Einstein's theory of relativity is considered creative. Not so in the Hebrew Scriptures! The Hebrew word for create, *bara*, is a very special term. It refers exclusively to activity performed by God (never humans) and immediately evokes a sense of awe and wonder. It must contain something of the miraculous and the mysterious (Exod. 34:10). Bible writers use *bara* sparingly to denote the pinnacles of God's achievements.

Bara creativity is characterized by a newness that is unprecedented, unforeseeable, valuable, transformational, and lasting. The New Testament Greek counterpart, *Ktizo*, retains the same meaning.

Bara creativity involves more than the creation of our physical world. It extends to the creation of the nation of Israel (Isa. 43:1), to righteousness and justice (Isa. 45:8), to cleansing from sin and psychological healing (read about David's cry, Ps. 51:10), to regeneration (2 Cor. 5:17; Eph. 4:24), and it leads inexorably to praise and worship.

That is, God's creativity includes not only physical, sociological, ethical, and spiritual kinds of construction, but also the construction of praise and joy. Our very topic!

For behold, I create new heavens and a new earth...be glad and rejoice forever in what I create; For behold I create Jerusalem for rejoicing (Isa. 65:17-18, NASB)

Bara newness is unprecedented (Isa 43:15-21)—the first of its kind, that which did not exist before, the unheard of.

Bara newness is humanly unforeseeable (Num. 16:30). It has the quality of surprise, of hidden things brought to light, of the unexpected and unpredictable.

Bara newness is valuable (Gen. 2:9; Isa. 41:17-20). It cannot be novelty for novelty's sake. It must solve a problem, serve a function, be workable, yet beautiful and fitting.

Bara newness is transformational in that it can become part of tradition and undergo transformation, re-creation (Gal. 6:15; Eph. 2:15).

Bara newness is lasting. It does not lose its luster after repeated examination and contemplation. It is a newness than never perishes.

I've thought much about *bara* creativity, and have tried to integrate its aspects into my own work. Could *bara* thinking benefit you too?

CHAPTER 13

Infusing Tension—One Over Four or Two

- 17 pages
- 40 examples

OUTLINE	REPERTOIRE
One Over Four	Holy Holy Holy
I/4 Possibilities for Holy, Holy, Holy	The Solid Rock
I/4 Possibilities for The Solid Rock	Great is Thy Faithfulness Amazing Grace
Other I/4 Song Possibilities	You Alone Be Thou My Vision
One Over Two	Firm Foundation As the Deer
A Rarer Possibility: IV/b7	Come Thou Fount Father I Adore You
Improvise!	Joyful, Joyful When I Survey
Expressive Dissonance	Open the Eyes of My Heart, Lord

Pieces often begin and end with a simple, major triad on scale degree I. In many cases it is the most foundational chord in a piece. *What if we could alter that sound and infuse it with more dynamism, tension?* Why do that? Our present culture has a preference for *more dissonance* than previous generations. The "one over four chord" certainly qualifies as an alternative. It has complexity, tension, and specifically relates to the I chord.

The "one over four chord" (I/4) can project emotional subtlety, but more importantly, power, energy, brilliance—precisely in situations where the less dynamic, simple triad would have been employed in the past. Let's explore how the sonority functions, and its possible meanings and feelings as revealed in various musical contexts. To begin with, make sure you understand the terminology below.

A Roman Numeral signifies a chord on a given scale degree.
An Arabic Number signifies a single bass note on a given scale degree.

The slash symbol I/4 (a generic symbol for all keys) means play a chord on scale degree 1, and a single bass note on scale degree 4. The slash symbol I/2 means play a chord on scale degree 1, and a single bass note on scale degree 2.

One Over Four

One Over Four Versus Fma9$^{(no3)}$ Explained. Two pop symbols can be used to describe our target sound. A slash symbol (like C/F) is most often used because it is the simplest to understand and perform. A second symbol, Fma9$^{(no3)}$, is more accurate theoretically, for it indicates the bass note (F) is the true root. But this symbol is longer, more complex, and therefore is used less often. "One over four chords" are bright sounding.

You won't find them in any hymnal, for their arrival on worship scene is relatively recent.

Example 13.1 Two Pop Symbols represent the "One Over Four" Chord (Key of C)

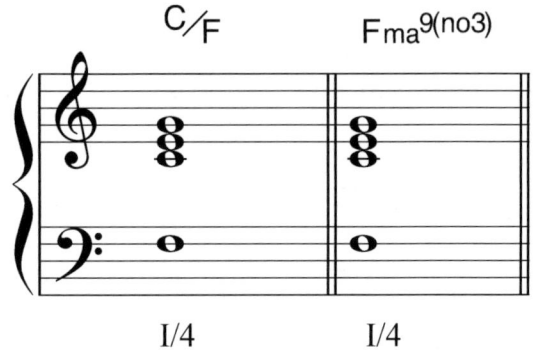

Does the sonority sound bright or "bold" to you?

Perhaps the sound originated as guitarists droned on a C chord while the bassist descended to an F (see below).

Example 13.2 **Play it!**

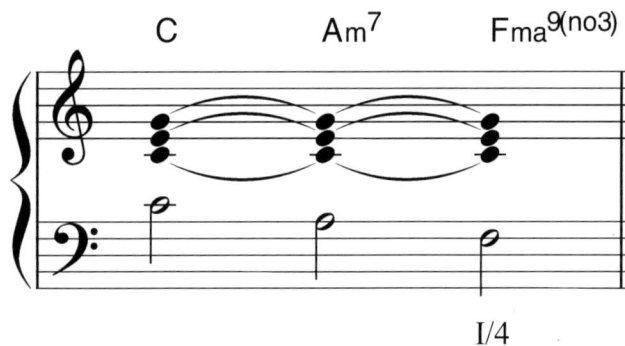

It has become commonplace in worship choruses for the I/4 sound to be part of a musical progression (as below). See it displayed as a triad drone and then as an open fifth (in the guitar key of E major).

Example 13.3 **Play it!** The Ninth (no3) is Situated in a Typical Harmonic Progression

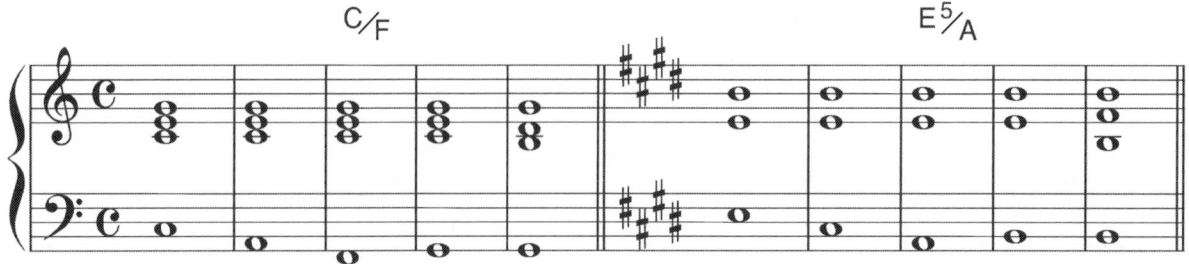

Any inversion in the RH can be employed—root, first, or second inversion (as below).

Example 13.4 **Play it!** Transpose it so that C, D, E, F, G, and A are in the Bass.

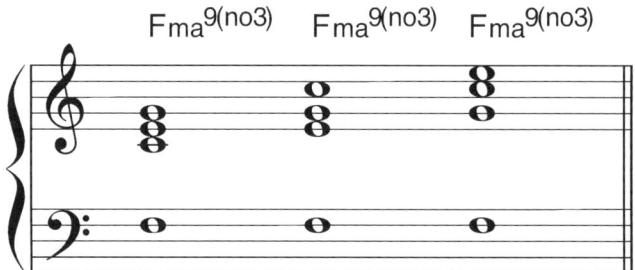

Notice, all the sounds fall easily for the your hand. The RH includes an upper structure, a ninth (G). The inversions move the ninth around in interesting ways.

Function. The most important thing to remember is that the bass note is routinely centered on scale degree four (4). Since the bass note commonly determines chord function, the sonority invariably functions as a IV chord, and resolves any of the ways IV chords normally do. Also remember: *the 'one over four chord" is regularly used as dissonant, tension-bearing substitute for a I chord.*

I/4 Possibilities for *Holy, Holy, Holy*

Example 13.5 Three Harmonizations of *Holy, Holy, Holy* .   Play it in C, D, E, F, G, A.

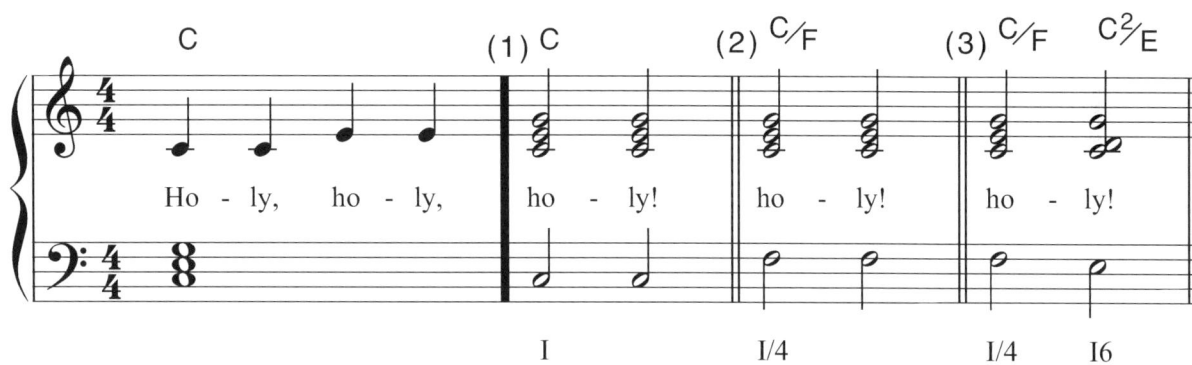

Note: (2) and (3) function as substitutions for the I chord and introduce tension. In (2), the I/4 chord may be perceived as having both a I and IV function (listen again). Because (3) resolves to I6, it has a stronger IV function. Below, let's expand (2) and (3).

Example 13.6   I/4 is Repeated, Descends a Third to the ii chord. Play in C, D, E, F, G.

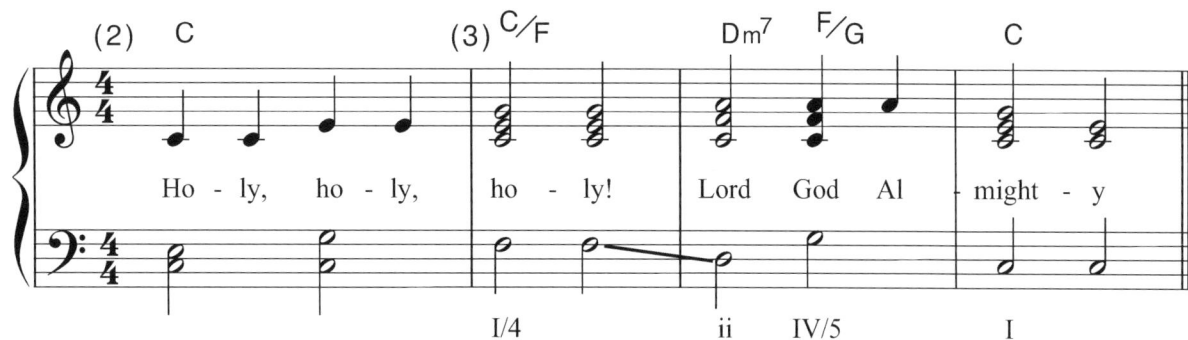

Example 13.7 I/4 Resolves to the I6 Chord.

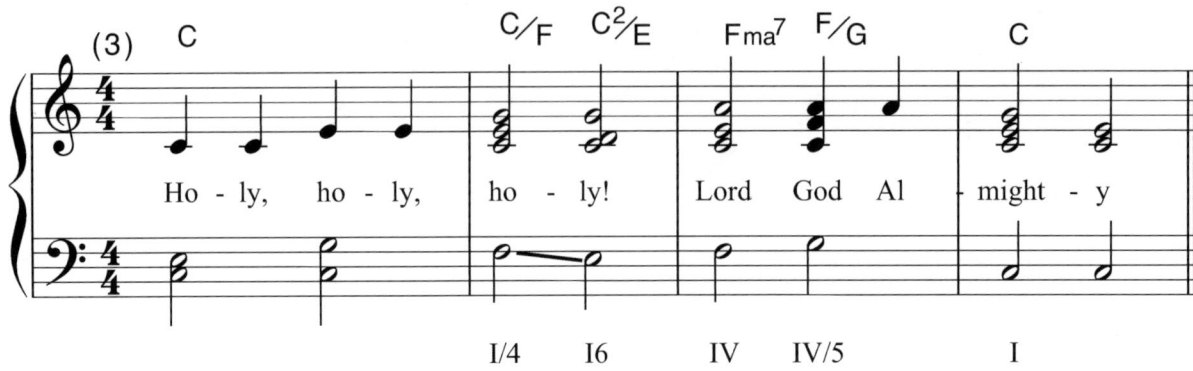

Now let's look how the I/4 chord could be applied to the last phrase of *Holy, Holy, Holy*.

Example 13.8 The I/4 Chord Resolves to a iii Chord.   Play it in C, D, E, F, G.

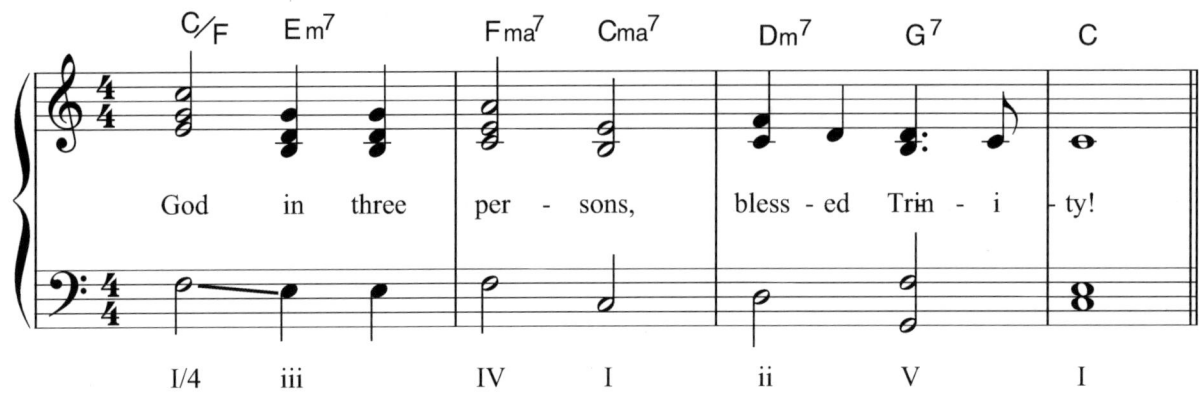

The I/4 (on the word "God") is the boldest, most dissonant chord in the phrase. It stands out most. It emphasizes the word "God." Do you agree? The high pitch helps too.

Example 13.9 The I/4 is Repeated using an Inversion, then Resolves to a I6 Chord

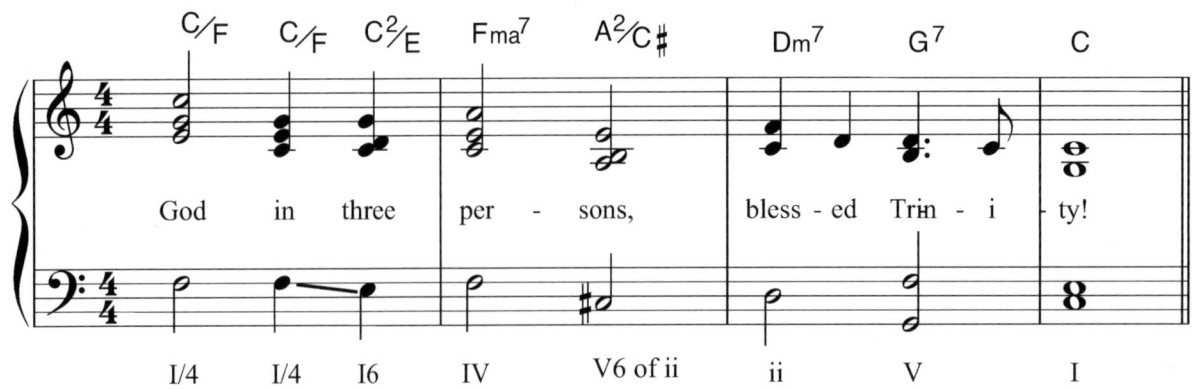

Try it! Play it in C, D, E, F, G.

Example 13.10 The I/4 is Repeated using an Inversion, then Resolves to V6 of ii.

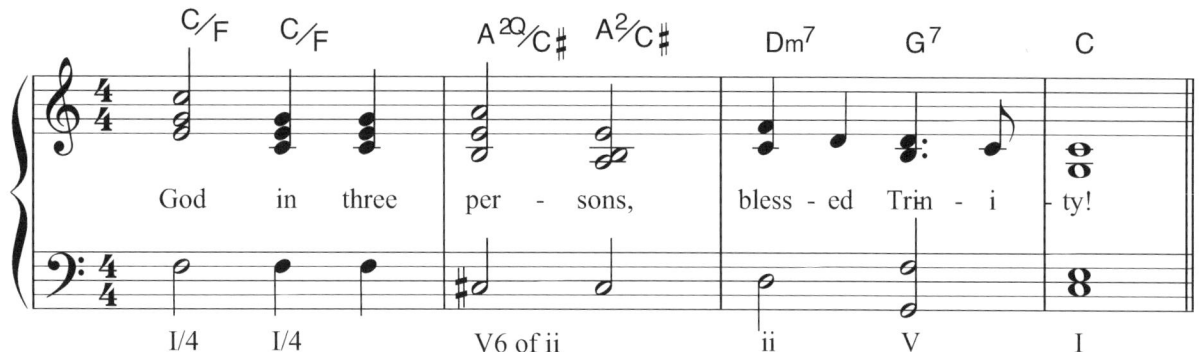

Include the third! The I/4 chord omits the third. However, if we include the third a major ninth chord results. The resulting sonority is more mellow and has less "bite."

Example 13.11 See the Fma9. A Major Ninth Results when the Third is Included.

Example 13.12 See the Wider Spacing of the Major Ninth Chord. Observe the Tenth.

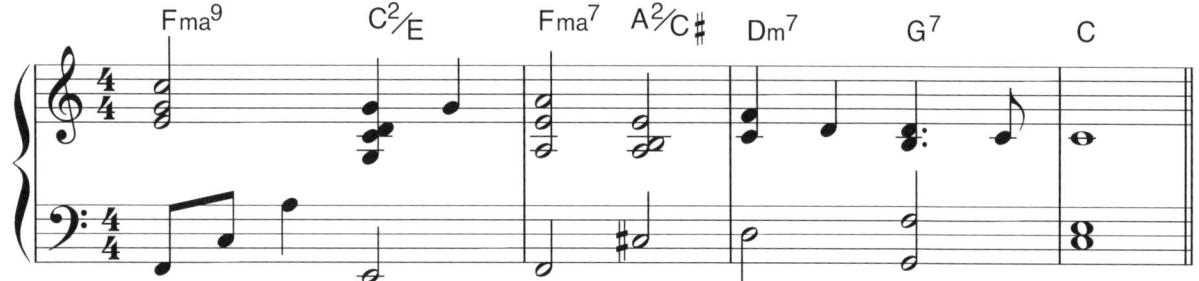

Again, when the third is included, the sound becomes warmer. When the third is excluded (as in the I/4 chord) the sound has more pungency.

I/4 Possibilities in *The Solid Rock*

The Solid Rock differs emotionally from *Holy, Holy, Holy*. Musically, it is more stalwart, thrusting, powerful, with many insistent, repeated notes. Can the I/4 successfully convey these qualities? Does I/4 inherently have a "word painting" tendency?

Example 13.13 The Bold I/4 Resolves to a Warmer Am9. Play in E, F, G, A.

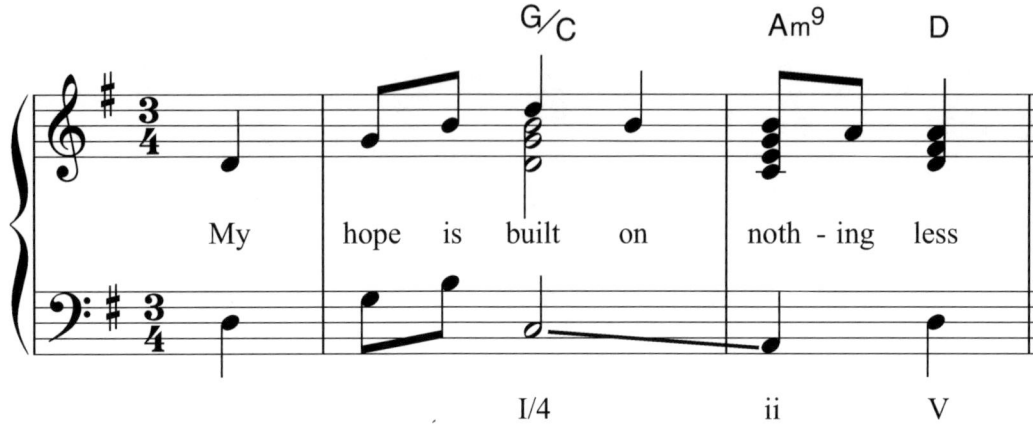

The inherent boldness of the I/4 is softened, contextually, by the warmer minor ninth.

Example 13.14 I/4 Resolves to a More Dynamic Half-Diminished Chord on C#.

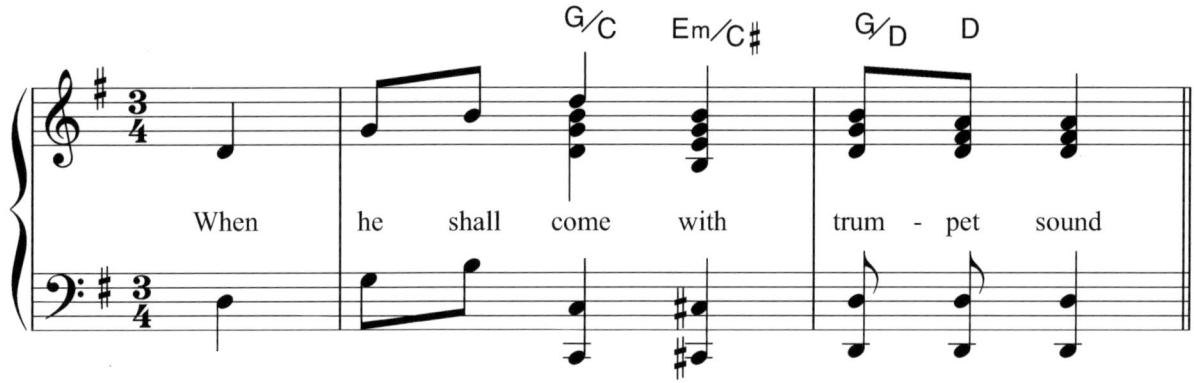

The bass octaves, the strong, rising, half-step bass movement, and the power of both the G/C and half-diminished seventh (Em/C#), all work together to project strength.

Example 13.15 Note the Arresting Quality of the I/4. *The Solid Rock.* Play it in F, G, A.

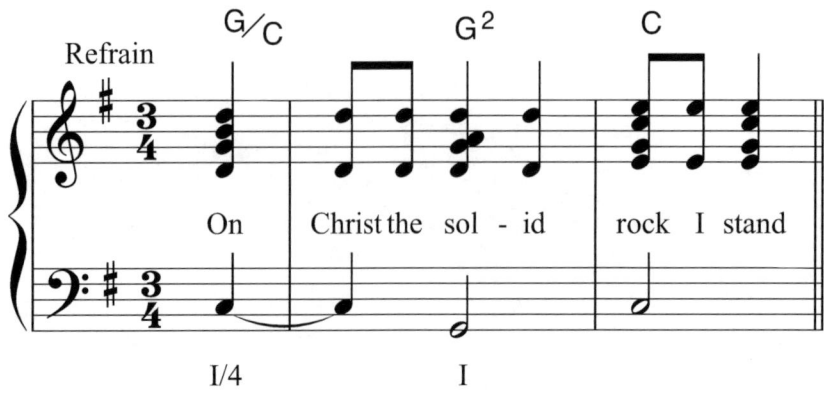

Example 13.16 The I/4 creates Harmonic Movement (G-D-G in the Bass)

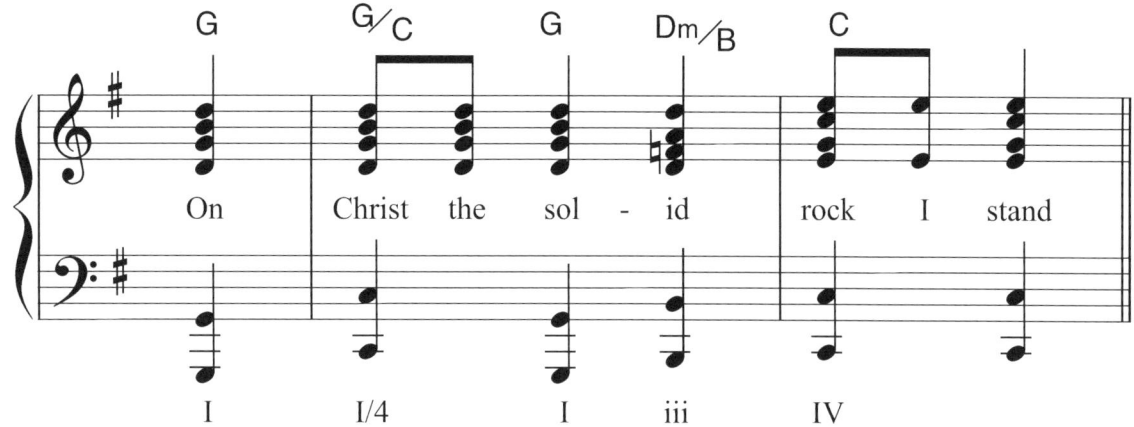

Example 13.17 Sustained Dissonance. The First 4 Chords are Identical in Sound Quality.

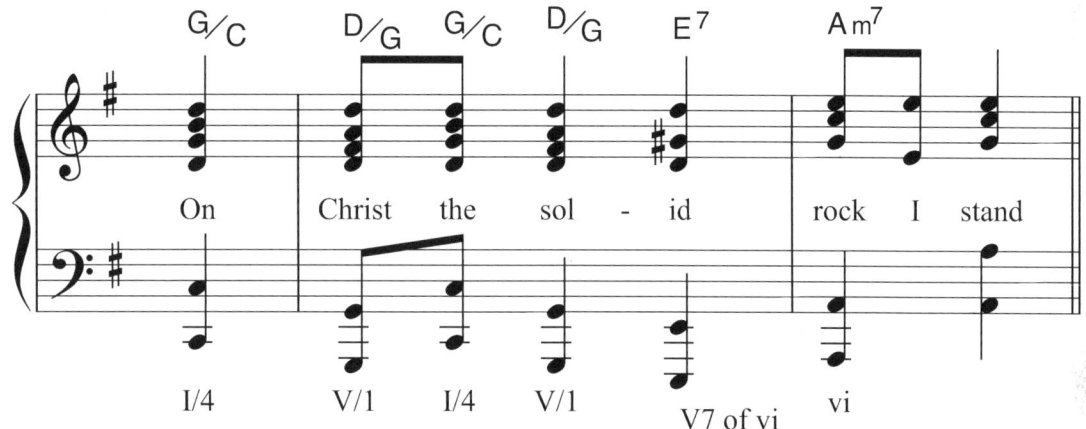

Think! Why is the example immediately above more powerful than the two above it?

Other I/4 Song Possibilities

Example 13.18 I/4 Resolves to I6 and V. *When I Survey the Wondrous Cross*

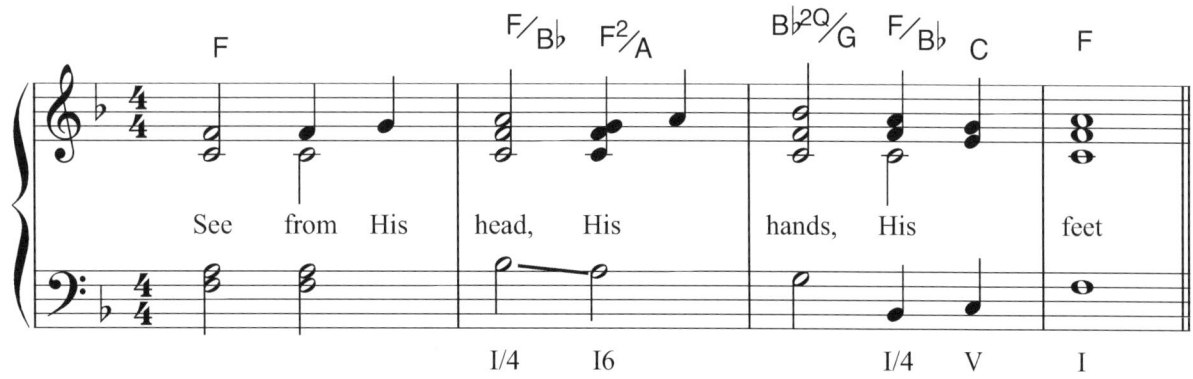

The I/4 dissonance on the word "head" might suggest pain and suffering.

Example 13.19 I/4 Resolves Smoothly & Graciously to I6. *Great is Thy Faithfulness*

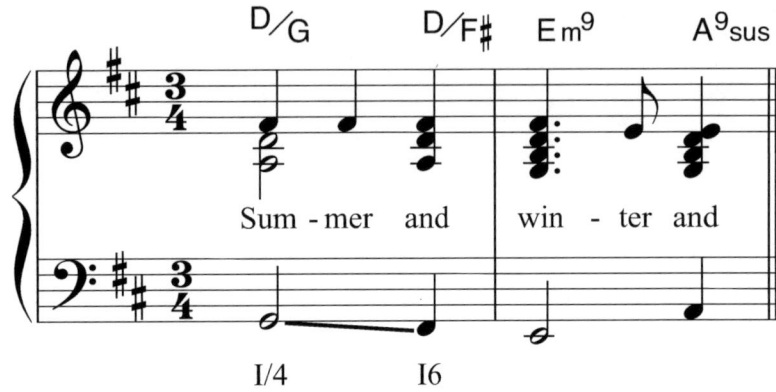

Example 13.20   Brilliant, Forceful I/4   Chorus of *Great is Thy Faithfulness*

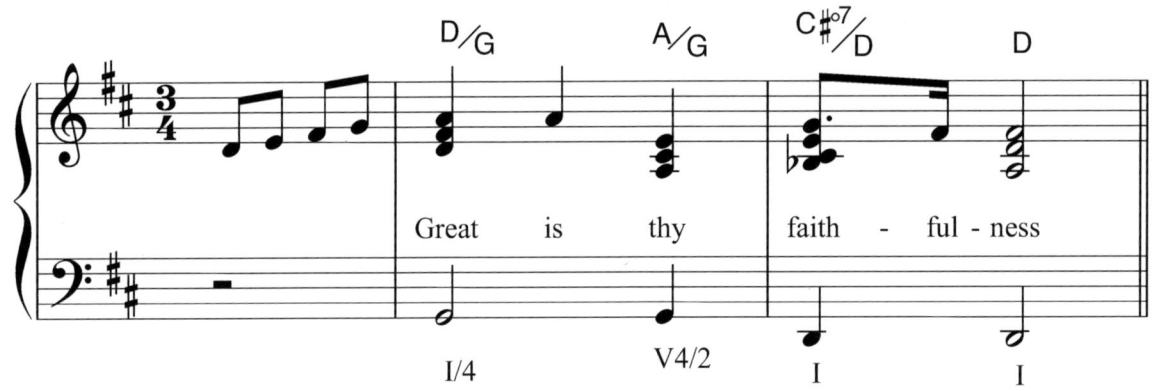

Does the bold complexity of the I/4 fit the word "Great"?

Example 13.21 Alternative Harmonization

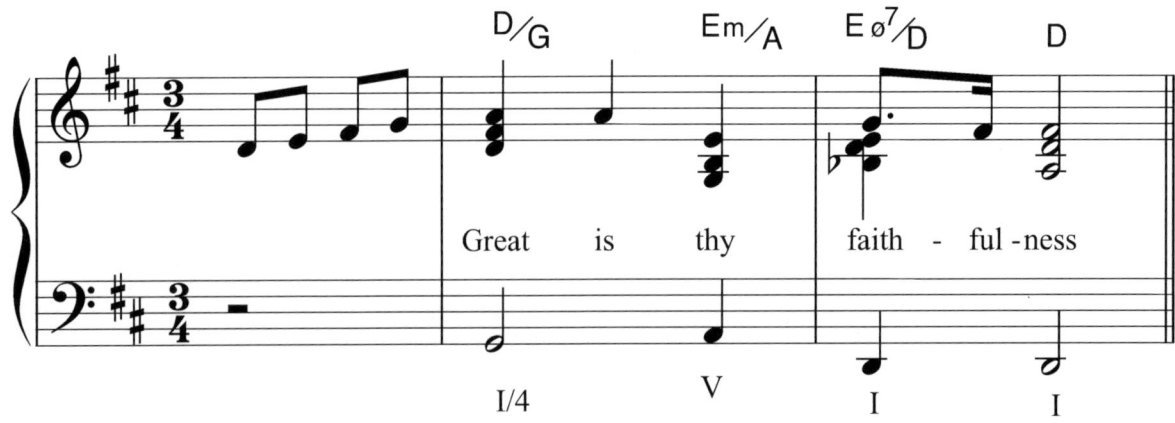

Below, the I/4 (E/A) rises a step (A to B) to the dominant chord (Bsus) at the half cadence. The I/4 could have resolved to any V substitute such as a IV/5 or a I6/4 chord.

Example 13.22 **Improvise!** *Open the Eyes of My Heart*

Below, in measures 2 and 4 we've expressed the 1/4 chord as a IV chord to emphasize its traditional-looking function. In m.2 the major ninth (no3) on IV moves to a I 6/4 chord (a second inversion F chord), which functions as a quasi V chord, before proceeding to the dominant (V). In m.4 it proceeds directly to V.

Example 13.23 **Play it!** *Firm Foundation*

Example 13.24 IV (I/4) Resolves to ii7. *Come Thou Fount*

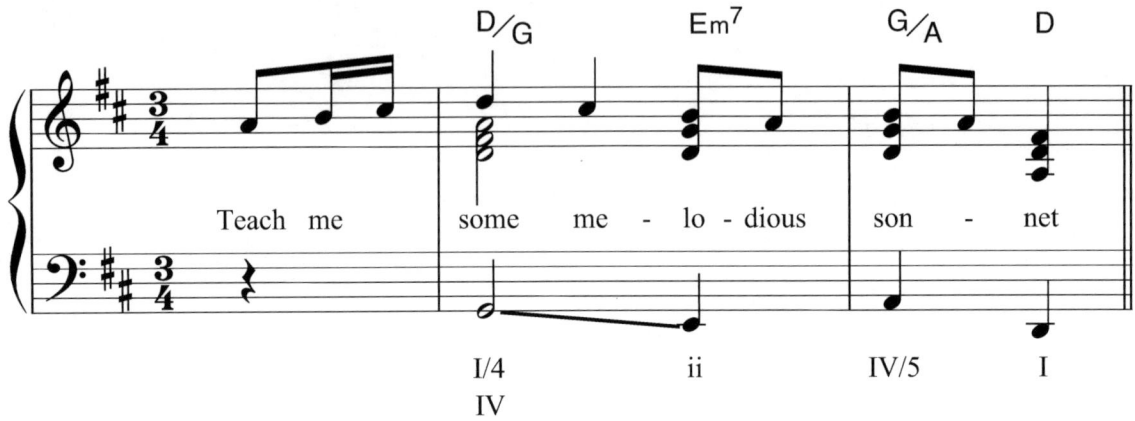

Below, the IV Major Ninth (no3) resolves to a simple IV chord. This relationship is a disguised version of the alternating rock "doubles" addressed in Book 1. It shows that the major ninth (no3), functionally, is actually closely related to alternating harmonies. The difference is that the I/4 chord resolves in any of the ways that IV chords normally resolve, whereas the V-I double is harmonically restricted to V-I.

Example 13.25

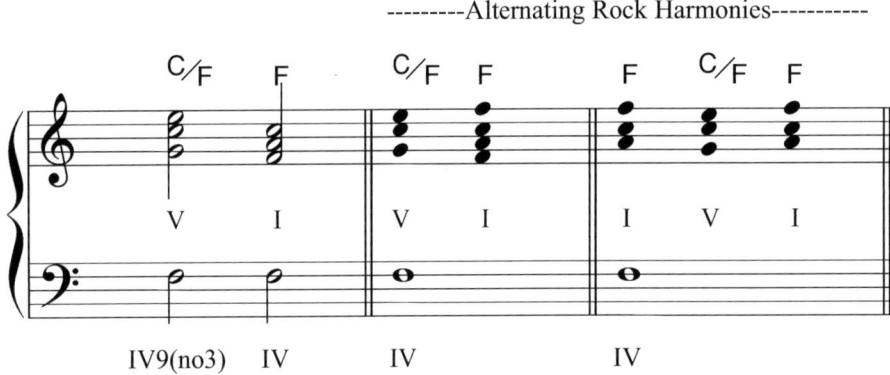

Measures two and three (above) are remarkably similar in function and sound to measure one. Now let's look at a worship chorus that demonstrates the relationship.

Example 13.26 **Play it!** The I/4 Resolves to a IV. *You Alone*

Use the exercise below to get the major ninth (no3) more firmly into your ear and hands. It traverses through the cycle of fifths (down a fifth, up a fourth).

Example 13.27 **Play it by Memory!** Play through the Major Ninth (no third) Cycle.

One Over Two

The "one over two" chord is in essence a minor eleventh with no third or fifth. Like the I/4, it can function as a dissonant, tension-bearing chord. However, it does not contribute as much tension as the "one over four."

Example 13.28

Two upper structures are present: a ninth ((E) and an eleventh (G). Inversions could occur in the RH. The chord falls easily for the hand.

Example 13.29 The I/2 can Substitute for a I Chord. *Joyful, Joyful* Play in C, D, E.

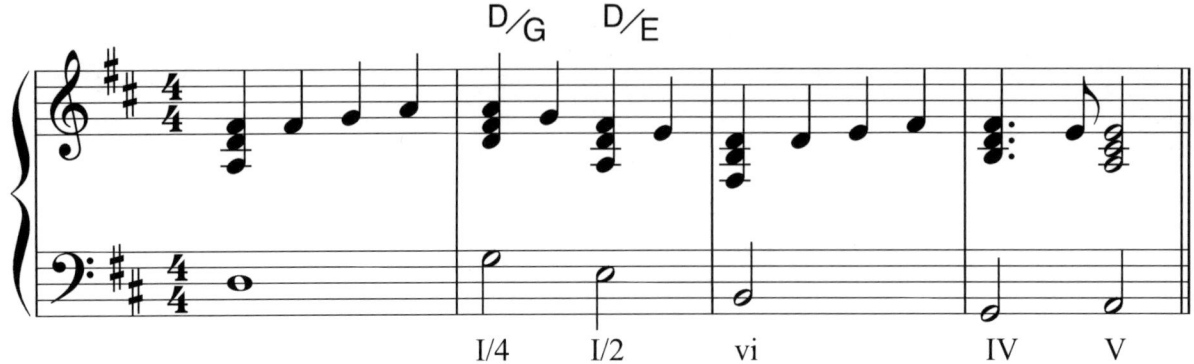

I/2 can function in the same ways a ii chord normally functions. Above it resolves to vi.

Example 13.30 The 1/2 Chord Resolves to V (like a ii → V). *Come Thou Fount*

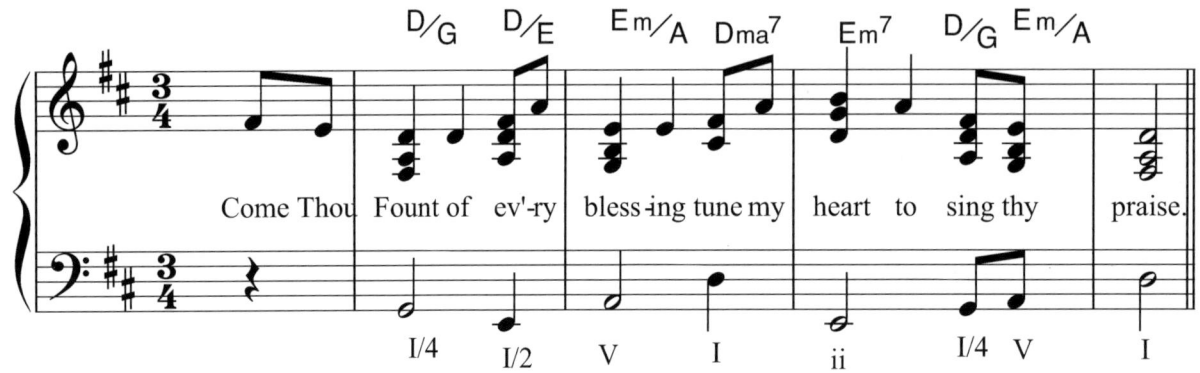

Example 13.31 *Father I Adore You* Employing I/4

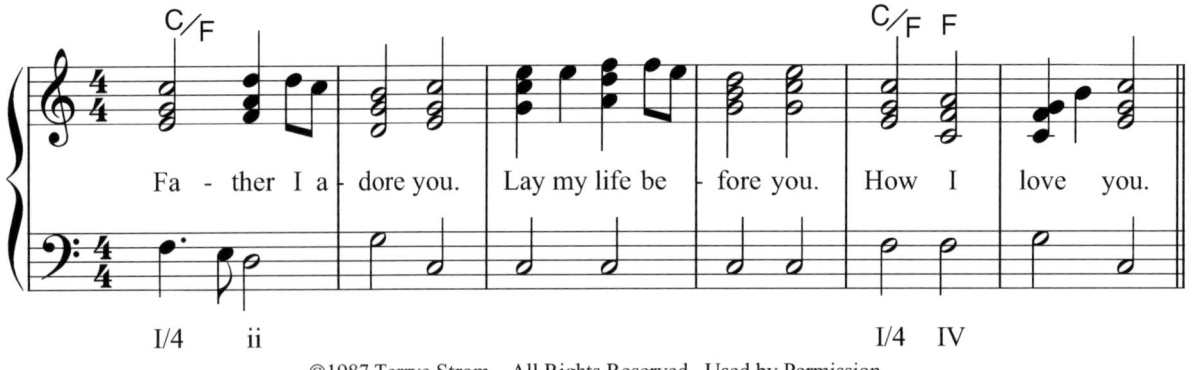

Example 13.32 *Father I Adore You* Employing 1/2 Instead. Play it in C, D, E.

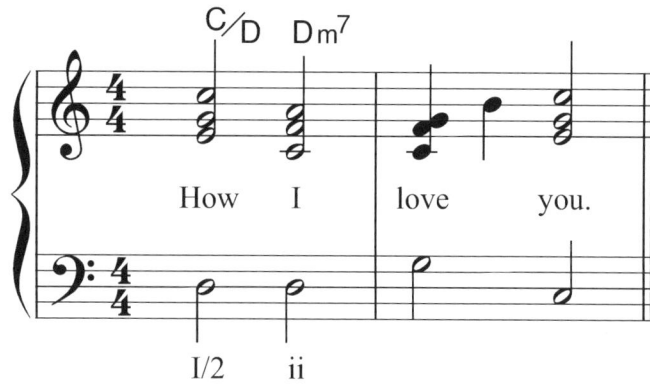

Example 13.33 *As the Deer* Employing I/4

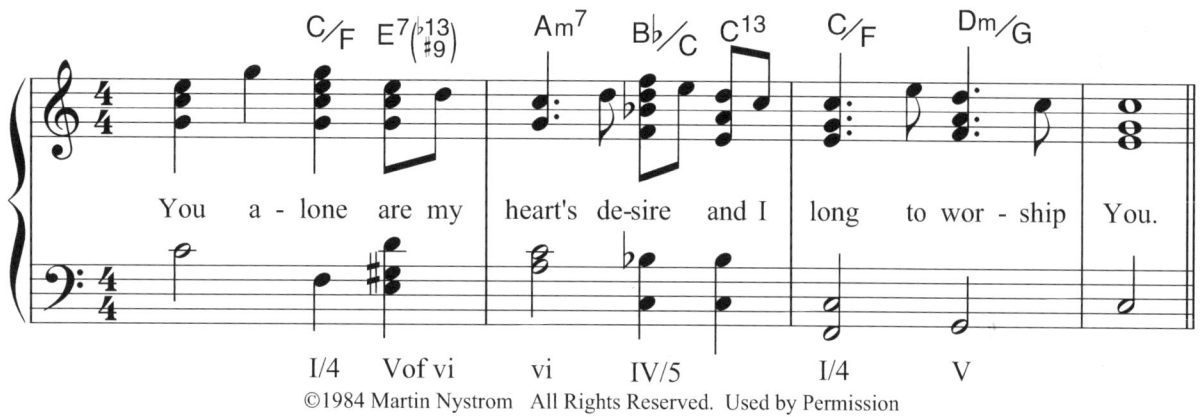

Above, I/4 fits nicely into the rich, ballad texture.

Example 13.34 *As the Deer* Employing I/2 Instead

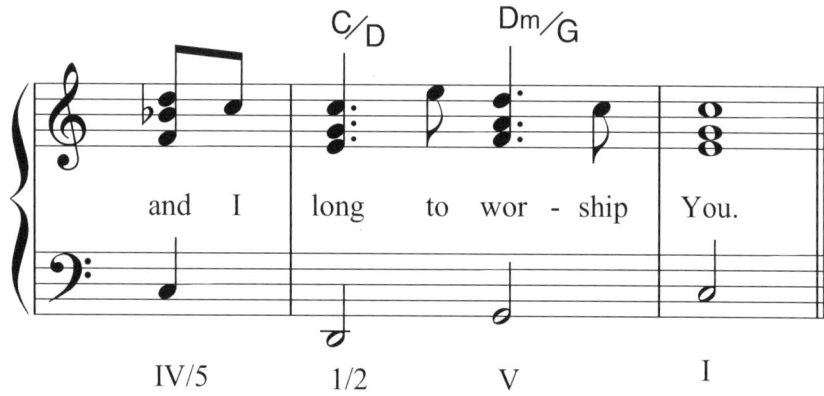

Example 13.35 *To God Be the Glory* Employing I/4, I/2, and 5/6

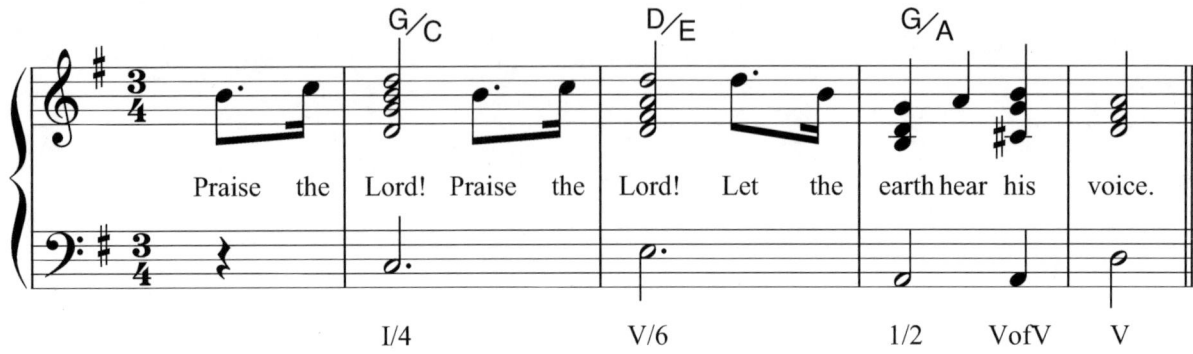

Note: the V/6 chord, functionally, is the same as the 1/2 chord, but is pitched a fifth higher. In essence, we have a series of descending fifths (E – A – D or 6 – 2 - V).

Example 13.36 I/4 and I/2 at the Half Cadence. *Amazing Grace*

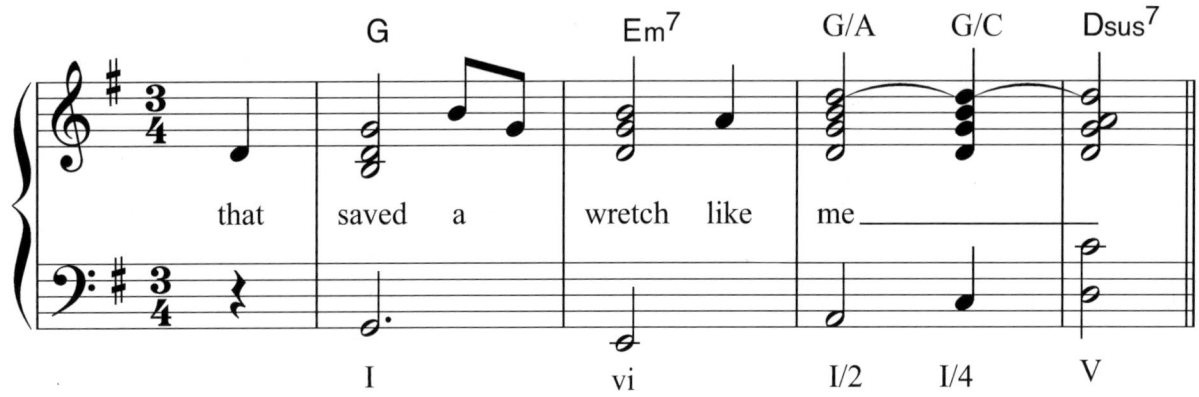

Example 13.37 I/4 and I/2 in *My Faith Has Found a Resting Place*

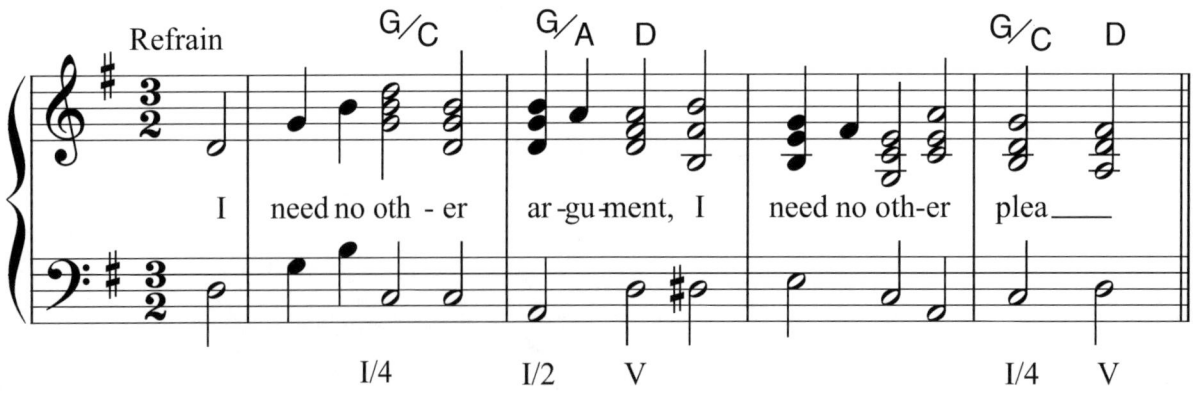

A Rarer Possibility: IV/b7

Example 13.38 *Be Thou My Vision* Employing IV/b7 (Constituted like a I/4)

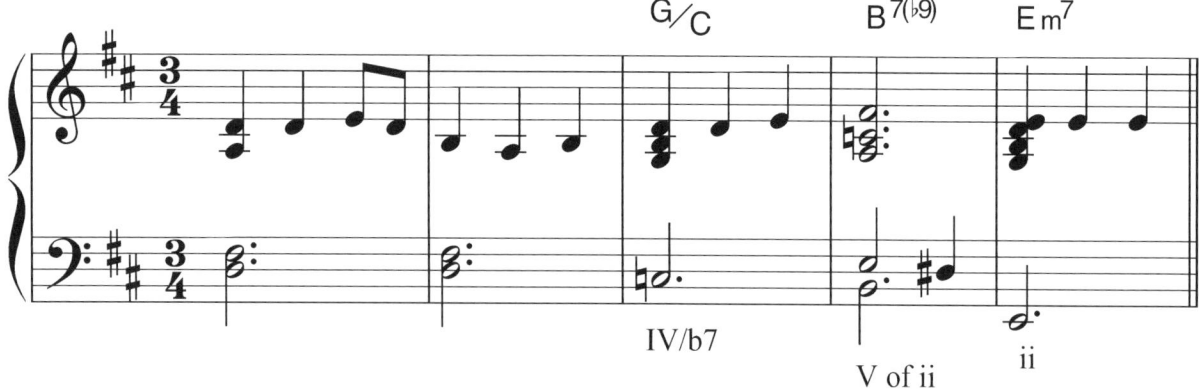

Example 13.39 *Shout to the North and the South* Employing IV/b7 and I/4

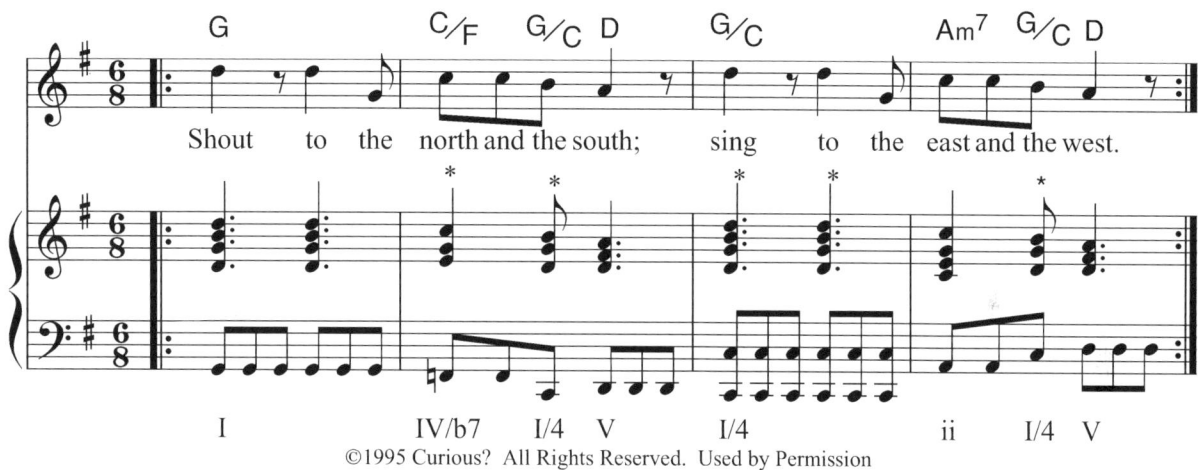

Improvise!

Example 13.40 **Improvise/Write** *(The Solid Rock)*

Create a lead sheet with both Pop Symbols and Roman Numerals that utilize alternating rock harmonies as well as the I/4 and 1/2 chords.

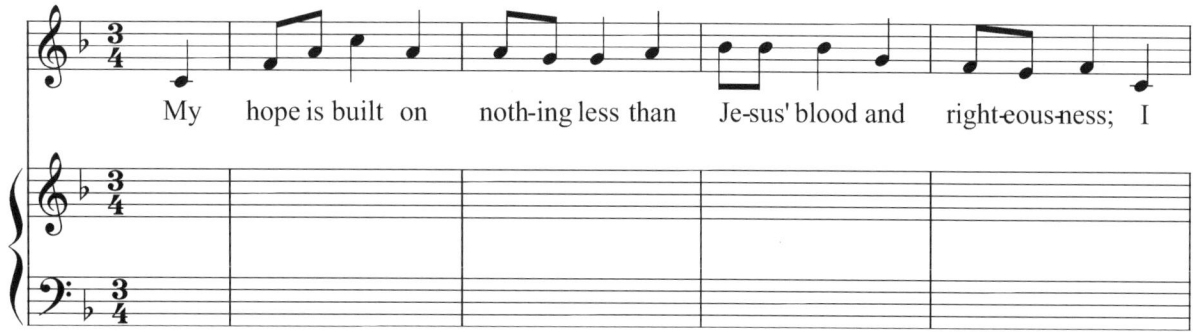

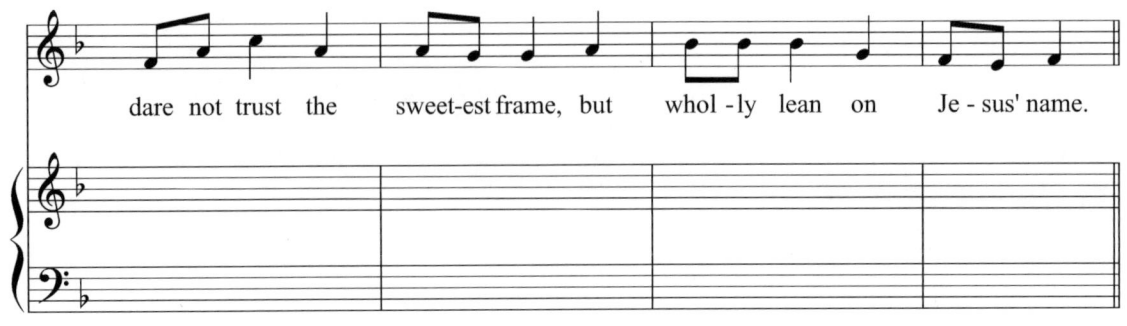

dare not trust the   sweet-est frame, but   whol -ly lean   on   Je - sus' name.

Refrain

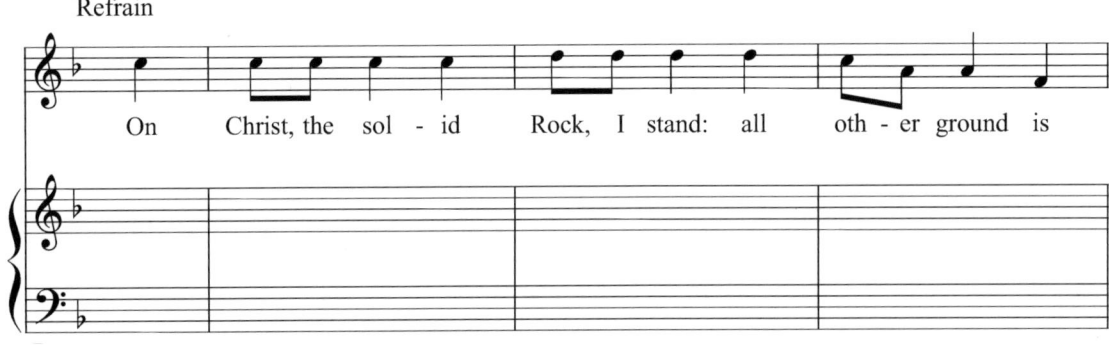

On   Christ, the   sol - id   Rock, I   stand: all   oth - er ground is

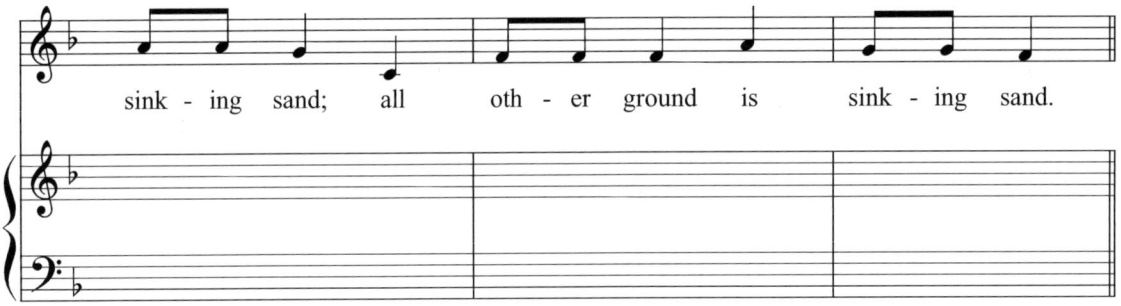

sink - ing   sand;   all   oth - er   ground   is   sink - ing   sand.

Expressive Dissonance

Book 2 deals with the appearance of recent chord structures in worship music. Of all the harmonic structures that have been highlighted in Book 2—added seconds, quartals, sus chords, and IV/5—I/4 is the most dissonant. Have you acquired a taste for dissonance?

The chapter has demonstrated ways that I/4 and I/2 can function, and that a major triad on scale degree I can be substituted with the I/4 or I/2 chord, thereby generating more musical tension.

I am not certain our abstract title "Infusing Tension" (though "tension and release" is a major music theory topic) best summarizes this chapter. The focus on and projection of harmonic complexity, brilliance, resonance, boldness, seems more on point, for "one over four" has elements of the kaleidoscopic.

In any case, experience shows that I chords have a crucial role. Therefore one can imagine that "one over four or two" chords could have a significant role in situations where more brilliance and complexity is desirable.

Thoughts on "Glory and Honor"

If you are an aspiring worship keyboardist, you cannot do better than to study and reflect on the book of Revelation. Fourteen of the twenty-two chapters deal with the primary struggle, worship. Who is to be worshiped, God or Satan?

Study will show that a pair of words often go together: *glory and honor* (see 4:9, 11, 5:12, 13, 7:12, 21:26). They project the highest esteem and respect due God and the Lamb.

Suggestion. Since this pairing of words is so frequent in heaven's worship, wouldn't it make sense to have them on our lips (and take them to heart personally) as we play and lead worship?

Wouldn't it be wonderful if our hands could find a way to project the musical image of "glory"? To my way of thinking, this is one of the ways that I/4 may help us. Through its sonic complexity, brilliance and boldness, it is one way to sound the note of "glory."

PLAYING KEYBOARDS IN A WORSHIP BAND

Playing in the Worship Band

Stylistically, the chapters that follow take a sharp turn in a different direction. The previous chapters addressed "what is possible" when playing the piano *by yourself* at home, or when playing or leading worship from the keyboard alone *by yourself*—for instance, you have more freedom, especially harmonically.

However, playing in a worship band requires rethinking your role—*how* and *what* you should play. It involves finding a part that works with the other players and serves the whole.

The 100% Rule. If we have four instruments in our band, it should be obvious that all four players cannot have the dominant, lead part at the same time. There has to be a give and take. If one person is allotted 60% of the "pie," the other three have to share the remaining 40%. There is only so much musical space available. Player roles can change from piece to piece. In a guitar-driven piece, the keyboardist may provide only minimal background support. In an intimate piece, the drummer may just play brushes. In the "break down" the drummer may play alone. Or, the entire band may sit out as the congregation sings a cappella.

The groove. When playing or leading alone, "rubato" (an elastic, slight speeding up or slowing down of the tempo) is easy to employ and can be effective. But in a band, it's more difficult. In contemporary worship the groove becomes more important.

The "groove" is the combined, in-sync effort of the rhythm section players when beat and rhythm come together coherently. Often it means not speeding up when you become excited or slowing down in soft, tranquil passages. So, when practicing at home, consider using a metronome. Study your own rhythmic tendencies (we all have them)–otherwise you may not know them. Likely, some day you will be required to play in sync with a track at church, given current technology. Consider these essential guidelines for playing the keyboard in a worship band.

Keyboard Guidelines

Listen to the drums, bass, and guitar parts!

1. If the kick is busy, then the left hand of the keyboardist needs to be simple. Listen to the Hi-Hat. It tells you the "feel." Do you hear 8ths or 16ths?
2. If the bass is busy, then the keyboard LH needs to be simple. *And vice versa.* Trade off!
3. If the guitar is busy, then the keyboard needs to be simple. *And vice versa.* Trade off! If the guitar strums throughout, play more.

You will find these principles being observed in the recorded examples played by the band in the following chapters.

If you have two keyboards on stage, one should be less busy (or play pads).

A Major Challenge. One of the most formidable challenges facing keyboardists is to have sufficient mastery of their instrument, and in addition, the extra capacity to not only listen to themselves, but also (at the same time) *listen to the band.* A seasoned, LA session player shared with me, "With my left ear I listen to myself. With my right ear I listen to the band."

REALLY TUNE INTO THESE THOUGHTS. TAKE THEM SERIOUSLY.

About the Band Pieces. In the chapters that follow, a notated piano part is provided, so you can learn it and play along with the band. For *Amazing Grace, I have Decided to Follow Jesus, and Joyful, Joyful We Adore Thee,* the harmonies are for the most part traditional—similar to those you would find in a hymnbook. The keyboard parts are pegged at the intermediate level.

Every Time I Feel the Spirit, a bravura, performance-oriented, keyboard-driven piece, is quite different stylistically. The advanced-level piano part employs intense, dissonant, harmonic extensions not found in hymnbooks, bluesy fills, and sophisticated syncopations at a break-neck tempo. In order to provide a more manageable learning and practice environment, the tempo in the "piano only" track is reduced appreciably.

Piano Pedals. Piano pedals are not indicated in any of the pieces. Listen to the piano tracks for the appropriate amount of pedal.

CHAPTER 15

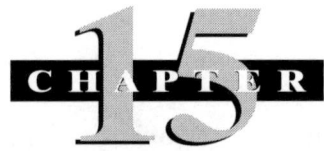

Amazing Grace: Gospel Shuffle

Two scores are provided: (1) piano notation (2) band chart.

Four tracks are provided: (a) vocal, band, piano; (b) band with piano; (c) piano only; (d) band without piano.

Suggestions. Learn the piano part (c). Play the piano part with the track that omits the piano (d). Also, experiment. Create your own original version and play along with the band.

Shuffle Rhythm Introduced. For the first stanza, even eights are employed. For the second stanza, shuffle eights (uneven, swung eights) occur. Note also the gospel licks in measures 21 and 29-30 of the second stanza. Measures 30-31 have a tidbit of Country. Shuffles are another feature of the contemporary worship scene.

Example 15.1 *Amazing Grace* (Keyboard Score with Even Eights followed by Shuffle Eights)

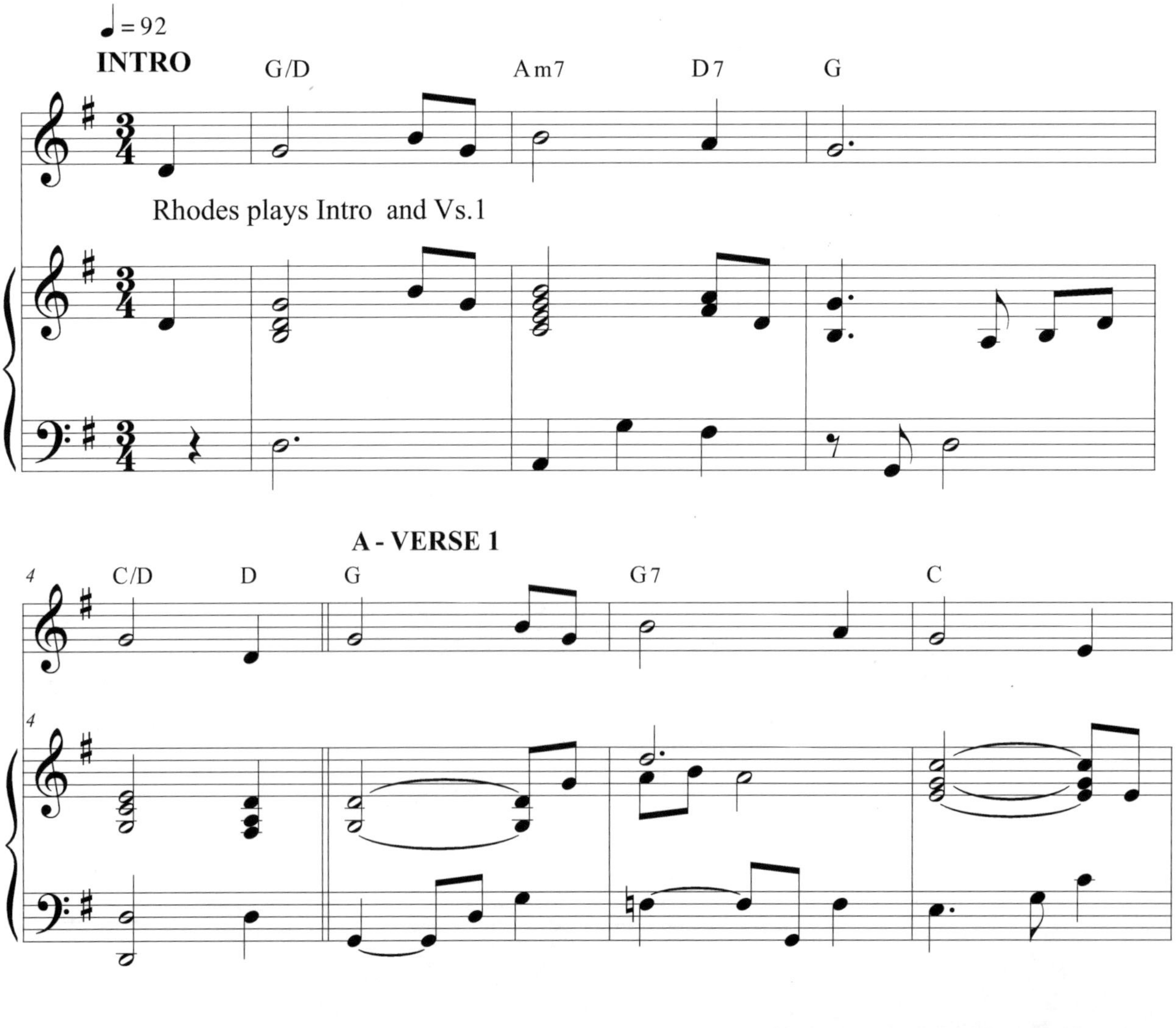
♩= 92
INTRO
G/D
Am7
D7
G
Rhodes plays Intro and Vs.1
A - VERSE 1
4
C/D
D
G
G7
C
4

B - VERSE 2

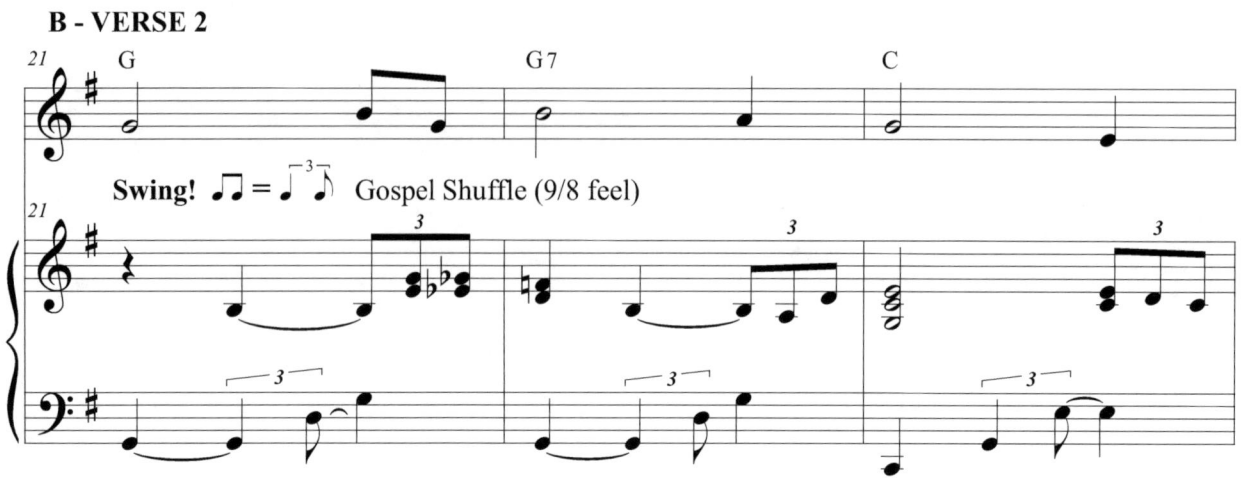

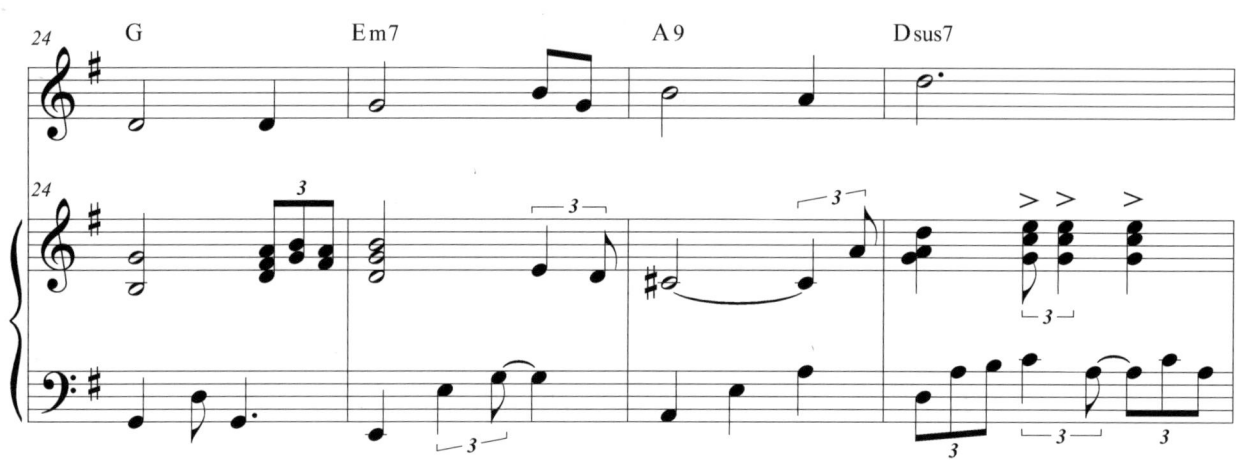

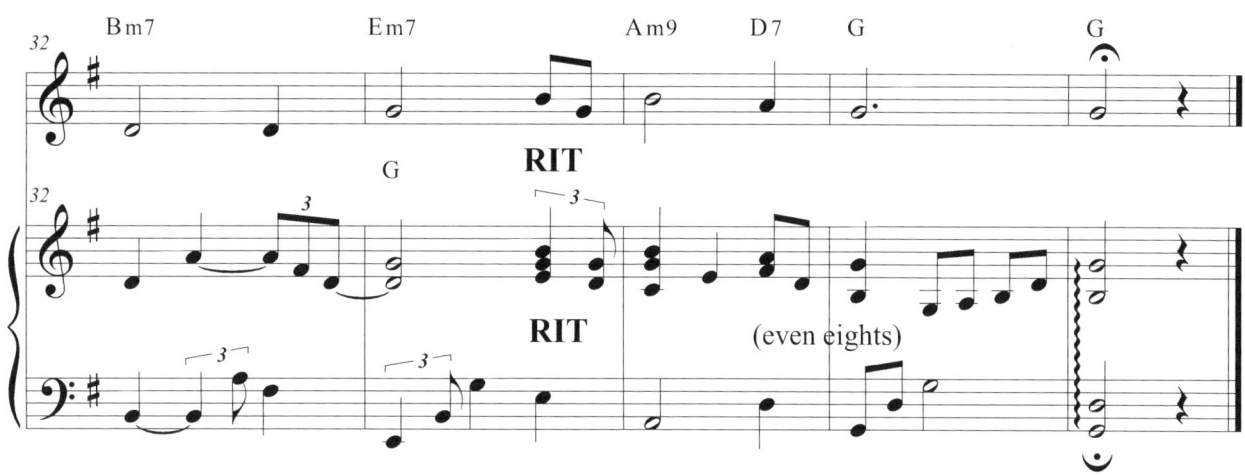

Example 15.2   *Amazing Grace*   (Band Lead Sheet) Play Along! Create your Own Version.

CHAPTER 16

I have Decided to Follow Jesus: Country

Two scores are provided: (1) piano notation (2) band chart.

Four tracks are provided: (a) vocal, band, piano; (b) band with piano; (c) piano only; (d) band without piano.

Suggestions. Learn the piano part (c). Play the piano part with the track that omits the piano (d). Also, experiment. Create your own original version and play along with the band.

Country Shuffle. Country licks in Country Shuffles have their own distinctive way of relating to added second chords. Look at beat 3 of measure 9, it has the sound of a F2 chord (the G resolves to an A on the next measure). Similar situations occur in measures 4, 23, and 31.

Example 16.1 *I Have Decided to Follow Jesus* (Keyboard Score)

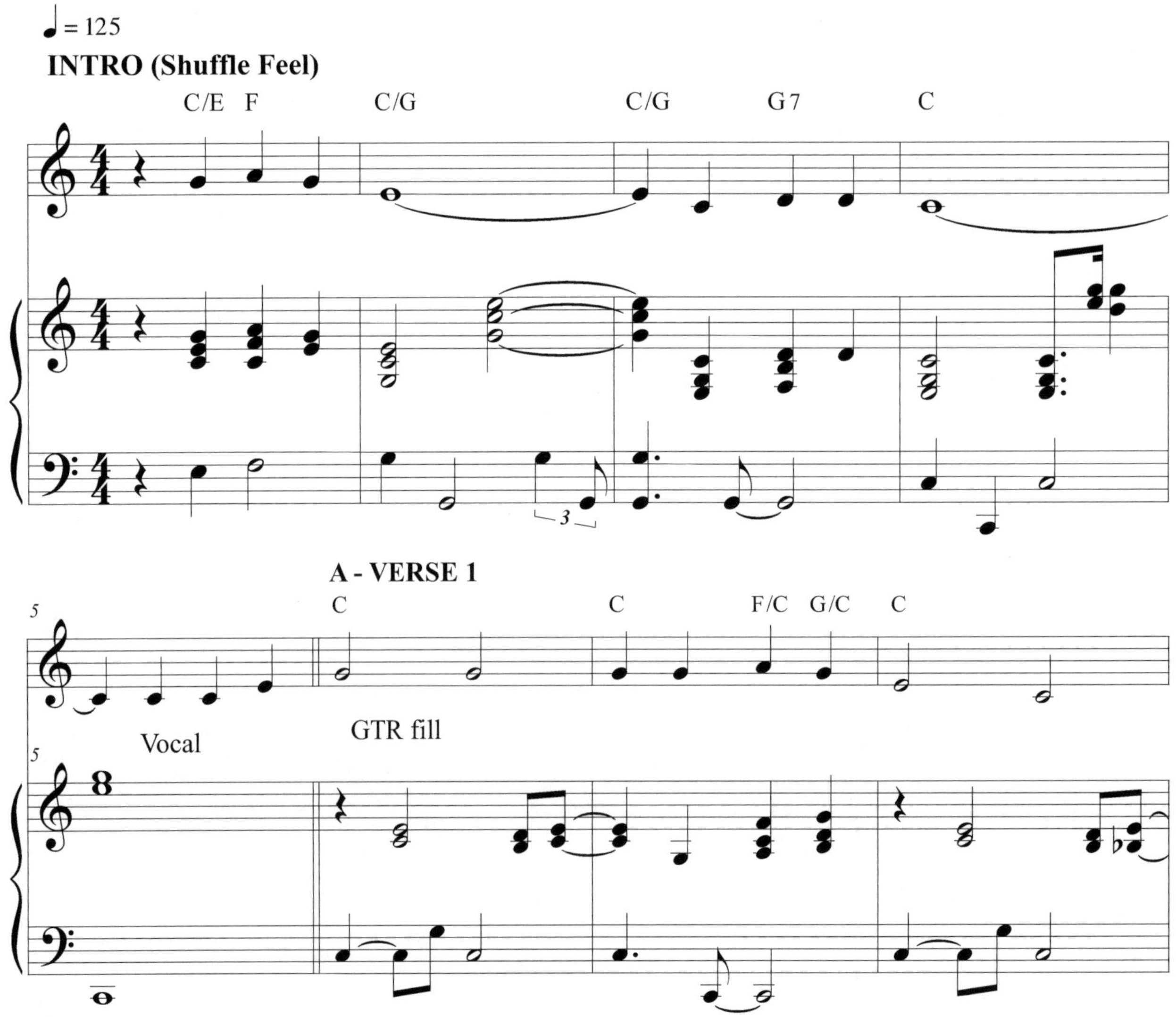

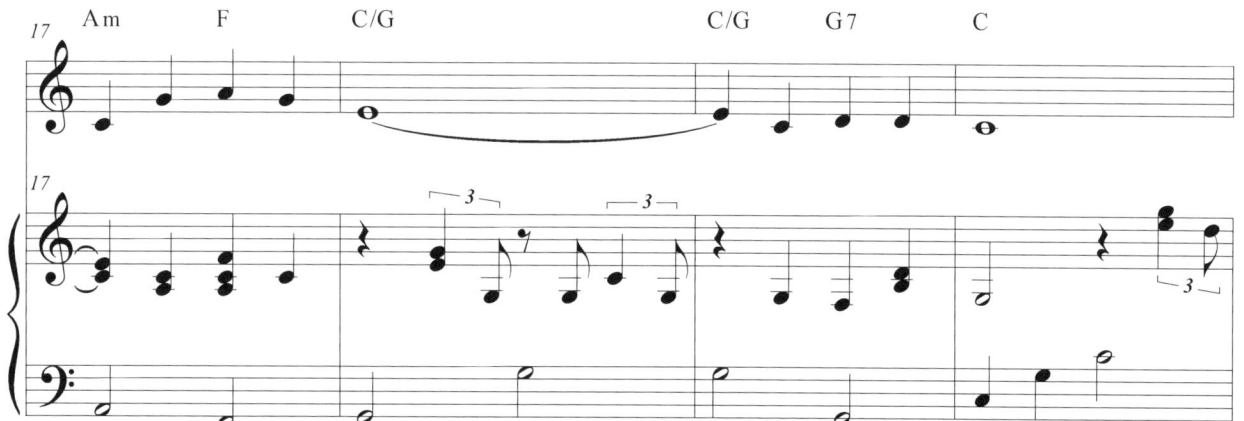

B - VERSE 2

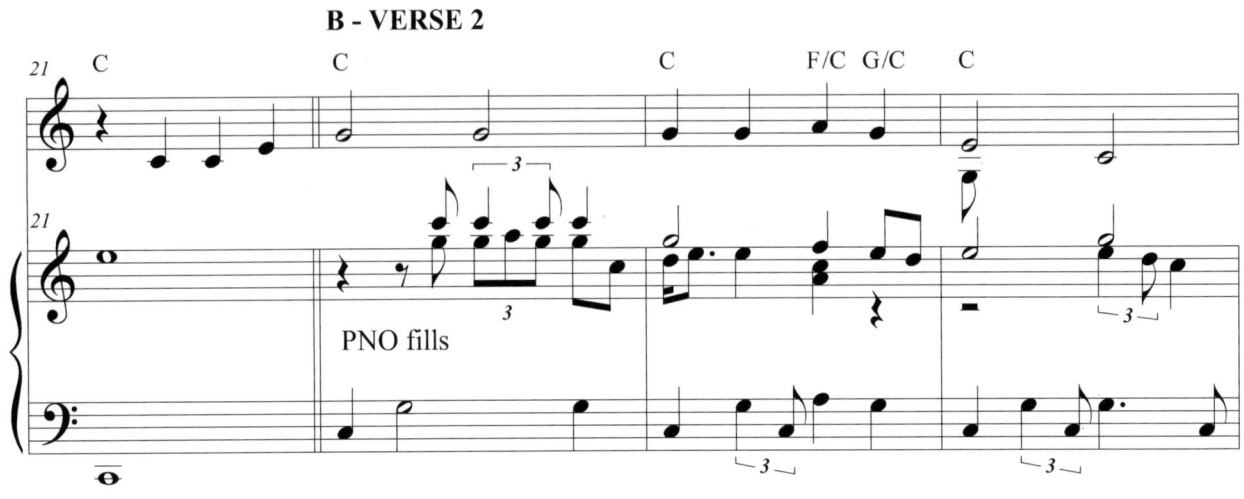

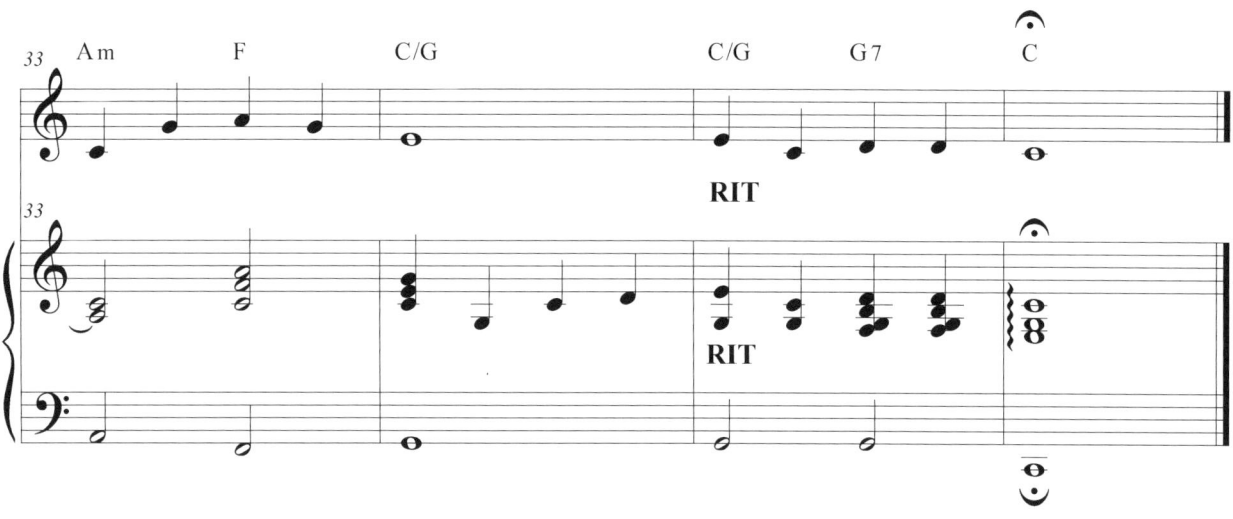

Example 16.2 I Have Decided to Follow Jesus (Band Score). Create a Piano Part.

Joyful, Joyful We Adore Thee: Classical

Basic hymnbook harmonies are employed with a Classical-Baroque style. This keyboard part is slightly more difficult than the previous ones.

Two scores are provided: (1) piano notation (2) band chart.

Four tracks are provided: (a) vocal, band, piano; (b) band with piano; (c) piano only; (d) band without piano.

Suggestions. Be sure to learn the piano part (track c). Play the piano part with the track that omits the piano (track d). Also, experiment. Create your own original piano part and play along with the band.

Things to notice. Where the RH is active (busy), the LH is simple (ms. 5-12, 25-28) and in a high register than does not step on the bass guitar part. In the same measures, contrasting lines are fashioned that complement the melody. Scalar "fills" (ms.16, 28, 36) are employed where there are "holes." In each case, the fills occur at the end of phrases, and a long half note (providing space) is in the melody. Also, the fills are fashioned to be easily performed, falling naturally and adeptly for the hand.

When improvising in the heat of the moment, ease of performance is important. Ideally, we want the obtain the maximum effect with the least amount of effort and avoid errors (session players call them "clams").

Example 17.1 *Joyful, Joyful, We Adore Thee.* (Keyboard Score)

A -VERSE 1

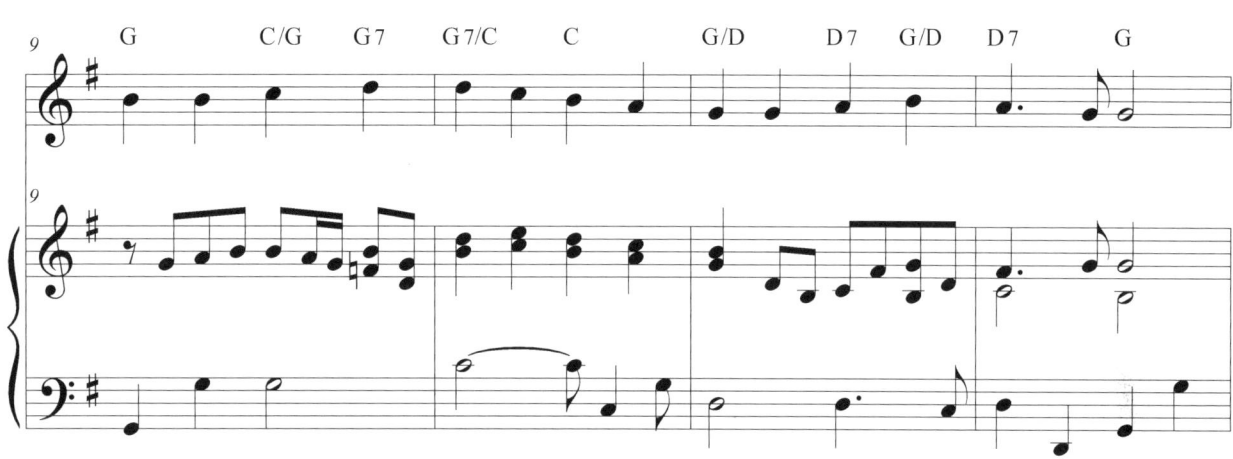

B - INTERLUDE

C - VERSE 2

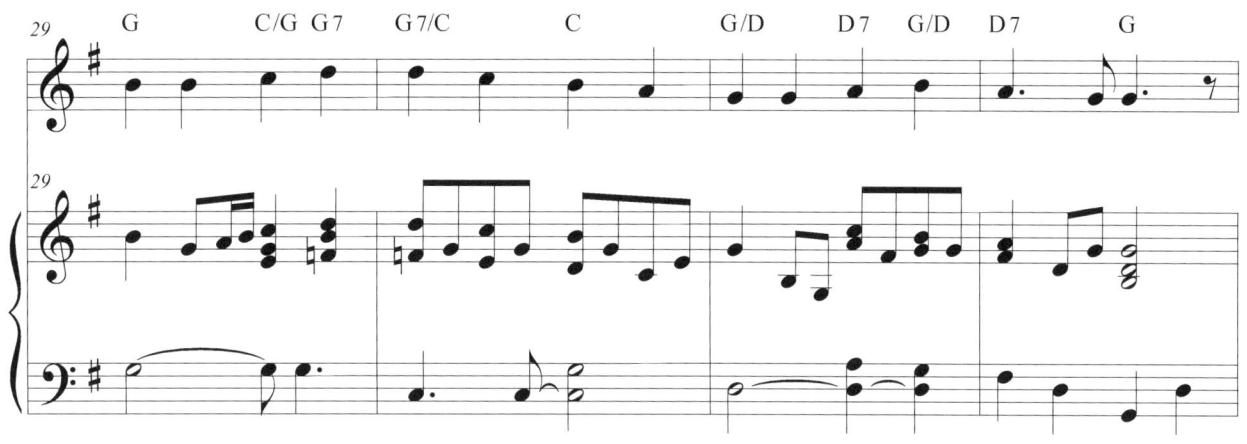

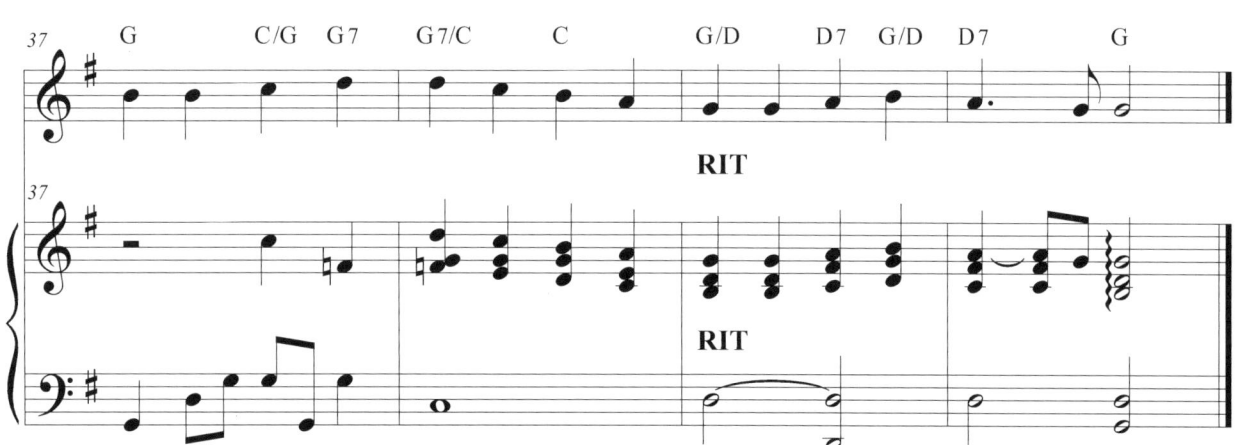

198

Example 17.2 *Joyful, Joyful We Adore* Thee (Band Score). Create a Piano Part.

Every Time I Feel the Spirit: Upbeat Gospel

One score is provided, the piano notation.

Four tracks are provided: (a) vocal, band, piano; (b) band with piano; (c) piano only; (d) band without piano (e) B3 organ.

Suggestions. Learn the piano part (track c). Play the piano part with the track that omits the piano (track d). Experiment. Create your own original version. Play along with the band.

Things to notice. This is more a performance piece than a worship piece. The vocal track is at a break-neck, fast tempo. The other recorded tracks are at a slower more manageable tempo to assist the learning process. You may wisely decide to practice the piano part at a slower tempo of 80bpm (beats per minute) and then move up to the recorded 95bmp. Slow practice is beneficial. Rootless chords in the piano part occur frequently (ms.1, 3, 4, 8, 11, etc.) and are *essential* in this arrangement. They help prevent the piano from stepping on the bass guitar part which is super active, and which roams around a wide pitch space.

Gospel harmonies. Bluesy thirds occur frequently in the accompaniment beginning in measure 1. They're termed 'bluesy thirds" because F natural (which is not part of the G scale) is a half-step lower than the expected F#. Below, see the movement.

Example 18.1 Bluesy Third in Melody

In measure 1 of our piece, a rootless D7(#9) occurs. The root of the chord (D) is omitted.

Example 18.2 Bluesy D7(#9) Chord

Let's unpack the above carefully. Although the D7(#9), or D7 with a raised or sharped ninth, should be spelled theoretically with an E# (m. 1), it is typically spelled with an F natural (m. 2). Notice also in m. 2, the D7(#9) embodies a major third (D to F#) and a minor third or tenth (D to F natural). This basic sonority also occurs at ms. 8, 20, 36, 40, and 47.

The combination of those two intervals (with the F# below and F natural on top) results in a wonderful, jangling dissonance which characterizes the sonority. I call it the "sweet and sour chord"—sweet major third on bottom, with a sour minor third on top. In m.3, the D7(#9) functions in a basic V – I progression. And the soprano part sounds bluesy.

Another bluesy progression is stated several times (ms. 12, 18, 32, 33). The F – Em – D movement, a bVII - vi - V progression, employs different inversions.

Example 18.3 Another Bluesy Progression in the Key of G

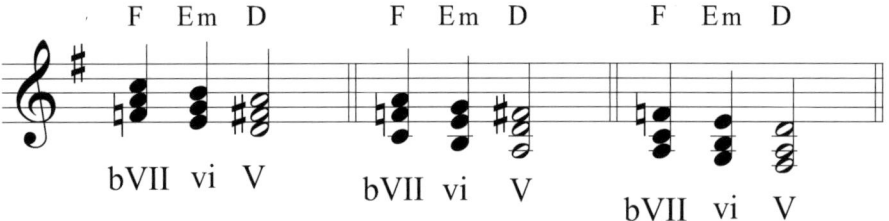

These two progressions (18.2, 18.3) significantly define the bluesy aura of the arrangement.

The transcription. The transcription is close to the original (but not perfect!) for at the time only the full band track—no piano only track—was available. Yet it should be serviceable. The arrangement was created, orchestrated, and performed by my colleague, Chris Wills. Where I have written even sixteenth notes, in actuality, often a gospel "shuffle feel" (with uneven sixteenths) is heard. Try to imitate that feeling.

Example 18.4 *Every Time I Feel the Spirit* (Keyboard Score)

CHORUS

VERSE 1

CHORUS

VERSE 2

CHORUS

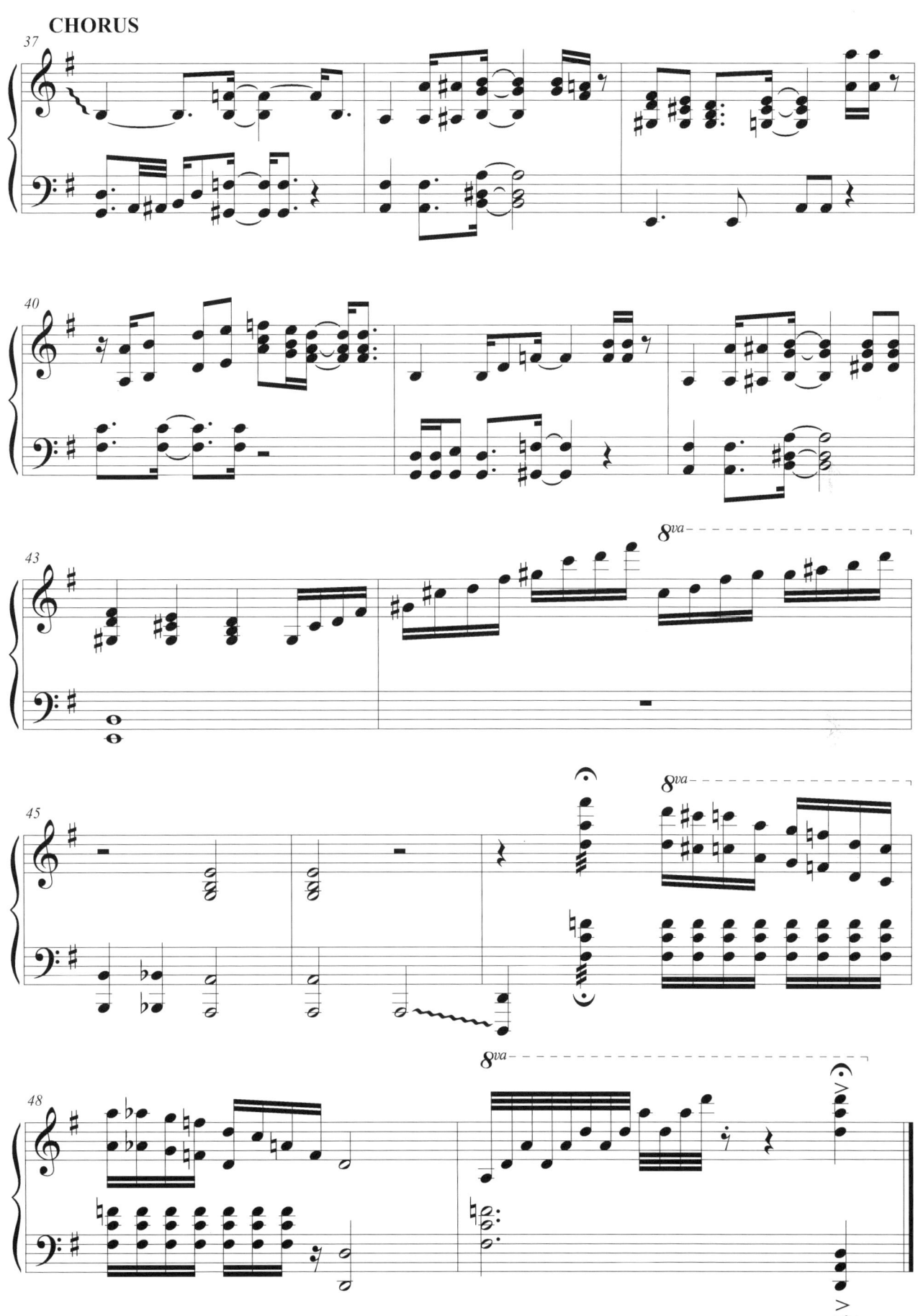

Other Books in Keyboard Series

(All Books Under $10)

Keyboard Worship Book 1 of 4
Learn, Integrate, Apply Basic Chords, Voicings, Progressions

This book deals with the basics of building a harmonic language, improvising, reading chord charts, and playing/leading by yourself or in a worship band.

200 Pages and 300 Online Tracks of Almost All Music Examples
Tracks for Playing with a Worship Band

Who is the Book for?
Intermediate worship keyboardists with a heart to serve for the glory of God
Classically trained pianists who want to improvise but don't know how
College piano proficiency and keyboard harmony classes
Piano teachers seeking to introduce worship songs, theory, improvisation

Basic Competencies Addressed
Get the shapes of triads and sevenths into your fingers
Learn new voicings and chordal pathways
Use Alternating Chords ("Doubles")
Become Free Let Go of the Melody
Techniques for Playing (or Leading) by Yourself
Techniques for Playing in a Worship Band

Keyboard Worship Book 3 of 4
Advanced Harmonic Techniques

This book addresses established harmonic techniques that are well known and appear in Broadway music, film scores, and Jazz, but are not well understood or used by most contemporary worship keyboardists.

In-Depth Panorama of Harmonic Possibilities
Advanced Level
200 Pages of Music Examples/Instruction and 300 Online Tracks

Who is the Book for?
College Undergraduate and Graduate Worship Keyboard Majors
College Undergraduate and Graduate Classical Piano Majors
Keyboardists with the hunger, drive, to train and perform for the glory of God

Goals

See your congregation sing with energy and conviction

Bring out the theology in worship songs

Create interesting bass/melody lines, captivating harmonies

Develop arranging and collaborating skills

Competencies Addressed

Learn to "text paint"—bring out theology in worship songs

Apply Secondary Dominants, Altered Dominants, Diminished, Half Diminished Sevenths

Employ tri-tone substitutions, half-step tensions, inner voice leading

Revoice extensions—evoke bold, nuanced colors

Devote all the powers of art to instill in classic hymns/worship songs vitality—spirit!

Create inspiring accompaniments for singers and instrumentalists

Keyboard Worship Book 4 of 4 (forthcoming)
Modulation, Intros, Outros, Turn Arounds

This book explores different ways to integrate and apply modulations, intros, outros and turnarounds.

200 Online Tracks Included

Advanced Level

Tracks for Playing Along with Worship Accompaniments

Musical ideas embedded in well-known worship songs

Who is the Book for?

Worship leaders and keyboardists seeking to fashion effective transitions

College Undergraduate and Graduate Keyboard Majors

Competencies Addressed

Ways of achieving free-flowing, seamless worship

Short and long modulations within and between songs

Modulations involving songs in different keys and with different meters

The value of Sus substitutions in creating modulations and intros

Emotionally meaningful modulations, intros, outros, turn arounds

All book sales donated to a children's orphanage in India
("Vikasitha Ministries")

A Personal Note

Looking at outward circumstances only, it would seem very unlikely that I would be a music professor, no less a Ph.D., and be writing this or any book.

I grew up in Vancouver BC in a loving, musical family, located in a poor, lower-class district of the city. My dad had a grade four education and I think my mom made it to grade ten. My parents respected education, but had no concept of higher education. My dad, who could barely read, had a small auto body shop, straightened fenders and painted cars. After school my brother and I would bicycle to dad's shop and help him. We loved our dad!

So how did it happen that I became a Ph.D? I give major credit to my home church and our pastor, W.H. Brooks, whom I loved and admired. Religiously, and without fail, our family attended sunday school and every morning and evening service. Pastor Books brought in a lot of missionaries and guest preachers (some were really good) that opened up the world to me.

Nurtured and lifted up in this enlightening environment, I can remember, as a teenager, having one thought as I tried to contemplate my future. This one phrase stuck in my mind: "I want to make a contribution!" I had no idea what that might be.

My avid interest in music came mostly from my dad and an incident that happened at church. Though my mom loved music and could play the piano, dad was the chief inspirer of music in our home. He sang, played, built instruments, and started tape recording my brother Don and me singing, well before we reached school age.

I began taking piano lessons at the age of 7 or 8, but when I was 12 a guy my age, Franklyn Lacey, came to our Sunday evening service and improvised on the piano. He stunned and amazed me. I went home and started working on it. Within a year I could play like Franklyn. I developed some piano solos and got to play one during the Sunday evening offering.

Dad sensed I needed a teacher who could help me. I will never forget the first meeting I had with Rowlie Hill, the best-known Christian piano teacher in the city. Teaching at his home, Rowlie said, "Play something for me." I played him my most expressive solo, with runs up and down the keyboard. "Very good," he said. Then he put music on the piano, "Read this." Immediately I broke down and wept uncontrollably. I said, "I can't do it…I just can't do it." It was so embarrassing to be a thirteen-year-old and to sob so uncontrollably. But I couldn't help myself. Years later Rowlie told me, "Right then, I knew you were a musician because of the way it affected you." That's one of the reasons, incidentally, why I've always been sympathetic to improvisers who struggle to read.

Soon after, I *really needed* to read! Our church invited me to play the piano (along with the organist) at our evening song service which was always packed with about 600 people. The ability to play a piano solo may have appeared impressive to our people, but I don't think they had any idea how raw, ignorant, and unprepared I was.

It was scary! I never knew what songs they'd pick. My anxiety rose as the service time approached. I'd get up there and "hope" I could play the key in the hymnbook. I knew some better than others. I didn't want to make a fool out of myself. I could read a little, but not fluently or securely. I mostly listened to the harmonies played on the organ and doodled on the first stanza. By the second and third stanza I had a better idea. The sheer terror of Sunday nights motivated me to learn how to read music—and fast!

The Sunday nights I wasn't playing, Rowlie drove all the way across town to our home (that always impressed me), and picked me up so I could be the accompanist for his youth choir. While driving me home, Rowlie would impress upon me the importance of serving in the church.

Around that time, I met Tom Keene, his most gifted student, also a christian. Tom and I went to high school together for a year, talked music every lunch hour, and became life-long friends. Unaware of any keyboard books, secular or sacred, we began taking down recordings note-for-note—records by Ted Smith (who played for Billy Graham), and other guys— and played them back note-for-note.

"What were our lives like those days?" We played at different services and youth meetings, at Youth for Christ competitions, and accompanied trios and quartets. Tom got to play on a 30 minute "live" radio program every Sunday night on CJOR. It was a big deal! In the summers, I began playing for small-city, evangelistic tent campaigns, Barry Moore city-wide crusades across Canada, and eventually a Leighton Ford/Billy Graham two-week crusade in Vancouver which filled up our Empire Stadium with 30,000 people.

Tom went on to Junior College in Washington, transferred, graduated from Biola where I now teach, and became a LA studio musician. He's arranged and performed on more than a 1000 recordings, and wrote the band arrangements in this book, improvising the piano parts.

I went the academic route. How it happened was amazing and may be important to you. While I was a music student at the University of British Columbia, the department head, Dr. Marquis, called me into his office: "Barry, have you thought about graduate school?" I was shocked as I wasn't sure I was of that caliber. "Think about it. Talk to your parents. We'll need a little money for applications. If this seems right, come back and see me."

I came back excited. This is the truth. Dr. Marquis had me sit down beside him at his office desk. He chose the schools and filled out the major part of the applications for me in his own hand writing while I looked on. I don't know why he did it. Maybe he sensed I was so ill-informed that I needed help. He'd peer at me through his glasses, "This grad school is rich and has money. Let's apply there."

It has always amazed me that someone, in this case a non-believer, would take such a personal interest in me. Why me? He changed my life! Actually, I think the Lord was leading him to do it. I say that, because I want to encourage you that God has a wonderful plan for your life. Believe it! It may come about in unexpected ways.

Because of Dr. Marquis, I was awarded a TA and scholarship to attend grad school, with free tuition, room and board, plus even some spending money. Altogether, I went on to become a university student for ten years at four different universities (two in Canada and two in the States). I loved the university environment and have never left it.

A final, touching story.

For several decades I did not make any contact with our old teacher, Rowlie Hill. Many years later, I looked up Rowlie and his wife, Clarice, and we had lunch together. He was so excited to see me. We had a great time. Rowlie really dressed up and looked his very, very best, but I could see he was old, fading, and becoming weak.

A year later Rowlie died. Clarice and Rowlie never had children. Clarice told me that Rowlie always talked about Tom and me as, "his boys." She said that he prayed for us daily for decades. To this day, it stirs me to think about it. I felt badly. I had no idea. Why had I not made contact all those intervening years?

If Tom and I have had any success, any ministry worth anything, I believe that Rowlie Hill, our old teacher, had a big part in it.

So these are my last words. Teachers, love your students. Pray for them unceasingly, even if they don't acknowledge you, or look you up.

Announcements and Resources
at *WorshipInfo.com*

Worshipinfo.com

Worshipinfo.com is the "headquarters" for announcements concerning the *Keyboard Worship* Series.

Downloadable mp3 Examples

Free, downloadable mp3 files for the *Keyboard Worship* books are available at worshipinfo.com. Approximately 90% of the music examples are public domain and presented without any limitations. For the remaining 10%, the copyrighted examples, licenses were obtained for the published books. However, to comply with copyright restrictions regarding the audio files, full mp3 accompaniments are provided, but the melodies have been omitted. Nevertheless, since both the melodies and melody accompaniments are notated in the books, this should not be a serious drawback.

Book Four

When *Book Four—Modulations, Intros, Outros, Turn Arounds*, becomes available, an announcement will be made at worshipinfo.com. Worshipinfo.com will be our announcement headquarters.

Other Forms Projected for the *Keyboard Worship* Series

As time and energy permits and technological challenges are overcome, announcements will be made of the following forms of the *Keyboard Worship* series, when and if they become available:

    A. Midiculous Version

    B. Ebook Version

    C. Youtube Lessons

What is Midiculous.com?

Midiculous software allows those who do not read music notation to hear and view the music examples being played on an 88-note keyboard displayed on your computer screen. As you hear the music examples played, you will see the piano keys being depressed visually in real time. You can slow down or speed up the examples, change keys, view the chord symbols, and play along. This exciting software is free to users (visit the site). It should enable *Keyboard Worship* to reach out and bless a large group of keyboardists who play by ear but read music notation hesitantly or not at all. Our expectation is that the book version along with the midiculous version, together, will reinforce each other and help ease the learning process. For that reason, the development of a midiculous component is a high priority.

Browse Worshipinfo.com

An abundance of downloadable materials, worship articles, worship PowerPoints used in my university teaching, and other sundry tools, are available free of charge—approximately 185 files in all. Additionally, the web sites of our Biola worship faculty (guitar, piano, bass, drums, voice, technology) are posted.

Finally, I want to draw your attention to two other keyboard books by friends of mine: *Worship Piano* by Bob Kauflin (Hal Leonard, 2017), and *The Complete Church Pianist* by Debbie Denke (2011).

APPENDIX I
Chord Catalogue

Pop chord symbols are not fully standardized—alternatives exist. This book will be employing (mainly) the symbols in **bold face**, yet you should be aware of other alternatives.

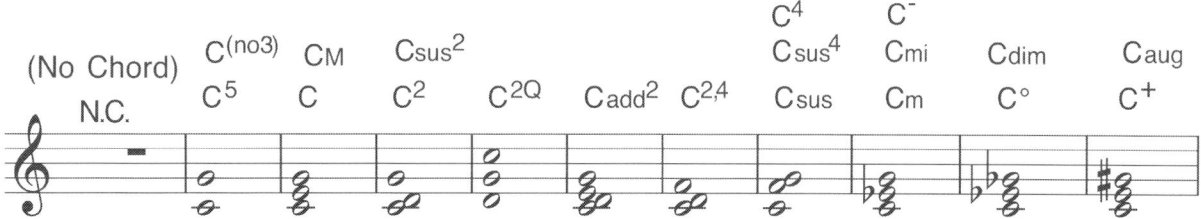

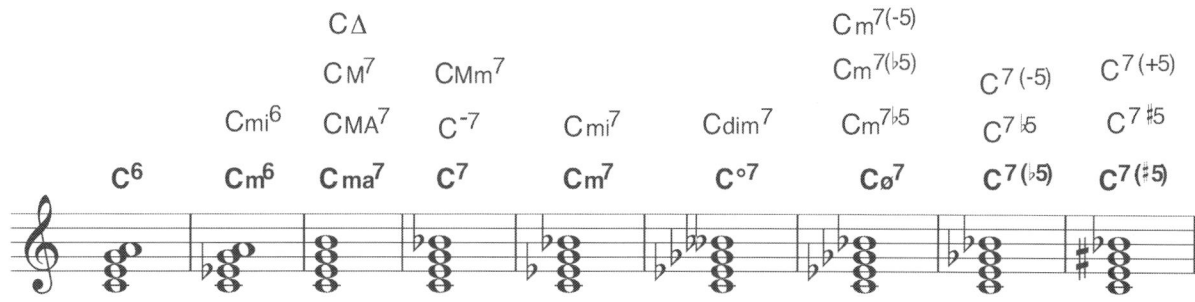

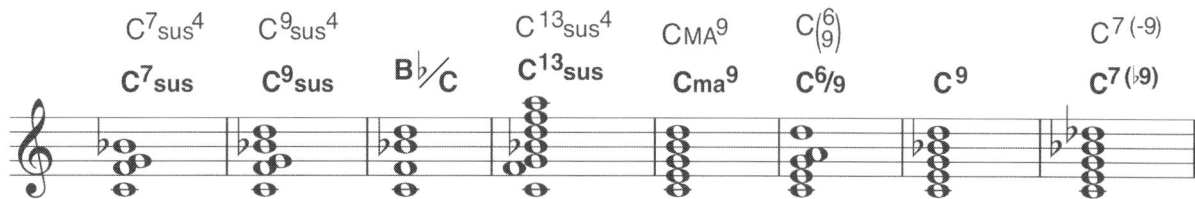

Alternatives to Traditional Harmony

Traditional harmony, expressed by the C chord (135), is composed of thirds, or what is termed "tertian" harmony in classical theory books. Traditional harmony is undergoing an expansion today in contemporary worship music. Sonorities such as 125 and 145 are assuming major roles. These alternatives, which lack the 3rd of the chord, have a more ambiguous sound—they are neither major or minor in quality.

Example 1 Traditional C Chord Compared to Two Contemporary Alternatives

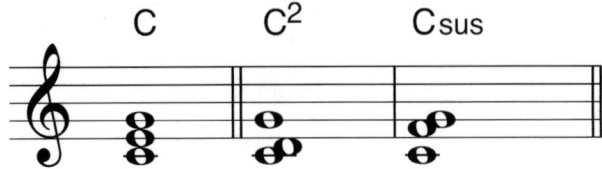

Inversions/Doublings

In measure two, the right hand notes are permutated or inverted. The lowest note becomes the highest note of the next chord. Beat one is in root position. Beat two is in first version. Beat three is in second inversion.

In measure three, various voicings (spacings) occur. The note C of chords two and three is doubled. The fourth chord triples the C (the root).

Example 2

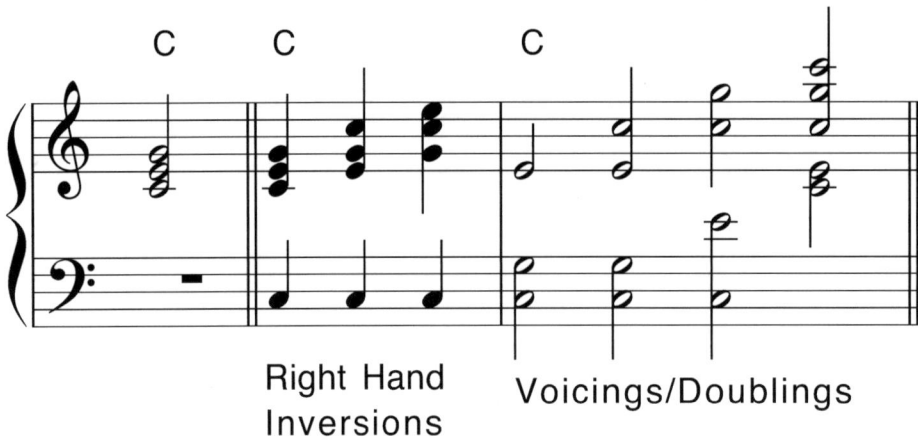

Right Hand
Inversions

Voicings/Doublings

Diagonal Slashes

The C/E designation (below) means: play a C chord and a single bass note on E. When slashes are used, the note below the slash always refers to a single note (not a chord). Slashes allow for a division of labor in a band. For example, the guitarist could play the C chord, and a bass player the single note E (an octave or two lower than written).

Example 3

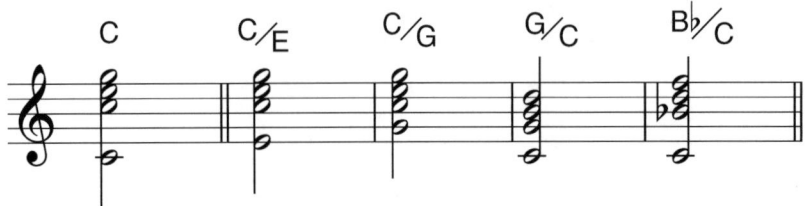

More Than One Spelling

Occasionally a symbol can have more than one spelling. Each pop symbol refers to a fixed sound, but not necessarily a fixed spelling. Chords could be spelled more than one way and yet employ the same symbol. What counts is the number of half steps.

Example 5

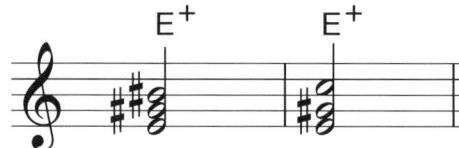

The spelling with thirds (m.1) is the default, theoretical spelling, but depending on the musical context, an alternative spelling (m.2) may be appropriate and easier to read.

Example 6

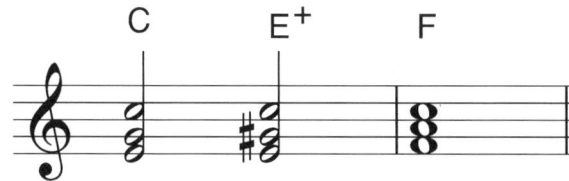

APPENDIX II
Pop Symbols vs. Roman Numerals

Since harmonic issues inevitably arise in keyboard improvisation, you'll find some harmonic explanation below—especially for those not familiar with basic music theory.

Two Worlds—Two Languages

In this book we use music language that is commonly accepted in both popular and classical music circles. Popular/Commercial musicians use pop symbols whereas classical musicians are taught to think in terms of Roman Numerals.

Triads

There are some advantages to Roman Numerals. Below is the C major scale and the triads that result from each scale degree when the collection of notes in the major scale is employed.

Example 1 Triads Derived from the C Major Scale

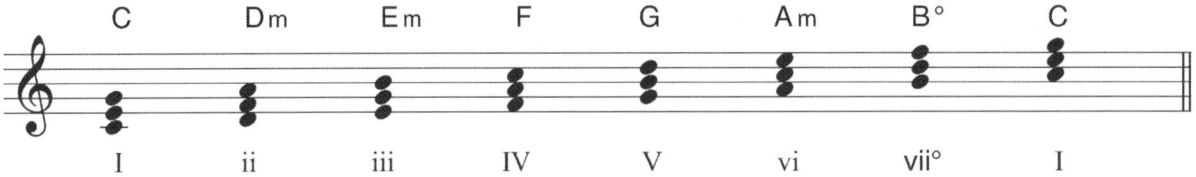

Note that the chords on scale degrees I, IV, and V are major (upper case). Scale degrees ii, iii, and vi are minor (lower case). Scale degree vii is diminished. This chord pattern holds for all major scales (Db, D, etc.), not just C major.

Thinking in scale degrees has a number of advantages, as demonstrated by the example below which transposes a progression of chords from C major to E major.

Example 2 Pop Symbols and Scale Degree Symbols Compared

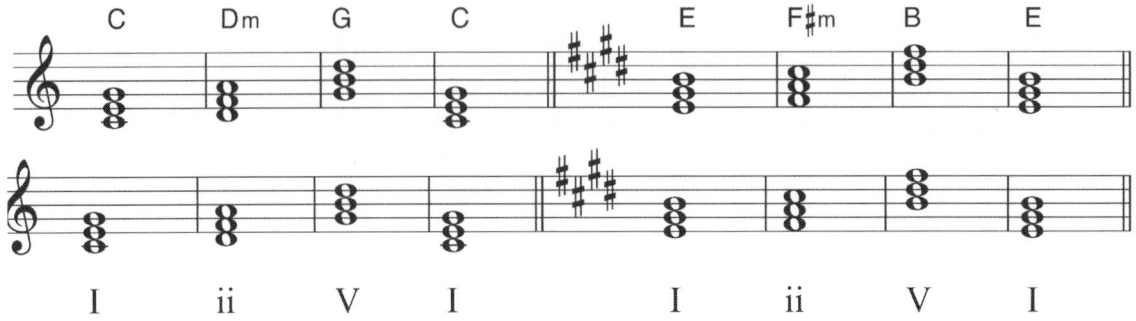

First, note that Roman Numeral designations are more efficient than the pop symbols. The entire line of chords above can be explained by four Roman Numerals whereas eight Pop symbols are required. A single set of Roman Numeral symbols serves both keys.

Second, Roman Numerals help us to think in principles—in generalized ways that apply to all keys.

Third, Roman Numerals give us more information. We learn that the progression of chords 5-8 (above) is the same as 1-4, functionally. This is important information, for in the act of improvising we need to be thinking "in music"—thinking of the function of chords on the fly! Knowing function is vital.

Example 3 Roman Numerals and Triadic Inversions

The symbols for inversions are calculated by the intervallic distance between notes. Below the intervals for each triads are represented above the chord. The symbolic abbreviation commonly used is represented below the chord.

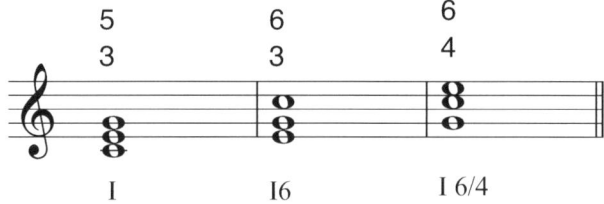

Sevenths

Example 4 Sevenths Derived from the Major Scale

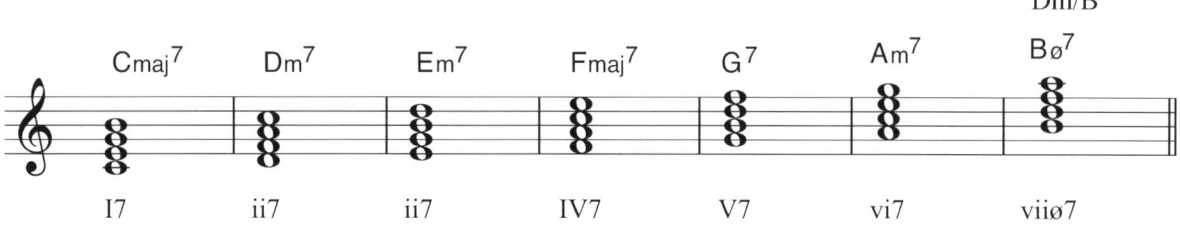

Example 5 Representative Inversions of Seventh Chords

A. Scale Degree One: Inversions of a Major Seventh

B. Scale Degree Two   Inversions of a Minor Seventh

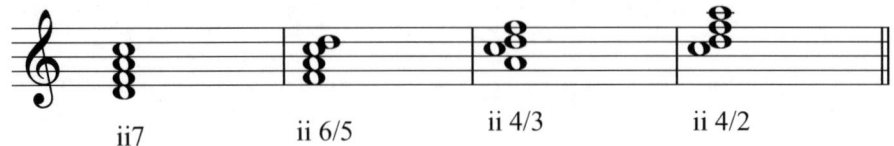

C. Scale Degree Five   Inversions of a Dominant Seventh

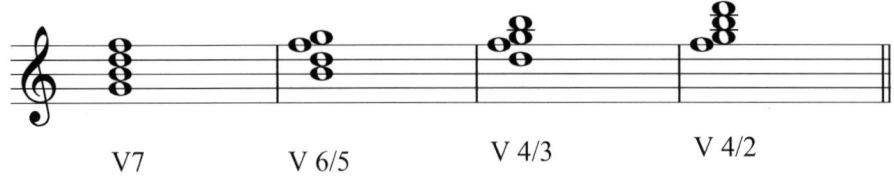

Determine the Root and the Inversion

In traditional music theory, chords are built on stacks of thirds. The lowest third determines the root. Once the root is known it is relatively easy to determine the inversion. If you can understand the logic of the symbols below, you are on your way to understanding how Roman Numerals operate..

Example 6

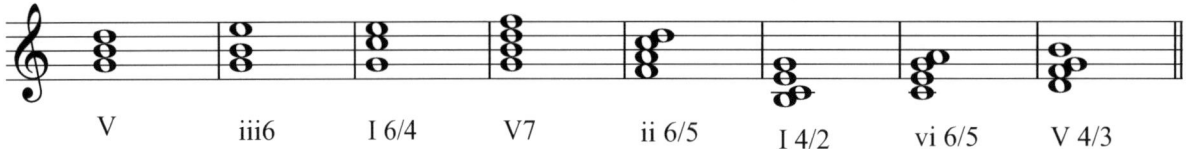

APPENDIX III
Nashville Numbers

Nashville Numbers to the rescue! Nashville Shorthand is a technique for the rapid creation of worship charts and arrangements that can be understood and performed quickly and securely—notation on the fly. Chord changes, bass lines, and rhythmic aspects of songs are indicated on a number chart. Numbers substitute for the Pop Symbols found in praise charts. The system is so easy and intuitive that musicians can begin to apply it in minutes.

Especially suited to songs with simple harmonies. Nashville Numbers tend to work especially well when songs have a simple harmonic structure (like many worship songs do), and are in major (not minor) keys. Nashville Numbers are not limited stylistically to Country music. They are applicable to a wide variety of music styles—even complex music can be transcribed. Our attention, however, will be focused on simple, easy-to-read charts for worship situations.

Nashville Numbers Resemble Roman Numerals. The Nashville Numbers resemble Roman Numeral analysis, but are more compact, accessible (more easily learned), and more intuitive for performance. They're being taught in evangelical worship schools today. *The basic prerequisite is that players must know the major scale.*

Advantages of Nashville Numbers over Pop Symbols.
(1) Number charts can be played in any key and be used to modulate to any key because the numbers (unlike chord letters) remain the same regardless of the key. Let's say you want to lift the key on the last repetition of a song. No problem! With a number chart you can accomplish that instantly without rewriting anything.

(2) Players learn something about chord function—how chords relate to each other in chord progressions (e.g. ii – V – I). Worship players become more educated.

(3) Your worship team may need to "take down' music when an internet chart is not available or inaccurate. "Takedowns" (Transcriptions) are easier to complete using Nashville Numbers. Why? You don't have to know the key of the song (helpful when you don't have perfect pitch). Rather, think in an easy key like C major. On the other hand, if you are transcribing with Pop Symbols, and the key is too high for your congregation, you'd have to rewrite the chart a second time! Nashville Numbers avoid that. Like Roman Numerals, the Nashville Numbers can be read and performed in any key.

(4) Charts are briefer (take less space), and can be transcribed more quickly.

Symbols for Scale Degrees & Triads

First, numbers are assigned to the notes of the major scale.

Example 1

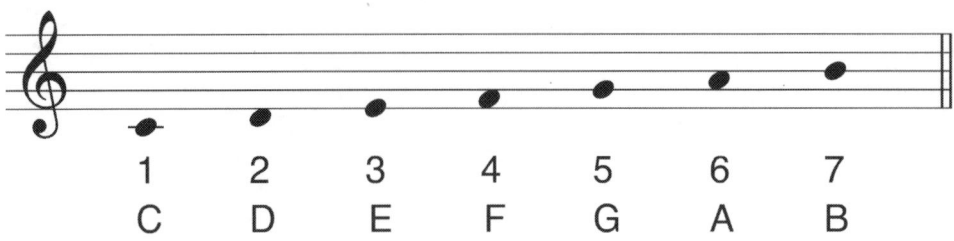

| 1 | 2 | 3 | 4 | 5 | 6 | 7 |
| C | D | E | F | G | A | B |

For all Major chords = use only the number (e.g., 1 4   5)
For all Minor chords = use the number and a minus sign (e.g., 2- 3-   6-)
For all Diminished chords = use the number and a small circle (e.g. 4° 7°)
For all Augmented chords = use the number and a plus sign (e.g., 3+ 7+)

For example, the notes of the major scale yield these chords for scale degrees 1-7.

Example 2

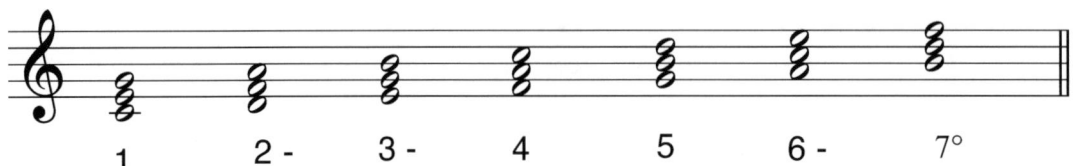

1   2 -   3 -   4   5   6 -   7°

Major triads require only a number; all minor chords have a number and a minus sign, and all diminished chords have a circle. It is not necessary for band members to know by memory, for instance, that the 2, 3, and 6 chords, derived from the major scale, are minor. But they do need to know the major scale.

Moreover, using this method, chords outside the diatonic scale (chromatic chords) can be clearly expressed.

Example 3 Chromatic Chord occurs on Scale Degree 2

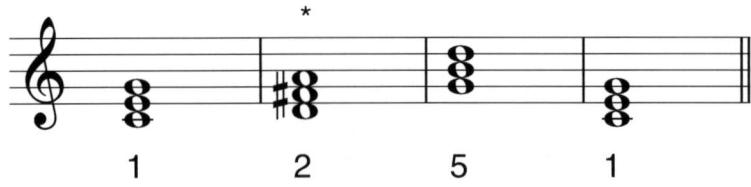

1   2   5   1

Notice above, the D major chord has no minus sign. Below, in line one a minor 2 chord occurs, whereas in line two, a major form of the 2 chord in C major is expressed.

Example 4

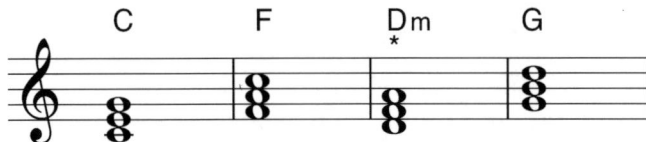

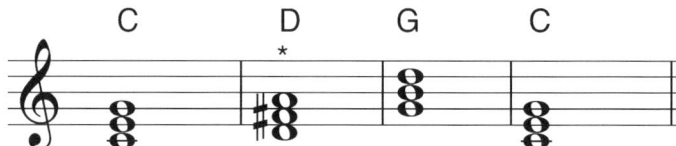

The Nashville chart for the 8 measures would look like this.

```
1   4   2-   5
1   2   5    1
```

Let's delve more deeply into the rules and processes governing the Nashville method.

Rules of Action

A. One number per measure. Each number denotes a measure of music. That is, write a chord for each measure whether or not the chord actually changes.

B. One line per phrase. In order to make musical phrases stand out visually, use a separate line of numbers for each phrase. Since most phrases are four measures long, you will generally have 4 numbers per line.

C. Set off extra measures to the right. Below, there are 4 measures plus an extra measure to the phrase on the second line—perhaps an extra measure for ending the piece. Set the fifth measure well off to the right.

```
1   4   2-   5
1   2   5    1        1
```

Example 5 *God is So Good*

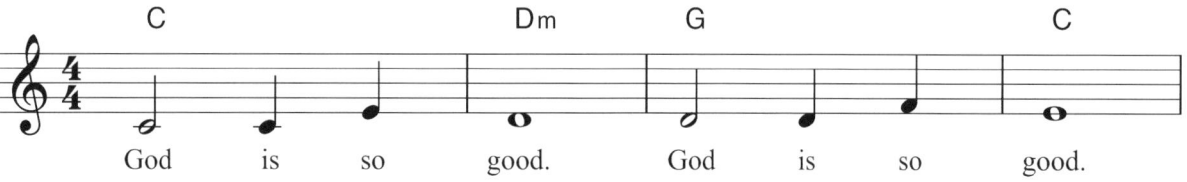

See the Nashville Numbers for *God is So Good*. Notice the time signature is also stated below. Always display that too.

```
4/4      1 2-  5  1
         1  4   5  1
```

D. Use parentheses to indicate split measures

Example 6 Measure 2 is a Split Measure *(Angels We Have Heard on High)*

An - gels   we   have   heard   on   high

Measure 2 has two chord changes instead of one. Therefore it is called a "split measure." Split measures can be expressed by using a parenthesis.

Parentheses indicate the split measure: 1 (5 1)

Meaning: the second measure consists of 2 beats of a 5 chord and 2 beats of a 1 chord.

E. Use dots to indicate other ways measures can be split

                        . . . .
4/4 time   (1   4) = 3 beats of 1; 1 beat of 4
                      . .   .
3/4 time   (1   4)   = 2 beats of 1; 1 beat of 4
                    . . . . . .
6/8 time   (1   4   ) = 3 beats of 1; 3 beats of 4

Make sure the dots are large enough to be read easily.

F. Use time signatures or dots in parentheses for changes of meter

1. Time signature: 4/4 time to 3/4 time to 4/4 time =   4/4 (1 4) 3/4 2   4/4 5   5

                                                                        . . .
2. Dots with parenthesis: 4/4time to 3/4 time to 4/4 time =   (1   4)   (2)   5   5

G. Comparison of Nashville Numbers Versus Roman Numerals

Nashville Numbers indicate the scale degrees of chords and bass lines.
Roman Numeral analysis computes the vertical distance between the notes in chords.

Example 7 Nashville Numbers Versus Roman Numeral Analysis

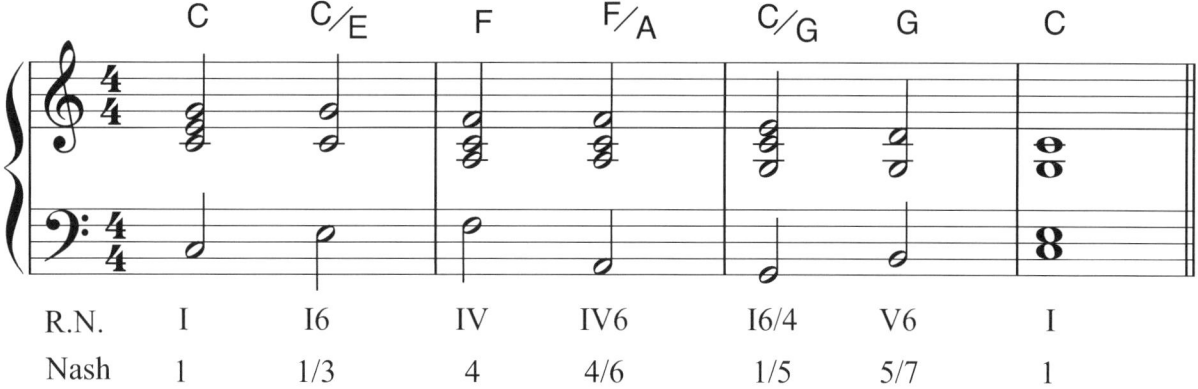

R.N.	I	I6	IV	IV6	I6/4	V6	I
Nash	1	1/3	4	4/6	1/5	5/7	1

H. Use slashes for bass lines and/or chord inversions

Example 8

Slashes are used for the bass notes above: (1   1/7) (1/6 1/5) (4   4/6) (5/7   1)

I. For pick-ups, use the abbreviation "PU" followed by a bar line

Example 9 Nashville Number Demonstration *(Amazing Grace)*

Notice, the rows and columns of numbers are aligned for easy reading. Also, the numbers are not jammed tightly together. Wide spacing aids the communication process.

		PU			
3/4	1 |	1	1	4	1
		1	2	5sus	5
		1	1	4	1
		6-	(1/5 5)	4	1

Example 10 Nashville Numbers for *Father I Adore You*

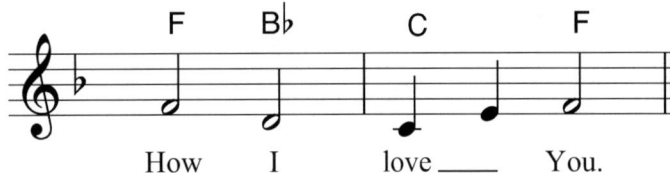

The phrases above are two measures long. So each line should ideally be two measures long.

4/4
(1 2-) (5 1)
(1 4) (5 1)
(1 4) (5 1)

Example 11 Nashville Numbers for *Away in a Manger*

Once they are written, how would you efficiently communicate the numbers above verbally to a band? See below for the answer.

J. For rapid communication, call out the numbers to your band

To communicate quickly, say the following:
Four measure phrases
Line one: eleven, twelve minus
Line two: fifty-one, twenty-five
Line three: eleven, twelve minus
Line four: fifty-one, parenthesis 2 minus 5, then 1

1	1	1	2-
5	1	2	5
1	1	1	2-
5	1	(2- 5)	1

K. Use a flat or sharp sign before (or after) the number for chromatic chords and/or bass lines

Lowered (flatted) 7^{ths} and 3^{rds} occur quite often. So do chromatic bass notes (as below).

Example 12   Chromatic Chords in C Major

	C	Bb	F	C
4/4 time	1	b7	4	1

	Eb	F	Fmin/Ab	G
	b3	4	4- / b6	5

Example 13 Same Example Expressed in Conventional Notation

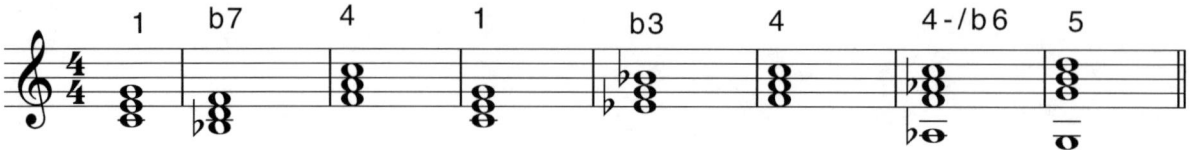

L. Use a horizontal parenthesis for rhythmically "pushed beats"

Example14 Demonstration of a Pushed Beat in Melody *(Sure Foundation)*

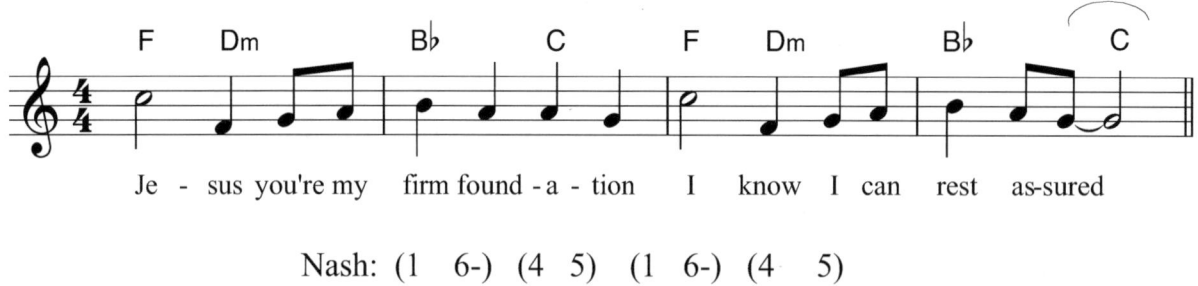

Je - sus you're my   firm found -a - tion   I   know   I   can   rest   as-sured

Nash: (1   6-)   (4   5)   (1   6-)   (4   5)

M. Sus chords, 7ths, and Various Chord Extensions

Sus $= 1_{sus}$, or 1_{sus4}, or 1_4
Dominant 7th $= 1_7$ or 1_{x7}
Minor 7th $= 1_{-7}$
Major 7th $= 1_{ma7}$
Dominant 9th $= 1_9$
Dominant 13th $= 1_{13}$

Note. Subscripts are often used instead of superscripts.

N. Use standard abbreviations for sections of pieces

I = Introduction
V = Verse
C = Chorus
Tag = Tag
D.S. and D.C., Repeat, and Coda signs

Key Points

(1) More educative. Players learn something about chord function.
(2) More versatile. Charts addressing various styles can be played in any key and be used to modulate to any key.
(3) More brief, speedy, compact. A Nashville Number chart uses less space and can be created more quickly than a Pop Symbol chart.   The learning curve is easy. The basic requirement is that players must know the major scale

Made in the USA
Monee, IL
10 May 2026

49872262R00125